IN THE STRUGGLE FOR FREEDOM

IN THE STRUGGLE FOR FREEDOM

by

VLADKO MAČEK

Translated by

ELIZABETH AND STJEPAN GAZI

THE PENNSYLVANIA STATE UNIVERSITY PRESS
UNIVERSITY PARK AND LONDON

Copyright © 1957 by Josipa Maček
Library of Congress
Catalogue Card 68–8182

CONTENTS

CHAPTER		PAGE
I	Childhood	13
II	The Land and Its Rulers	24
III	A New Idea	36
IV	Growth of the Croatian Peasant Party	49
V	War	60
VI	Birth of Yugoslavia	76
VII	Early Struggles With Belgrade	92
VIII	The Murder of Stephen Radic	107
IX	At the Head of The Croatian Peasant Party	119
X	Prison	142
XI	The Boom of the Party	158
XII	Reconciliation	177
XIII	The Gathering Storm	196
XIV	Crisis and Coup	209
XV	War and Fascism	224
XVI	Prison Again	239
XVII	In Exile	261
	Index	277

MAPS

(between pages 264–65)

Croatia in the Tenth and Eleventh Centuries
Croatia, Bosnia, and Republic of Dubrovnik, 1397
Croatia, Dubrovnik, and Venetian Dalmatia, 1606
Croatia and Slavonia, 1914
Croatia per St. Vitus-Day Constitution of 1921
King Alexander's Banovinas of 1929
Banovina of Croatia, 1939
Croatia under the Axis, 1941

To the Memory of the Croat Peasant Leaders

Ante and Stephen Radić

IN THE STRUGGLE FOR FREEDOM

CHAPTER I

Childhood

ON A BEAUTIFUL summer morning many years ago, I was playing in the backyard of my parents' home when I heard a loud, sharp report. I ran out into the street and saw the rifles of a number of gendarmes fire over my head, wrapping me in thick black smoke. It had all lasted a few seconds. Mother came running, took me in her arms and carried me quickly into the house. In the safety of our room a moment later, I climbed onto the window sill. All was now deserted. A solitary peasant lay quite dead on the pavement. Near him a gendarme stood calmly, his rifle posted near his foot.

More than seventy years have passed, but the image of that peasant—his white linen shirt and trousers, his blue waistcoat, his long fair whiskers and bloody head—has remained engraved in my mind. At the sight of him, I had cried out in terror, anxiously asking my mother why the gendarmes had killed the poor man. Instead of an answer, she lifted me from the window and told me to pray with her for his soul—and then forget what happened. I prayed obediently but I did not forget.

Several days later, I repeated the same question to a 14-year-old peasant girl: Why had the gendarmes killed the peasant? With her apron, she wiped tears from her eyes and replied: "They killed him because he stood up for our rights!"

I was only four or five years old and I did not know what our rights were, much less what it meant "to stand up for them." Nor could the girl explain the sense of her words, which she had heard from her elders. But in my young soul I sensed perhaps for the first time that our rights were something great and important, since people were willing to die for them.

I was born on July 20, 1879, at Jastrebarsko, a small town some 20 miles south-west of Zagreb, capital of Croatia.

My father, then a civil engineer in the public service, had come to Croatia from nearby Slovenia as a young man. The son of a Slovene peasant, he had lost his mother when he was only three years old, and his father at 16. Left to his own resourcefulness, he diligently progressed in his studies at Graz, graduating from high school and then from the Institute of Technology. After obtaining his diploma he entered the service of the autonomous government of Croatia as an engineer.

With good spirits and ready willingness, he conscientiously carried out his duties: maintenance of all the old roads and bridges and, if need be, construction of new ones, as well as the erection of public buildings where called for in his district. Cheerful by nature he had learned early to face life realistically, and he showed little interest in problems not directly linked with his own existence. His personal demands were few and modest; his main concern was the well-being of his family. Notwithstanding his own frugality, he never tired of helping those who appealed to him for material aid. I frequently heard him say, "If all men were like myself, there would be no poverty in the world. No one would be in need, if people worked and saved as I do. And should extraordinary circumstances prevent anyone from doing so, it would be easy to bring him help, provided everybody who possessed something were ready to contribute his share to aid those in need." Father spent his later years with his grandchildren in my household, and died at the ripe age of 88. It has always been one of my more painful memories that I could not be at his death-bed. I was in prison.

Mother's heritage was both peasant and noble. My maternal grandfather, an Austrian officer, was the son of a peasant, while his wife belonged to a branch of the Polish nobility who had emigrated from their homeland. I remember both of them very well, as Grandfather died when I was 16, and Grandmother lived for another twenty years. A few drops of her noble blood apparently stirred in Mother's veins, for throughout her life she remained a lady. In contrast to Father, who tended toward simplicity, she nourished ambitions to attain a higher station in life, waging a constant war to keep her children among the best and most refined in regard to clothes, behavior and schooling. When she died at 70, I was 43, but she always considered me, much to my regret, a disobedient child. Neither my habits nor my dress nor my choice of friends received her approval. One day, for example, I had to attend a funeral, an occasion which in Mother's eyes definitely called for a top hat. I refused to wear one, adding I could do very well without it for the rest of my life. She smiled somewhat ominously, but said in a calm voice, "You will wear one yet, believe me." When she died ten years later, I had quite forgotten this little disagreement. How great, then, my astonishment when I read in Mother's will the clause ". . . and from my dear son Vladko I expect that he will attend my funeral in appropriate attire, including a top hat." I complied with her last wish, of course, remembering with regret many things— minor to me—that I might have done to please her while she lived.

In my childhood, Jastrebarsko, though a county seat, was but an ordinary village. After seventy years I can still see the quaint one-story houses, which, except for a few public buildings, were built from hard oak, covered for the most part with rye straw. With delight, my thoughts fly back to my early childhood, recalling the peaceful life I lived with Father, Mother and a brother, a year younger than myself, in the midst of a most charming and idyllic country.

Jastrebarsko, lying at the foot of the Plessivica Mountains, is bounded on the north by numerous picturesque villages, embedded in a green maze of alternating vineyards and orchards. Just south of the town an expanse of virgin forest began, which extended more than a dozen miles to the banks of the Kupa River. Many a summer afternoon or autumn day I spent with Mother, picking strawberries or gathering mushrooms, near the edge of the dense forest—scarcely a hundred yards from our home. Or again I accompanied Father north into the country of vineyards, fruits and grapes yielding sweet fresh juice. In the cold winter months, we gathered near the hearth in the warm room, watched the red flame licking at the logs and listened to the fascinating stories about the fairies, witches, vampires and ghosts who inhabited the forest, the orchard and even our very house.

Although village life can hardly be called monotonous, the changing seasons requiring their special tasks, I always enjoyed the many welcome interruptions provided by religious and other holidays. These village festivities, with their special charm, customs and old traditions, shall always be cherished in my memory.

In early spring, as soon as the snow melted, preparations were made for Easter. I remember the excitement of Palm Sunday, walking solemnly to church at my mother's side, carrying in my hand a branch of evergreen, together with a few willow branches covered with tender new buds. All the churchgoers brought similar branches but I was especially fascinated by the village lads who carried branches so big they looked like trees. When my own branches had received their blessing in church, I brought them home with care, where Mother stuck them into the corner of the frame of Our Lady's picture in our room. And then, in summer, when the sky suddenly darkened and the distant rumbling of thunder was heard approaching, one broke off a small part of the branch and threw it into the fire, believing firmly in its power of protection from lightning.

Throughout Holy Week, the persistent clinking of the mortar and pestle could be heard all over the house, and I knew that sugar, walnuts, hazel-nuts and poppy seeds were being ground by busy hands, to find their way eventually into many delicious cakes. Later, on Easter Eve in the community pasture outside the village, the village boys began to build a gigantic pile of dry logs and branches, some twenty feet high. After stuffing the pile with straw, they waited until the next morning to set it afire before sunrise. This blazing tower was called *vuzmenjak*—Easter. Though but a small child, I was unable to sleep that night before Easter Sunday for fear of missing the marvelous moment when the *vuzmenjak* would be lighted and its blazing flames would shoot fiercely into the morning sky. My parents were still fast asleep when Ann, our servant, approached my bed on tiptoe, whispering softly into my ear, "Come quick." In no time I was up and ready to go. We arrived at the community pasture just in time to watch the young people gathered around the flaming *vuzmenjak* join their fresh voices in the glorious hymn "Rejoice, O Queen of Heaven. . . ."

After the *vuzmenjak* had burned, Ann led me home. Taking off my shoes, I lay down on the bed fully clad, while Ann carried a basket, filled with ham, smoked sausages, white bread and red colored eggs, on her head to early mass, to have its contents blessed. The festivities continued with wonderful excitement until Easter was over.

A few evenings later, loud songs could be heard from all parts of Jastrebarsko, announcing: "Colored Easter is over, Green George has come, with new branches a foot long and grass a span tall. Give him gifts, give gifts to Green George. . . ." Boys and girls proceeded in separate groups through the streets, one child in each group decorated with branches to personify Saint George. They held big baskets to be filled by the villagers with smoked bacon, bread, eggs and home-made cheese. On one occasion, my brother and I participated in these exploits without Mother's knowledge. When we came home, we displayed our "loot" with great pride: a sizable slab of bacon and a dozen eggs. But, to our astonishment, Mother did not share our enthusiasm. On the contrary, she reproved us sternly, saying that this was simply ordinary begging, and insisting that we return everything to its owners. My father, himself the son of a peasant, smiled indulgently and confessed that his first earnings, too, were the results of such an expedition on Saint George's Day.

Saint John's Day was again celebrated with bonfires: the Croats are very fond of them. On the eve of that day, a fire was lighted, like the *vuzmenjak* though considerably smaller, and the village lads competed in jumping over it. Too small to take part in this privilege, I eagerly awaited the day when I would be permitted to do so. My ambition was never satisfied, for when I was old enough I had already left the village; and the city ignored the fire of Saint John.

Christmas, of course, outshone all the other holidays. On Saint Barbara's Day (December 4), a handful of moistened wheat grains, evenly divided, was placed in two bowls. After a couple of days in the warm room, the seeds sprouted tiny germs and were moved to the window sill. Exposed to daylight, the germs grew and developed lovely green blades, up to six inches long. If the crop was good in the bowls, so it would be in the fields next summer.

Saint Barbara's had hardly passed, when my mother began to make chains and miniature baskets from red, blue, gold and silver paper to decorate the Christmas tree. She worked at them for half an hour each evening, while we children watched the daily progress of her dainty products in wonder. After Mother had gilded hazel-nuts, walnuts and little apples, everything for the tree was ready. In those days, we were ignorant of the ready-made tree decorations of later times. The tree itself was hardest to get; there was no possibility of buying one. Anyone who wanted a pine tree was forced to steal it from Count Erdoedy's forest. Thus inevitably on Christmas Eve I discovered a lad standing in our kitchen with a Christmas tree, stolen the previous night and brought to our house. Warming himself near the hearth, the young man waited to be given a tip and a glass of brandy by my mother. Even today, I wonder how Mother, with her puritan morality, did not consider the theft of the tree a sin. Most likely, it was because she had not cut it down with her own hands.

We were never alone at Christmas. My grandparents usually came to stay with us. In the evening, we all assembled in the dining room, where no light had been allowed until the familiar rituals were over. First Father entered the room with two candles; then Mother, carrying a white tablecloth and the Christmas bread, baked with snow white flour and milk. Mother spread the cloth on the table and placed the bread in the center, between the two candles and the two bowls with their green wheat, planted on Saint Barbara's. After she had added a few red apples, a cup of honey and one of salt, we children left the room to bring in the straw, prepared beforehand and lying in a heap outside the door. The whole floor was strewn with straw a foot high, before we settled down to eat supper, which was copious, though without meat. After supper the candles on the tree were lighted, Christmas carols sung and presents exchanged. My brother and I, accustomed to early bedtime hours, were overjoyed for that night we were not sent to bed at all. When we could not fight off sleep any longer, we settled down for the night, fully clothed, on the straw under the table.

At the age of six I entered Public School, where I became acquainted with other boys of my age. Girls were taught in separate classes by a woman teacher, and we had no contact with them; we considered them inferior, and could not lose our dignity by associating with them. Apart from a few children in city clothes, whose parents were public officials and artisans, the public school was attended by peasant children from Jastrebarsko and its surroundings who dressed in typical native garments. In summer, they wore white linen shirts and pants, enlivened by a red or blue belt, and a blue or black waistcoat. Their foot-wear was a kind of moccasin, called an *opanak*. Over their shoulder hung the indispensable leather bag, its outer cover embroidered with bright red wool. In winter, they wore an additional overcoat made from homespun cloth, called a *surina*. Some children, from well-to-do families, also wore boots, as well as a sheepskin coat and cap. During the warm season, both peasant and artisan children went to school barefoot. Only two or three of us, all children of officials, were an exception. I particularly disliked this distinction, and soon found a remedy for it. I simply took my shoes off on the staircase outside our apartment, hid them carefully from my mother, and went to school barefoot. Mother eventually discovered my ruse and made a big affair of it, accusing me of bringing shame on her. Nevertheless, Father yielded to my insistence and bought me moccasins; in my second school year, I even got regular peasant boots. Now I had at least one thing in common with my peasant friends.

I soon felt a great respect for them. They often brought various toys to school, which they had carved themselves with a simple knife, called *kostura*, while guarding their cattle. We admired their flutes, miniature sleighs, ploughs, harrows and other agricultural tools, all carved down to the last detail. The teacher confiscated all the toys and locked them up in a glass-fronted book-case. Toys, he declared with pedagogical emphasis, did not belong in school. But one day, a school inspector visited us and our teacher showed him these samples of peasant craftsmanship with unconcealed pride. I remember the superintendent looking them over with great care. The boys who had so ably carved those toys later provided their own necessary household and farm tools with equal skill.

In elementary school, I gained my first impressions of what might be called politics by witnessing and even sharing the Croatian antagonism against the Magyars. As children we derived great pleasure from writing on fences or even on the blackboard "Long live Croatia," "Down with the Magyars" or similar slogans. Of course, all this was nothing more than a small scale reflection of the general national struggle, which we children were not yet able to understand.

When I was ten, my father was transferred to Zagreb, and with a heavy heart I took leave of my beloved village, my peasant friends, and above all, the unforgettable forest. Ten years later, when I visited my birthplace again, I found the village and the countryside greatly changed. Many of the old wooden homes had been replaced by brick houses, and the straw roofs were few and far between among new tile-covered dwellings. The forest, not escaping the march of time, had receded a mile or so, giving way to prosperous fields and green meadows.

Although Zagreb is not very far from Jastrebarsko and at the time had only 30,000 inhabitants, I felt I was in a completely new world. There were no orchards behind the houses and, of course, no forest. I disapproved heartily of the well waxed, shiny parquet floors in our apartment, because now I had to take off my shoes and put on slippers as soon as I came home. The worst problem seemed to be my total failure, at least at first, to find a place among the city children. In my opinion, they were either too aloof or too undisciplined; fights unknown in the village were a matter of course here. It also took me quite a time to acquire the necessary routine in the commonly used forms of courtesy toward the grown-ups. In the village it was not only considered polite, but an obligation to lift one's hat in reverence to all older persons and to sing out in a sonorous voice the familiar "Praised be Jesus and Mary." In the city it was not customary to greet unknown people at all, while our loud "Praised be Jesus and Mary" degenerated into a somewhat more subdued and servile "I kiss your hand."

I spent only a few months in elementary school in Zagreb before entering the gymnasium. The educational system in Croatia (and for that matter in most of Central Europe) required all children to complete four years of elementary school. Then those who could afford it went on to the gymnasium for eight years of study. The first half of this period was termed lower gymnasium, the second half upper gymnasium. Completion of the lower gymnasium qualified the pupil for normal schools as well as secondary schools of forestry, agriculture and military science. Moreover, it qualified those who turned to practical life for various subordinate civil service positions (such as postal or railway service). The eighth and last year of the gymnasium terminated with an examination, called the *matura,* in which the students had to give evidence of their accumulated knowledge in every subject treated in the past eight years. Having obtained the *matura*—a level of education approximately equivalent to American high school plus junior college—the young people could enroll at the university or seek positions in the postal, railway, or internal revenue offices.

I was profoundly impressed by the austere gymnasium building several centuries old, adjacent to Saint Catherine Church, a fine example of baroque art, by the imposing number of professors, and the vast collection of books, ranging from the dull Latin grammar to the beautifully illustrated volumes of natural science. At once, I was aware that the time of play had passed and the time of work begun.

My schoolmates came partly from Zagreb, partly from the country regions, more or less distant. About half of them were peasant children, but instead of sheepskin coats, moccasins and red bags, they wore cheap city clothes. Most of them were housed in the Archbishop's Seminary, which served as a nursery for prospective priests. The school work, especially Latin grammar and, after the third year, Greek grammar, required all my time and effort. Those two subjects remained my Achilles heel throughout my gymnasium years.

At the age of 14, when I entered the upper gymnasium, I had already acquired a general grasp of the Croatian political parties and their aspirations. But, before proceeding any further, it might be well to sketch very briefly the history of Croatia.

CHAPTER II

The Land And Its Rulers

          *T*OWARD THE END of the 6th century A. D. the Croatian* tribes left their lands beyond the Carpathians, migrated South and West into the territory between the Drava River and the Adriatic Sea, and soon created a well organized state with somewhat flexible boundaries. The Croats moved into a region which had become the meeting ground between the Roman and Byzantine cultures, but, as time went on, they leaned more and more heavily toward the West and in the Great Schism they sided with the Roman Catholic Church.

 Until the beginning of the 12th century, Croatia was ruled by kings chosen from her own nobility. Then, in 1102, a pact with the Hungarians was signed in which the Croats agreed to crown the King of Hungary as King of Croatia on their own territory. This connection, somewhat analogous to the relationship between Great Britain and her Dominions, was termed the "Personal Union." For eight centuries, until 1918, the political life of the Croats was closely connected with that of their Hungarian neighbors.

 The Turkish invasion of Europe and their many advances during the 14th, 15th, and 16th centuries induced the Croats

---

 * "Croat" is a Latin name adopted by many Western languages. The Croats themselves have retained the original *Hrvat* and *Hrvatska:* Croatia. The same designation (mostly in its variant spelling *Horvat*) is also used in other Slavic languages and in Magyar.

and, somewhat later, the Hungarians to place themselves under the protection of the Hapsburg dynasty, and the Hapsburg Emperor added to his impressive array of titles those of the King of Hungary and King of Croatia. The arrangement, however, was of little avail to the Croats, for the Turkish invader conquered most of their country, leaving but a small fraction of the former state which contemporaries sadly called *Reliquiae reliquiarum olim regni Croatiae.*

The Venetians also invaded Croatian territory, occupying Dalmatia, the Eastern Coast of the Adriatic. Liberated from Venetian control by Napoleon, Dalmatia, too, ultimately was added to the Hapsburg lands. At the Congress of Vienna, it was "temporarily" subjected to Austrian administration, though *de iure* recognized by Austria and Hungary as an integral part of Croatia. The territories between the rivers Sava, Drava and Danube and the Northeastern part of the Adriatic had been restored to Croatia after the withdrawal of the Turks in the 18th century, while the rest of her former lands remained under Turkish domination, incorporated in the provinces of Bosnia and Hercegovina.

On the whole, the relations beween Hungary and Croatia remained unchanged during the seven centuries following the pact of 1102. Both countries were governed by their respective aristocracy, who pursued similar interests; they intermarried frequently, so that kinship in many cases was close. The situation was hardly ideal, however, since the different clans entertained many bitter quarrels, that led to frequent bloodshed and sometimes even civil wars of a sort. But these hostilities did not in any way affect the union between Croatia and Hungary, since both parties to these feuds usually included both Hungarians and Croatians. Thus, after the death in 1526 of the last Hungaro-Croatian king, Louis II, in battle against the Turks, the Croatian aristocrats were divided among themselves, some supporting the pretender, Ferdinand of Hapsburg, while others encouraged "the son of the Hungarian country,'" John Zapolya; the Hungarian nobility were divided in much the same way. With the help of his brother, the German Emperor Charles V, Ferdinand at last emerged victorious after the death in battle of Zapolya's principal supporter, the Croatian aristocrat Kristo Frankopan. The ensuing Hapsburg policy failed to satisfy both Croatians and Hungarians and they planned a revolt. Again their interests were common; at the head of the illfated, ruthlessly crushed conspiracy were Peter Zrinski, a Croat, and his son-in-law, Ferenc Rackoczy, a Hungarian.

Matters changed radically after the American and French Revolutions. Along with the new ideas of freedom and enlightenment came the consciousness of belonging to a social and cultural unit transcending the clan and provincial feuds. The nationalism of the peoples of Central and Eastern Europe was on its way.

At the time, hardly more than half of Hungary's populations were Magyars; the balance consisted of Slovaks, Rumanians, Ukrainians, Croats and Serbs. Nevertheless, the ruling Magyars abolished Latin as the official language and imposed the Magyar tongue on the whole country. The ancient name of Hungary, which had identified the state without revealing any national character, was eliminated in favor of *"Magyarorszag,"* land of the Magyars. As the name Hungary (*Ungarn, Hongrie,* etc.) continued to be used in most foreign tongues, the rest of the world began to confuse the notions of Hungarians and Magyars which it believed to be identical. The Magyars went even further, and claimed Croatia to be simply a part of the *Magyarorszag*.

The antagonism between the Croats and the Magyars, quick to arise and quick to spread, came to a head in the tumultuous summer of 1848. The Magyars, led by their great patriot Louis Kossuth, planned a revolt against Hapsburg domination. But the Croats knew of Kossuth's chauvinism; he had asserted boldly that he "could not find Croatia on the map." For the first time in seven hundred years, Croatia and Hungary stood at opposite sides of a chasm. Far from encouraging the Magyar insurgents, the Croatian *Sabor* (Parliament) declared war on their neighbors on July 4, and General Josip Jelačić, a Croatian officer known for his opposition to the Magyars, who had been acclaimed the *Ban* (Viceroy) of Croatia, led Croatian troops into Hungary. Franz Josef, assisted by Russian troops under the command of General Paskevich and by Jelačić's Croats, suppressed the Magyar rebellion and thereupon introduced absolutism and centralism throughout the Hapsburg dominions.

Severe at the outset, like all dictatorships, the post-Metternich regime relented after a few years, dwindled and gradually lost all effectiveness. This became increasingly evident after the defeats of the Austrian army at Solferino in 1859. The need for modifying the structure of the Hapsburg Empire became pressing.

During those critical years, the outlines of the Croatian political parties appeared. First to take shape was the Union Party, supported mainly by the aristocracy. As elsewhere in Europe, they had lost their feudal prerogatives in 1848, and now they believed that the absolutist tendencies of the Hapsburgs could be checked only through a tight union with the Hungarians. Hence the adherents of the Union Party were dubbed simply *"Magyarons."*

The second party was founded under the name of the National Party and was headed by Josip Juraj Strossmayer, bishop of Djakovo, whose primary aim was to bring about a reform of the Hapsburg Monarchy on a federalist basis. Broad-minded, rebellious, erudite, Strossmayer exerted a profound influence on Croatian political thinking. He strongly affirmed the idea of the unity of Southern Slavs—Slovenes, Croats, Serbs and Bulgarians—the so-called "Yugoslav" idea, as a first step toward the unity of all Slavic nations. He strongly opposed all attempts to send a Croatian delegation to the Imperial Council in Vienna, unless such a delegation were entitled to take part in all common affairs with rights equal to those of all other nations of the Monarchy. It was this party's hope that the "Austrian" Slavs, namely the Czechs, Slovaks, Slovenes, Croats and Poles residing in Austria, would have a majority over the Germans and Magyars in the Parliament and would thus be able to defend their interests.

At about the same time, a third party was formed, the small Party of Rights, under the guidance of Ante Starčević, a stern, unyielding man, who saw a solution of the problem only in an unconditional recognition of Croatia's historical rights to state sovereignty. He put forth the slogan, "Neither Vienna, nor Budapest"; his party advocated that the Croats should arrange their affairs directly with the King. But as Franz Josef did not seem disposed either to open separate negotiations with Croatia or Hungary or to federalize his Empire the question remained unsettled until 1867.

After Austria's defeat in the war with Prussia, Franz Joseph signed a pact, the *Ausgleich* of 1867, which recognized the absolute sovereignty of Hungary. The Parliament in Budapest, concerning itself with matters on Hungarian soil, became equal to the one in Vienna which controlled the Austrian territories. The common interests—foreign affairs, finances and the army —were to be dealt with by delegations from both parliaments. The Magyars were given a free hand to bargain for a settlement with Croatia as they saw fit. An Austrian statesman is said to have summed up his ideas of the newly established Dual Monarchy in a remark to the Magyar delegation: "From now on you watch your hordes and we shall watch ours." The "hordes" were the people of all nationalities under the Hapsburg dynasty except the Germans and Magyars: the Czechs, Poles, Ukrainians, Slovenes and some of the Croats in the Austrian sphere; in the Hungarian sphere the Slovaks, Ukrainians, Rumanians, Serbs and, of course the ever-rebellious Croats.

The Magyars were quick to realize that their own security

THE LAND AND ITS RULERS 29

would be endangered if they did not make some concessions to the Croats. To assure a favorable outcome of negotiations with Croatia, the King nominated Baron Levin Rauch, a Croatian aristocrat, *Ban* of the Kingdom of Croatia, Slavonia and Dalmatia. Rauch immediately introduced a somewhat dubious electoral law which gave him a majority in the Croatian Parliament and, with consent of that majority, signed the *Nagodba*, a pact between Croatia and Hungary analogous to the *Ausgleich*.

According to the *Nagodba*, Croatia regained certain rights and attributes of an autonomous state, and the Croats were explicitly recognized "a political nation." The autonomous Croatian *Sabor* became legal, with the *Ban* and his government responsible to the *Sabor*. Croatian was declared the one official language not only in autonomous Croatian affairs, but also in the so-called "joint Hungarian" matters on Croatian territory. Only the Croatian flag was authorized on Croatian territory. For autonomous affairs, the use of the coat of arms of the Kingdom of Croatia, Slavonia and Dalmatia was legalized, while in all matters falling under joint administration a combination of the coats of arms of Hungary, Croatia, Slavonia and Dalmatia represented both countries. However, the city and harbor of Rijeka, nominally a Hungaro-Croatian condominium, was in practice brought entirely under Hungarian control. And Dalmatia, an integral part of Croatia on paper, remained under the direct administration of Austria until the dissolution of the Empire.

By the 1890's when I began to take an interest in politics, the three original Croatian parties had undergone some confusing changes since the days of absolutism. Now they were divided and distinguished mainly on the basis of their approach to the accomplished fact of the *Nagodba*. The old Union Party, joined by some of Strossmayer's partisans, had changed its name to that of the National Party; this change failed to confuse the people, who kept on calling them *Mag-*

yarons. The *Magyarons*, on the whole, were satisfied with the existing state of affairs and they were permanently in power. Strossmayer's old National Party had rallied around the influential newspaper *Obzor*. The *Obzor* party recognized the *Nagodba* as a historical fact, but not a particularly good fact, and called for its revision. Starčević and his Party of Rights, on the other hand, declared the *Nagodba* null and void, since it had been approved by *Sabor* members chosen in staged elections, who had misrepresented the will of the people.

It should be mentioned here that the Magyars, from the very beginning, rather foolishly tried to violate even the limited autonomy the Croats had acquired. In 1883, for instance, openly defying the obvious text of the law, which ruled that Croatian was the only official language in all joint affairs on Croatian territory, they added the corresponding Magyar text to the Croatian lettering on the metal plates designating certain official buildings in Zagreb, one of which happened to be the Treasury Department. This infraction of their rights provoked demonstrations among the Croats in the capital and elsewhere; defying the police, the people removed the illegal signs. Although it was obvious that the Croats were merely insisting on their rights, the government decided to restore the plates and make a big military fuss out of the occasion. The *Ban*, Count Pejačević, refused to comply and resigned. He was succeeded by the special Imperial appointee, Ramberg, who had the powers of the *Ban* without being responsible to the *Sabor* for his actions. Ramberg, to show his power, had the signs restored for 24 hours and then replaced by plates without any inscription at all. The mute plates continued to adorn the buildings until the fall of the Empire. The incident was characteristic of that era.

Ramberg governed for about half a year, until Count Karl Khuen-Hédérváry was nominated *Ban* of Croatia. Khuen, although born in Croatia, had received his education in Hungary, and considered himself more of a Magyar than a Croat.

Barely over 30 years old when he became *Ban,* Khuen announced his program with the ambitious slogan: "Order, Work, Law."

Although the Croats saw an affront in the very nomination of a man of Khuen's background and disposition, Khuen managed to stay in power for twenty years, a feat unequaled before or afterward. His task, to be sure, was greatly facilitated by the electoral law, which limited the suffrage to persons who paid a minimum of 25 florins of direct tax a year. That sum, worth about $10 at the time, was a great deal more than the average peasant's tax, but restriction did not apply to officials of the state, autonomous or municipal administration. These were automatically entitled to vote, and they included all persons in public service, even municipal guards, janitors, *per diem* clerks and copyists. All of these people were economically dependent on the regime and hence unwilling or unable to vote against it.

Moreover, even those peasants and artisans who could vote felt so far removed from the ideologies of the parties and the issues of the day that they were largely indifferent to the outcome of elections. The political candidates, therefore, adopted a rather peculiar fashion of campaigning, the notorious "electoral goulashes": Immediately before the election they gave a large party, cooked stew and served wine to the voters. People ate the goulash, drank the wine and voted for those who paid the bill. The simple theory was that since the new administration was not likely to be very different from the old one, a man might as well get a drink out of the deal. The people were not far wrong. The effective opposition was reduced to a handful of independent intellectuals, mainly lawyers and priests, and a few hundred students. If now and then the peasantry did join movements of resistance, the affair usually degenerated into a riot, which more often than not had a tragic end. One of them was the occasion of my first meeting with a peasant who had stood up for our rights, related in the previous chapter.

Apart from its manifestly unfair political rule, the Khuen regime produced many positive results. Khuen surrounded himself with capable men, raised the Croatian judiciary system to a high level, improved public education quite effectively and contributed greatly to the development of the national economy. Yet, despite all his merits, he was judged only from the political viewpoint. We gymnasium students thought it not only patriotic but also fun to write on walls and fences whenever possible, "Down with Khuen- Héderváry."

During the Khuen regime, Serbian propaganda in Croatia increased notably. In the Turkish wars, many parts of Croatia had been completely ravaged, and the Turks populated these regions with people of the Eastern Orthodox faith. There were some Serbs among them, but most were people of Latin stock called Vlachs; that name soon became a common designation of *all* new settlers. When the Turkish frontier had been pushed back to the region south of the Sava River, Croatia became host to many Orthodox people. They cannot all be traced back to the settlers established by the Turks; many came of Croatian families who, under the Turkish occupation, had foresworn Catholicism and adopted Orthodoxy. The Turks preferred the Orthodox to the Roman Church, because the Patriarch of the former had his seat in Constantinople and was thus under Turkish influence.

When the French Revolution stimulated the national consciousness of these Orthodox believers, they awoke at first to Croatian patriotism. But an historical incident shifted this trend: In the 17th century, the Serbian Orthodox Patriarch, Arsenije Crnojević, had led some 30,000 Serbian families to southern Hungary and eastern Croatia. There they were granted complete religious freedom under the guidance of their Patriarch, who resided at Srijemski Karlovci. This event stimulated Serbian nationalism in Croatia which, through the in-

THE LAND AND ITS RULERS   33

fluence of the Serbian Orthodox Church, affected all Orthodox believers.

Count Khuen did not hesitate to strengthen his position against the Croats by favoring the Serbs from Croatia, who in their turn became his strongest support. He incited Serbian nationalist tendencies, became their powerful protector, and thereby widened the incipient rift between the Croats and the Serbs.

The most vehement protest against Khuen's pro-Serbian policy came from the Party of Rights and especially from its leader, Starčević. He went so far as to deny the existence of Serbs in Croatia, calling them Orthodox Croats "seduced by Vlach priests." This sounds no more fantastic than the assertions of certain latter-day Serbs that the Croatian nation does not exist and that all Croats are merely Catholicized Serbs.

In the autumn of 1895, the twelfth year of the Khuen regime, the beautiful modern edifice of the Croatian National Theatre and the new gymnasium in Zagreb were completed. Khuen chose the occasion to show off his success in "pacifying" Croatia and arranged a solemn official visit of the Emperor and King Franz Josef to Zagreb. There were extensive preparations for an exceptionally magnificent reception but they were conducted in such a spirit as to invite incidents of protest. When the triumphal arch had at last been erected in front of the Zagreb railway station, the Magyar colors were waving briskly in the wind beside the Croatian flag. This sight revolted the whole city until several courageous students pulled down the foreign and illegal emblem. The police lost no time in hoisting it again, but throughout the capital people sensed that something was afoot.

I stood on the square before the university, the center of most political manifestations. I was 16 and I waited impatiently for what promised to be most exciting demonstrations, ready to do my best to contribute to the disturbance. Nothing of the sort happened. Instead, about 200 students, dressed in traditional uniforms, had assembled and now began to march in perfect order, carrying the University banner, in the direction of the Jelačić Square. They had stopped right in front of the monument to *Ban* Jelačić, when one of the students produced a Magyar flag, drenched in kerosene, from beneath his coat and set it afire among shouts of "Glory to *Ban* Jelačić," and "down with the Magyars." (*Ban* Jelačić, it will be remembered, with his Croatian troops, had helped crush the Magyar revolution in 1848.) No disturbance occurred, much to my disappointment, and the students dispersed as calmly as they had assembled.

That bold act attracted quite special attention, because it had happened while Franz Josef was visiting Zagreb. Immediately after the incident, about 60 students were arrested, brought to trial and sentenced to several months in prison. During the hearings all the students behaved courageously, but one of them, Stephen Radić, later the founder of the Croatian Peasant Party, particularly distinguished himself by his great courage and his detailed knowledge of Croatian constitutional rights. Accused of being the principal instigator of the demonstration, he received the heaviest sentence, six months of rigorous confinement. All the condemned students were automatically expelled from the University of Zagreb; after having served their prison term, many of them left to continue their studies at the University of Prague, followed by some younger students who had had no part in the flag-burning exploit. Their stay in Prague furthered greatly the feeling of Slavic solidarity among young Croatian intellectuals, and thus influenced considerably the future development of Croatian politics.

Just when, in Prague, new vistas were opening for the young generation of Croatian students, a split occurred in the Party of Rights, by now the most popular of them all. Even today, the reasons for this split are not quite clear to me. At any rate, the founder and head of the party, Ante Starčević, was old, and the time had come to choose his successor. The two foremost aspirants were Fran Folnegović and Josip Frank. In the ensuing polemics, they called each other traitor, basing their accusations on words uttered publicly in speeches on this or that past occasion. When Starčević died in February 1897, the division in the party had become irremediable. I attended the funeral of the deceased leader and felt painfully embarrassed, listening to the caustic speeches of the antagonists. Not confining themselves to pay homage to the memory of Starčević, they accused each other across his open grave.

From then on, the two factions, Folnegović's Party of Rights and Frank's "Pure" Party of Rights, opposed each other. Folnegović died soon after Starčević, and his party was left without a leading personality. It accepted some of the "progressives" of the Prague group, adopted some of their political views, entered the Croato-Serbian Coalition and finally, with the dissolution of the Hapsburg Monarchy, was dispersed among other Croatian parties. Frank's Pure Party of Rights showed more vitality. However, lacking the firm leadership of Ante Starčević, it divided itself again, one faction becoming a mere instrument of Austria, the other serving the Great-Serbian policy. But that was later on.

CHAPTER III

A New Idea

At 18 I successfully passed the *matura*. Now I was ready to choose a career. I had already made up my mind to devote my life to the struggle for the liberation of Croatia and the Croatian people, but to do this without restriction one had to have an independent existence. The best course to take, therefore, was to enter a university and continue my studies. Should it be theology, philosophy or law? One had little choice, for those three faculties were the only ones taught at the time at the University of Zagreb. The religious education I had received from my mother inclined me, while still at the gymnasium, toward theology. Grown up, however, I became convinced that I would never make a model priest. The other two faculties led one one way or another to official service, which meant to serve the regime blindly. Agronomy, forestry or science would have been more to my taste, but these were out of the question—first because the requisite schools did not exist in Croatia, and second because, even assuming I could complete my studies abroad, such an education again would have led ultimately to civil service.

After careful deliberation I decided to become a lawyer, although that profession did not hold much attraction for me. Nevertheless, law was practically the only profession in which one had some freedom to act politically and even to oppose the government—providing, of course, one was not primarily interested in making money.

To practice law a doctorate was required in addition to the regular studies at the Faculty of Law and Government; beside the usual juridicial studies of civil, criminal, constitutional and international law, those who wished to obtain the degree had to pass examinations in finance, administration and political economy. So I proceeded to digest the dry and dull Roman and Canon Law along with other required subjects. I became a doctor of law early in 1903.

At the university I found the students divided politically into two broad groups. One group reflected the ideas of one or another of the three traditional parties. That is, some found the relations with Hungary according to the *Nagodba* of 1868 wholly satisfying; some recognized the compromise as an accomplished fact, but urged its revision in favor of Croatia; and some advocated the non-recognition of the *Nagodba* and the eventual separation of Croatia from Hungary. Only naturally, the first two programs could not satisfy the radical impulses which have always characterized the younger generation. Therefore, within this broad group of students, it was Starčević's thesis which prevailed. Since his party was then led by the Zagreb lawyer and politician Josip Frank, the faction was commonly known as Frankists *(frankovci)*, a name which stuck even long after Frank's death.

The other group of students not connected with any of the three parties had just been formed. This group received its ideological direction from the students of the University of Prague, or more precisely from Professor Thomas Masaryk, who was to become the first president of the Czechoslovak Republic after the First World War. They rejected the old Croatian political values based on history, and spiritual values based on a millenium of religious traditions, and called themselves "progressive."

Neither of the two trends satisfied my own political ideals.

The first appeared hopeless to me. Basing its principles exclusively on historical documents, it seemed incapable of successfully facing practical issues. And since the second group proposed that the progressive way of dealing with social and political problems was to neglect, or even deny, our traditions and our historical and spiritual values, I wanted none of it.

Possibly I would have lost all active interest in politics, had I not in that critical period met Ante Radić, the father of the Croatian Peasant Movement—a man who in my opinion was the first to perfectly understand and interpret the role of the Croatian, and perhaps of the entire East European, peasantry.

To the Western World, the term "peasantry" may need some explanation and clarification.

Although the East European peasant makes his living in the same manner as an American farmer—by tilling the soil—the difference between the two is great. There is, first of all, an obvious economic difference. An American farmer as a rule owns and works more land, and he operates with the help of modern machinery and all kinds of gadgets and inventions. The peasant of Eastern Europe still works his land with oxen and horses—without modern agricultural equipment, without even such simple aids as artificial fertilizers. The American farmer is, as a rule, a specialist: America has dairy farms, wheat farms, poultry farms, and fruit farms; and the individual farmer is mainly concerned with only one product.

The East European peasant, on the other hand, produces everything he needs on a comparatively small amount of land —not only all the food for his family and animals, and most of his clothing (even light footgear)—but also a great deal of his everyday household equipment. The few things that the peasant does not produce at home (boots and hats, for instance) are produced by small artisans in the small neighboring towns only a few miles away. The same type of small artisan takes care of his other simple needs. Local carpenters and woodworkers make all his furniture, carts and barrels; and the local blacksmith shoes his horses, puts felloes on the wheels, and supplies all the other hardware the peasant may need. Briefly, then, East European peasants take care of their needs in a very old-fashioned autarkic manner.

But the most important difference between the East European peasant and the American farmer (also the West European *Bauer*) is spiritual. While the Western farmer is tied to his own land only (and even that land changes hands comparatively often), the East European peasant is irrevocably tied to his whole environment and particularly to his village. The ties to his own land and village are not only those of his own time but also the unbreakable ties of the centuries of past and, God willing, the centuries of future for his children and grandchildren. The peasant lives in the same spot in which his ancestors have lived for centuries before him. He and his neighbors have identical needs, customs and hopes; they have the same philosophy and the same outlook on the world—an outlook which can be traced back for ten or more centuries.

Serfdom was abolished in Croatia in 1848, and in the 1860's the Military Frontier, too, came gradually under civilian administration.* These social changes altered the economic system in a significant way. The barter system, under which the peasant had maintained his self-sufficiency, gave way to a financial system of trade. The peasant now had to pay ready money for many products which had previously been manufactured at home. And money was extremely scarce in the peasant household, because there was no market for agricultural products. The peasants inevitably suffered one economic crisis after another. No solution to this acute problem could be found, unless it was, as they told me themselves, to tighten their belts. When this, too, failed, the peasants fell easy prey to the

* The regions of Croatia, gradually liberated from the Turkish power, though added again to Croatia, fell under a special imperial administration, the Military Frontier, instituted to create more efficient defenses against sporadic Turkish invasions.

insatiable provincial banks and "savings" associations which mushroomed all over the country. It is difficult even to speculate how they would have solved their problems, had not the First World War broken out. It shook the national economy and caused a great inflation, which helped the peasants settle their debts.

And yet, it would be quite erroneous to assume that the economic factor was the only one in bringing forth the peasant movement which broke the ground for the Croatian Peasant Party. There was a more profound cause, the major, the haunting, depressing evil of the era: the underprivileged social position of the peasantry.

The abolition of serfdom had left the former masters in want of free labor. They adapted themselves to the changed conditions and became civil officials, administrators or judges. The officers of the former Military Frontier also entered the civil service as soon as the civilian system was introduced. This new caste continued to regard their former serfs or subordinate frontiersmen with contempt. It should perhaps have been expected that a class long privileged would not surrender freely its acquired social advantages. But I shall never be able to understand how those peasant children who were now able to go through school and become judges, administrators, doctors, teachers or perhaps only subordinate clerks, copied their former lords and officers in showing contempt for the peasantry, hence for their own parents, brothers and sisters. City dwellers all, they were now a section of the "gentry" (*gospoda*) and they would not associate with a common peasant. The bourgeoisie joined their ranks. Any small artisan, merchant or peddler, who had recently migrated to the town from the country, considered himself incomparably superior to his rural brother who continued to wear his homespun linen pants, his moccasins and his sheepskin coat and who had remained home to till his peasant soil.

As late as the First World War, and even some time afterward, every village had a large inn which had two rooms, a smaller one for the "gentry" and a larger one for the peasants. Everyone in city clothes, from the judge down to the village merchant, had admittance to the room reserved for the gentry, but even the most intelligent peasant was denied that privilege. Thus the status of the peasant in Croatia strongly resembled the status of the Negro in some regions of the United States; but the humiliation hurt perhaps even more, for the peasant knew that most of those from whom he was segregated came themselves from peasant homes.

Nobody, of course, ever dreamed that the peasantry could have a say in Croatian national affairs, even though they comprised over 80 percent of the nation. The peculiar electoral law had made government employees largely decisive in the election of representatives to the *Sabor*. Prior to 1910, most of the peasants did not have the right to vote, since they were in an extremely low income bracket, and even those who could vote had no particular preferences. Since the elections were open (every voter had to appear before the electoral commission and orally state his choice of candidate), the trend of the peasant votes depended chiefly on whether the peasant, who was more or less permanently up to his ears in debt, was influenced more by the official authority of the district chief, the Church authority of the parish priest, or the authority of the village merchant's credit.

It would be unjust to deny that the Croatian political leaders—both in and out of power—were animated by a sincere patriotism. Their proclamations of love and solicitude for "the people of Croatia" truly came from the heart. But none of them apparently stopped to think who those people of Croatia actually were who formed the backbone of the nation.

Those were the conditions when Ante Radić entered the political scene at the turn of the century. With extraordinary lucidity he at once grasped the fundamentally simple fact: To exalt the Croatian nation, and at the same time neglect and even despise the Croatian peasantry, was nonsense. For the peasantry were essentially the only representative of the Croatian nationality. The nobility and the bourgeoisie of Croatia, exposed through centuries to foreign (partly German and partly Italian) civilization, had also accepted a foreign culture; as Ante Radić put it, they had lost their Croatian national soul. There were times when, anxious to enhance their refinement, the urban strata considered it in good taste to converse in German (especially in Upper Croatia) or in Italian (mostly along the Adriatic coast), relegating their mother tongue to communications with peasants or servants. In the first half of the 19th century, there was a renascence of the Croatian language among the bourgeoisie, but they could not bridge centuries of alien thinking and acting. Their ways and their ideas remained foreign. Nation, Ante Radić would say, is a word frequently and enthusiastically used by the gentry, and yet they keep on rejecting and despising what makes a people a nation: their traditional ways and thoughts, costumes, songs and dances—in short, their lives. And these are what the peasantry have preserved from time immemorial. Having safeguarded his language and his indigenous culture through centuries of neglect and persecution, the Croatian peasant has safeguarded the Croatian national individuality.

But in his enthusiasm Radić was never carried away from reality. He was painfully aware of the shortcomings of the Croatian village; he knew that much of the evil stemmed not only from the peasant's ignorance of the world in general, but also—and even more specifically—of the life of other peasants from different regions of Croatia. This ignorance, according to Radić, was the reason for the peasantry's lack of confidence in their own moral, economic and physical strength.

In 1898 Radić started his campaign against peasant ignorance by publishing, all alone, a review entitled simply *"Dom"* (Home). Through this paper he hoped to foster self-confidence and regular contact among the inhabitants of various rural

A NEW IDEA 43

regions. The idea was to let them know each other better and thus shake them out of their intellectual lethargy. The review was a 24-page, bi-monthly, one-man enterprise, for Radić assumed not only the work of editor and publisher, but was also its only contributor! He discussed amazingly diverse subjects, local, universal, spiritual or material, and no important event escaped his attention. His pedagogical method was peculiar: He would bring up a question, illuminate it from all sides, but leave it open without drawing a conclusion. The article would end with the suggestion, "Think it over and we shall continue our conversation next time." The "next time" never came; it was not necessary. Radić had attained his purpose. He had incited the peasants *to think for themselves* and draw their own conclusions. And they did. When people saw that the continuation of the discussion was not forthcoming, they sent him letters from all parts of the country expressing their own opinions on the matter. Ante Radić had been my professor at the gymnasium, and later on, as a young university student, I often went to see him again, happy to exchange my own ideas with him on a subject that interested us both. I vividly recall his enthusiasm over the many letters he had received written in a heavy peasant hand and expressing reflections in a clumsy handwriting. And I also recall the elation with which he noted that the peasant from the Hungarian border thought in the same way as the peasant from Bosnia or from the coast of the blue Adriatic. In this we both saw the best proof of the complete unity of the Croatian peasant mind.

The hundred-odd issues of the *Dom* alone reveal enough learning, patience and understanding to be considered a life's achievement. Yet the publication of the *Dom* occupied only a smaller part of Ante Radić's productive time. His most important work is a collection of material on the "Life and Customs of Southern Slavs," published over the years by the Yugoslav Academy of Sciences and Arts in Zagreb. To facilitate and systematize the study, Radić formulated a questionnaire of over a thousand items which had to be collected to cover the enormous field of research. It was this monumental work which established Radić—whose scholary background was in the province of Slavic languages and literature—as Croatia's leading sociologist.

It would take us too far afield to try to outline even the finest of Radić's many ideas. The peasant accepted them with eagerness, for they were not alien thoughts but only a written formulation of what had already been in his heart. Unfortunately those who could and were willing to read *Dom* were few. But there were small groups of faithful readers, people with the most open minds all over Croatia. With his simple newspaper, Radić had sown the seed that fell on prosperous ground and developed into the immensely powerful Croatian Peasant Party.

Thus Ante Radić, philosopher and teacher, with great skill gathered around himself what might be called a spiritual elite from among the peasantry. But this, of course, was not sufficient to create a strong political movement, capable of rousing the broad sections of people within the Croatian borders and serving as a beacon to the peasant world abroad. A man was needed who could move broad strata and gain general popularity. Such a man was Stephen, Ante Radić's younger brother.

Stephen Radić, too, was an intellectual of the first rank, perhaps even a genius. It was a strange destiny that willed that the man who was to lead the Croatian peasant to his political ascendancy was to be born almost blind. One of his eyes was completely dead. With his other eye he could see sufficiently to read script at a distance of one or two inches or discern the dim features of a person several feet away. He was blind for all purposes except reading; he knew hundreds of people only by their voices. To read he would move the book quickly left and right, up and down, holding it directly in front of his one eye.

He was an avid and prolific reader and had an extraordinary memory for details.

His character, in contrast to that of his brother, was dominated by impulse rather than by calm deliberation. With extraordinary ease he expressed his thoughts both in speech and in writing, never falling short of an appropriate answer when challenged. He was still at the gymnasium when he became the center of attraction as a result of an incident at the Zagreb Opera House. *Ban* Khuen-Héderváry happened to attend the presentation of the historical opera *Ban Nikola Zrinjski.* Suddenly Stephen Radić interrupted the play, shouting at the top of his voice "Glory to Ban Zrinjski! Down with the Magyar exponent Héderváry."

His impulses ran away with him on several other occasions. Despite this youthful buoyancy the principal and the professors of the gymnasium, and perhaps even Khuen himself, appreciated his talents and allowed him to pass the final examinations, though he was no longer a student of the gymnasium. In 1895, as a law student, however, he was expelled from the University of Zagreb and went to Prague. He did not join his fellow students who adhered to Masaryk's doctrines, labelling them foreign to the Croats, and he soon left Prague for Paris to enroll at the famous School of Political Science. The gifted young man passed all his examinations with flying colors, and carried off as the first prize a superb collection of historical and sociological books.

After his return to Croatia in 1902, Stephen Radić participated in an unsuccessful attempt to unify the divided Croatian opposition into one party which could confront the Magyar supremacy. By that time, he had come to share his brother's conviction that the political strength of the nation had to be sought in the peasantry alone. It was necessary first to build up the self-confidence of the peasants, and then to organize them to create an overwhelming political force.

The strength of the Croatian peasants, Radić pointed out, was based first of all on their number—four-fifths of the Croatian population.

Second, on their economic strength. There was little or no industry in Croatia at that time. Manufactured products, insofar as they were not furnished by village craftsmen, were imported from Austrian lands. State and community employees thrived thanks to a government budget derived mostly from peasant taxes, while the merchants derived their prosperity from dealing profitably in agricultural as well as city goods, which again were bought from or sold mainly to the peasants.

Third, on their cultural traditions. They have preserved an indigenous culture, based on ancient traditions which, together with their language, handed down through generations, form the essence of the Croatian nationality.

And fourth, on their moral value. To form a unity, human society must observe the moral laws which can be done only by an absolute faith in the God who had created them. "I have met quite a number of people," Stephen Radić would say, "who believed in God, and who nevertheless were scoundrels. But I have never met anyone who, without faith, was capable of a purely unselfish and sublime action." Just as they have preserved their national character against invasions of alien ideas, the peasants have kept the faith of their fathers in the teeth of the invasion of materialistic trends.

While Ante Radić had the profound nature of the philosopher, Stephen Radić, though erudite, revealed his greatest talents as an orator whose equal I have never heard. The name of political poet he had acquired was well deserved. His speeches, for the most part entirely extemporaneous, were poetry in form, content and choice of metaphor. It is a great pity that precisely the finest of his speeches are permanently lost, because they were addressed to audiences of only 20 or 30 people at small village meetings, where there was no one to write them down.

Radić continued to preach his gospel for many years, but its tenets are few and simple: The greatest value among men is man himself—aware of being a creature of God, valuing his own dignity and respecting it in others. Man is also a social being, and those who live by themselves and for themselves resemble wolves. The most intimate and important social unit is the family, closely attached to the home, especially among peasants. (Stephen Radić himself married very young, before he went to Paris, and on his return he bought a house—on credit, of course—in the outskirts of Zagreb, yielding to his strong desire to have his own home.) And just as a man is not a whole man without a home of his own, a people are not a nation without their own state. Hence the Croatian Peasant Party was not to be based only on the personal rights of the peasants, but also on Croatian constitutional rights.

At the time of the foundation of the Croatian Peasant Party, Marxian socialist movements were on the upswing all over Europe. Whatever Marx's materialistic dialectic may have meant to their leaders, its message to the ill-educated working classes was twofold, and in it they saw the essence of socialism. First, a just division of all property, and second, the negation of God and rejection of religion. From the very outset Stephen Radić made abundantly clear the sharp difference between the Peasant Party and this type of socialism. He coined two simple slogans. One repudiated the socialist materialism: "Faith in God and unity of the peasants." The other emphasized the eternal basic attachment of the peasant to the land and the home of his fathers: "Let's be ourselves, each keep what's his own, and united defend our Croatian home."

Preparations for the foundation of the Croatian Peasant Party were made toward the end of 1904, and the formal announcement was issued at the beginning of 1905.

Although I had remained in regular contact with the Radić brothers, I did not take part in the formal establishment of the party. Since 1903, when I had obtained my doctor's degree,

I had been practicing at the court. The law read that to become a judge the candidate—having finished his studies at the university and passed the requisite theoretical examinations—had to complete at least one year of court practice and then take an examination in practical juridical matters before a special commission of the Court of Appellation. To obtain access to the Bar, two more years of practice as a lawyer were necessary, which also terminated with an examination before the combined commission of judges and lawyers.

I had hardly begun my court practice when, after eight months, I had to abandon it for a whole year of compulsory military service. The usual length of service was two years, but this was reduced to one year for young men with the *matura,* provided they passed the commissioned officers' examination within that year. I was assigned to the 25th Royal Hungarian Home Defense Infantry Regiment. The Austro-Hungarian Empire maintained a "Joint Army" as well as the Austrian and Hungarian Home Defense. The official language in the Army and in the Austrian Home Defense was German and in Hungarian Home Defense Magyar. Although Croatia had been allotted to the Hungarian Home Defense, there existed on Croatian territory a special division in which the Croatian flag and the Croatian language were official. The Twenty-Fifth was one of its regiments.

I stayed in the service from the autumn of 1903 to the autumn of 1904. Having obtained my commission in the reserve, I returned to juridical practice. In the spring of 1905 I passed the practical juridical examination. I served thereupon as a judge for several months. I left this position to start the two-year lawyer's probation in the provincial town of Krapina. Neither as a probationary judge nor as a soldier was I authorized to participate actively in politics. But as soon as I had become a probationary lawyer at Krapina, I joined the Croatian Peasant Party and started my political career.

CHAPTER IV

Growth of
The Croatian Peasant Party

𝒮 INCE THE EDUCATED adherents of the Croatian Peasant Party could be counted on one's fingers, upon my joining it I was immediately accepted as a member of its central committee and never missed one of its sessions. I also arranged meetings with the peasants living around Krapina, the town where I lived, with a view of explaining to them the party's principles and aims.

Many adversaries made the task of organizing the Croatian Peasant Party difficult; virtually every non-peasant opposed it. Above all, the entire state administration was pitted against it. Although in 1903 Count Khuen Héderváry was, after numerous Croatian revolts, dismissed as *Ban,* there was no perceptible change in the administration. Khuen's successor, Count Theodore Pejačević, looked upon any form of opposition to the state as a crime; but to tell the peasants that their payment of taxes and military service entitled them to a voice in their own destiny was more than a crime, it was sheer madness. The entire police force was directed to use every means to impede the progress of the peasant movement. Although private meetings among small numbers of mutually acquainted persons were perfectly legal, the gendarmes intervened whenever they were notified of such a meeting among peasants. (Public assemblies which granted free admission could not be organized without a special police permit.) We therefore kept the convocation of these small gatherings secret; when the police finally learned about them, everybody had already left. This could easily be managed by peasants unknown to the police who were able to walk freely from one village to another. It became more of a problem to the few educated organizers, well known to the local authorities; we were shadowed as soon as we left our homes. As an assistant lawyer, however, I was often called away from Krapina, and took advantage of these occasions. With my chief's fast horses at my disposal I would drive to the village to which my official duties took me and tell a trustworthy peasant to arrange a secret meeting for the evening, when my work would be finished. The poor gendarmes, when they got wind of it, had to follow me on foot, sometimes as far as ten miles, only to arrive on the scene too late. Several times I was summoned by the chief of police, who warned me against "illegal" meetings. I calmly declared that if I were guilty of something illegal, it was up to him to bring a legal action against me. Of course, he could do nothing of the sort, and our interview would end with his plaintive remark: "It's easy for you, because I am the one who has to answer to my superiors and take all the blame for your doings!"

Stephen Radić, of course, was most dangerously exposed. He could travel nowhere by rail without being watched, and gendarmes often broke up his meetings, using rifles to disperse the audience. At such occasions Radić would shout: "You can only get me out of here in chains or dead!" This display of courage lifted the peasants' morale immensely.

In its persecution of the Croatian Peasant Party, the government had the strong support of the great majority of the intelligentsia, the middle classes, and above all, of the Catholic clergy. The influence exercised by the Church on the peasants was considerable, and a bitter political feud raged with incredible fury between the Peasant Party and the Catholic clergy in the party's first years.

The conflict was by no means based on religious divergences. The Peasant Party's slogan "Faith in God and peasant unity" clearly expressed its disapproval of modern anti-religious liberalism. Moreover, the party's program included the statement: "As to our religion and Church we accept it in its entirety as it has been handed down to us." This meant that the party would not seek to abolish the Concordat signed early in his reign by Franz Josef, which granted important privileges to the Catholic Church. (The Concordat had later been abolished by Austria and Hungary but had remained in force in Croatia.)

Why, then, this enraged propaganda of the Catholic clergy against the Peasant Party? The answer is that it was the instinctive defense of the educated classes who could not and would not accept the despised peasants as their equals, let alone permit them a decisive role in national politics. Before long, the priests were denouncing the party from their pulpits, even accusing the deeply religious Radić of atheism. Strangely enough, a Catholic clerical party, the Croatian Popular Party, had appeared right after the foundation of the Croatian Peasant Party, but few priests joined it. The majority of them, fearing the Peasant Party, preferred the two more numerous formations—the rather liberal party of Josip Frank, and even the new Croato-Serbian Coalition, led by avowed Croatian anticlericals and Orthodox Serbs.

These unscrupulous methods of persecution were modified only after 1911, when Dr. Ante Bauer, professor of theology and former opposition member of the *Sabor*, became coadjutor to the senile Archbishop Posilović. Bauer forbade the use of the pulpits for attacks on the Peasant Party. Outside the church, however, the clergy continued to fight the Party by all possible means, until the dissolution of the Austro-Hungarian Monarchy. After the formation of Yugoslavia the intelligentsia gradually changed their views.

Yet overcoming the fears deeply anchored in peasant minds was more of a challenge to the party than its feud with the government and the intelligentsia in all its complexity. Through the centuries of oppression, persecution and systematic intimidation, the peasants had developed a distressing sense of inferiority. For example:

One winter's night in 1906, I assembled about 30 people in the lonely mountain village of Lobor, which lies in the shadow of an old feudal castle whose noble owners died out long ago. I explained the aim and principles of the party, emphasizing the peasants' rights to equality in national life and the efforts needed to free them from the despotism of the functionaries and the exploitation of the merchants. When I had finished I asked them for their opinion. An old peasant of 80 replied candidly: "My son, all you say sounds well and good, but if old Count Keglević (the last master of the castle) heard you, he'd put you in irons up to your nose." He illustrated his words with a movement of his hand and then went on with resignation: "What's the use? A gentleman is a gentleman and a peasant is a peasant."

On the other hand the combined attacks of clergy and gentry sometimes provoked a positive reaction. My friend and later a fellow representative, Franjo Malčić, who was killed by the Communists, told me once how he had found his way to the Croatian Peasant Party.

"I had returned to my native village from military service," Malčić said, "when I first heard the name of Stephen Radić in church on Sunday. The priest heaped insults on the man. A short time later I went on an errand to our city hall. There I overheard conversations among officials about Radić. Again it was all abuse and insults. A few days later my father sent me to see a lawyer in Zagreb, and he, too, brought the conversation around to Radić, asking me, if he came to our village. When I answered in the negative, he exclaimed, 'That's good! If he ever shows up, drive him away with stones and pickets!'

"I came home, absorbed in thoughts, and asked my father if he had ever heard of Radić. He said 'no,' and so I told him what I had heard. He meditated for a while, pushed his pipe from one corner of his mouth to the other, and finally said: 'You know, son, if the priest, the lawyer and the functionaries are against him, he must be on our side.'

"Encouraged, I went back to Zagreb to see this Radić for myself. He had just sat down for lunch when I called at his house. Right away he asked me to join him, but I declined, telling him I would wait till he had finished. He took his seat at the table and before lifting his spoon made the sign of the cross. This humble gesture belied all the false accusations that he was an atheist.

"Radić and I talked for an hour. I asked him to come see me at the village, where I would recruit some of the more intelligent and serious men for a meeting. He came and talked to us. We all remained devoted to him and his teachings until his death and will belong to the Croatian Peasant Party to our last day."

The Croatian Peasant Party held several thousand meetings in the decade between 1904 and World War I. Twice a year in Zagreb its president, Stephen Radić, convoked the party's executive committee, composed mostly of peasants. After listening to their opinions and suggestions on current political problems, Radić would outline the specific tasks entrusted to the representatives of the various regions.

Each weekend Radić visited one of these regions to hold two or three small meetings. Unfortunately, I rarely had the occasion to accompany him on these trips. I did, however, have many opportunities to hear him address vast public assemblies of 30,000—sometimes 50,000—people. These public discourses, brilliant as they were, never attained the perfection of his more intimate speeches, delivered in small peasant cottages to 10 or 20 quietly listening men. It was there that he developed his pure ideology, unspoiled by the tactical considerations which arose later, when the party became a decisive factor in politics. The seeds sown by Stephen Radić and his collaborators took root so deeply that neither persecutions nor national disasters proved strong enough to wipe out the spiritual legacy of Stephen Radić.

In June 1903, King Alexander Obrenović was assassinated in his neighboring Kingdom of Serbia. His dynasty was replaced by the Karageorgević in the person of King Peter I. This change altered the line of Serbian foreign policy from friendship with the Austro-Hungarian Monarchy to collaboration with Russia. Belgrade's new anti-Austrian policy began to exercise a strong influence not only on the Serbs of Croatia and Bosnia but also on numerous Croatian intellectuals with anti-Austrian and pro-Slav tendencies. The Magyar opposition, the so-called "Kossuthists," fought against Austria, as did all the Serbian parties in Croatia as well as the Croatian Party of Right (Folnegović's partisans) and the progressives.

In 1905, these new allies of the Kossuthists organized a meeting in Rijeka presided over by Frane Supilo, a competent and energetic journalist, who acted as an intermediary between the Magyar opposition and the Croats. They agreed in the "Rijeka Resolution" that the task of the Croats was to fight at the side of the Magyars against Austria. Stephen Radić vigorously opposed this "Neo-Magyaron" policy, as did Dr. Frank's followers and the clericals. He foresaw—correctly— that the Magyar opposition, once in power, would be more intransigent toward the Croats than the Liberal Party then governing.

At the beginning of 1906, the Magyar opposition obtained a majority in the Hungarian elections, and in May the Croato-

Serbian Coalition won the elections for the Croatian Diet by defeating the National Party ("old Magyarons") who had held power for two decades. The Croato-Serbian Coalition had profited from the votes of all the employees in the joint Hungarian service and thus dependent on the new Hungarian government, as well as the votes of many autonomous functionaries. Most independent electors voted for the Coalition, because it had been in opposition.

The Croatian Peasant Party advanced several candidates without sucess. On this occasion, I went to the polls for the first time in my life and voted for the candidate of the Croato-Serbian Coalition, notwithstanding the political differences between our respective parties. The Croatian Peasant Party did not put up a candidate at Krapina, which left me with a choice between an "old" or a "new"' *Magyaron*. As the party rule was to vote for the worst man in the opposition rather than the best partisan of the regime, I did not hesitate in my choice.

After this election, the Croatian Delegation to the joint Hungaro-Croatian Parliament comprised only members of the Croato-Serbian Coalition. The friendship between the Hungarian Government and the Coalition, however, lasted but a short time. The Kossuthists promptly moved to legalize the Magyar tongue as the only official language on the state railways in Croatia. This was already a forceful fact, despite the clearly contrasting text of the Hungaro-Croatian Compromise. The obstruction of the Croatian delegation in Parliament prevented its acceptance as a law. Instead, Parliament issued a pragmatic sanction in favor of the motion which was put in force by an ordinance of the Railway Ministry. The result was exactly the same. To justify this violation the Magyars advanced the questionable argument that the State Railways did not come under joint Hungaro-Croatian affairs, but were exclusively a private property of the Hungarian State.

In 1908, I passed my practicing lawyer's examination and

left Krapina immediately. I settled down as an independent lawyer in the small town of Sveti Ivan near Zagreb.

The year 1908 marked the expiration of the mandate which had given Austria-Hungary the right to occupy Bosnia and Hercegovina for thirty years. The Monarchy soon proclaimed the annexation of these provinces. A new *Ban* of Croatia was nominated, Baron Pavel Rauch, who immediately dissolved the *Sabor* and called for new elections. He did not obtain a single deputy; instead, the Croatian Peasant Party saw three of its members elected, Stephen and Ante Radić and the peasant Vinko Lovreković.

Zagreb, meanwhile, witnessed the conviction on treason charges of a number of leading Serbian politicians, who were condemned to prison terms lasting up to twenty years. Shortly afterward, however, they were pardoned by a new *Ban,* Nikola Tomašić, formerly a pillar of the Khuen Héderváry regime but one of the leading intellectuals in Croatia, who realized that even a shaky compromise is preferable to violence.

Ban Tomašić also obtained the King's preliminary sanction for a more liberal electoral law. The new law lowered the requirement for voting from 25 to 5 florins income tax a year and in the poorest counties as low as 3 florins. The result was that four times as many people voted. The Croatian Peasant Party profited by this new law; it obtained 9 mandates in the elections of 1910 and 11 mandates in 1911. I was a candidate in both elections, but failed of election because the Croatian Peasant Party had not yet taken sufficient root among the people of my district. The middle class and especially the clergy still influenced the population against it.

I vividly recall an incident in the late autumn of 1911 when on foot I toured the Stubica district in which I was a candidate. With another party man, I wandered through rain and mud till I reached a solitary mountain village. About 30 persons had gathered to listen to my program. When I asked them for their comments, an elderly man said:

"What you said is all true and to say anything against it would be a sin. But you see, beside you, we have two other candidates. I listened to them near the church, and truly, no honest person could rebuke them either. How, then, can we poor men tell which of you is the right one? If I were sure who was the right one, believe me, I would carry him on my back across the mountain right into the *Sabor,* regardless of my age. But the trouble is we do not know for whom to vote." And, turning to the listeners he declared: "I suppose, boys, the best thing will be to vote for nobody. Those who think they know better, of course, ought to vote."

On election day, I noticed, with dismay, that no votes came from this village or from many others.

The collaboration of the Croato-Serbian Coalition with the governing Magyar chauvinist party of Kossuth did not turn out happily. A crisis ensued. Following the victory of the Coalition in 1906, the Croatian Diet was dissolved three times, bringing on the elections of 1910, 1911 and 1913. *Bans* came and went. *Ban* Nikola Tomašić had been succeeded by a former administrator, Slavko Cuvaj, who could not win the confidence of the Diet to which he was responsible by law. He had to abandon his office and be content to serve as a royal commissioner. After him, a high official from the Croatian Ministry in Budapest, Baron Nikola Škrlec, also served as a commissioner until he at last contrived a *modus vivendi* with the Croato-Serbian Coalition which led to his nomination as *Ban.* Meanwhile, the Party of Right of Frank split and a separate group was formed under Mile Starčević, nephew of the founder.

Throughout this period, the Croatian Peasant Party had struggled against both the governing Croato-Serbian Coalition and the two opposition parties in the Croatian Diet, that of Dr. Frank and that of Dr. Mile Starčević. Since Khuen's time, the two opposition parties used to agree that the weaker one should never put up a candidate against an apparently stronger one of the other party. This method allowed the opposition to win additional mandates, but did not prevent the deputies of these parties from attacking each other fiercely once they sat in the *Sabor*. The Croatian Peasant Party on principle rejected any advance electoral agreements. Stephen Radić maintained that all parties ought to vote independently, and that necessary compromises concerning national policy had to be arranged in parliament.

Such was the situation on the eve of the elections of 1913, when all the parties compromised except the Croatian Peasant Party. That year I was a candidate in the Dugo Selo district where the Croatian Peasant Party had triumphed in the two preceding elections. Again I had no luck, losing out with 1,000 votes against the 1,050 of my rival. I was not the only member of the party defeated, for its mandates fell from 11 to 3. This was the consequence of stringent preventive measures taken by the other parties. Wherever a victory of the Croatian Peasant Party seemed probable, the rest of the political parties formed a common front in favor of a single candidate. In the Dugo Selo district, where I was a candidate, six rival parties, (Croato-Serbian Coalition, Frank's Party of Right, Mile Starčević's Party of Right, and the clerical, socialist and unionist parties), had concentrated on one common candidate against me.

In retrospect, I can see that I did not fare badly after all. Despite the fact that the government helped our adversaries by permitting some of their electors to vote more than once at different polling places, I received almost as many votes as all other parties together. As we candidates, most of us defeated, gathered in Zagreb, we were a sad, dejected group. All of us, that is, except Radić.

"Excellent," he told his astonished listeners. "You know well, that before leaping over an obstacle you must step back a little to make a running start. You will see, at the next election we shall obtain a majority."

He spoke the truth. In the next election we won a majority in Croatia. But that was seven years later in newly formed Yugoslavia, and in the meantime millions of people throughout Europe were to be killed in war.

CHAPTER V

War

$\mathcal{E}$ARLY ON THE MORNING of June 28, 1914, I awoke in the grip of a strange disagreeable dream: I had seen two heavy metal coffins standing solemnly side by side, then turned away and wandered aimlessly through a maze of subterranean galleries. Not long before I had lost three cherished members of my family: my uncle, my aunt and my grandmother. I therefore feared that this dream might signify more deaths and mourning. When later I found myself in the trenches of war, the full meaning of the dream dawned on me.

In June 1914, I was still living in the small borough of Sveti Ivan Zelina, a few miles from Zagreb, practicing law. June 28 was a Sunday, the first day to provide a taste of the coming summer heat. Right after lunch, I went swimming in the narrow Lonja River nearby. When I returned that evening, my neighbor, the postoffice clerk, broke the news. The Archduke Franz Ferdinand, heir to the throne of Austria-Hungary, and his wife, the Duchess Sophie Hohenberg, had been assassinated at Sarajevo. Though I instantly realized that this would breed incalculable consequences, little did I imagine that it would provoke world war.

For a few days, Sveti Ivan Zelina and neighboring villages discussed the news excitedly. Then things gradually quieted down, and life took its normal course again. The newspapers led me to no conclusion; they merely reflected the oscillating political situation.

On July 25, I went to Zagreb on official business. After completing it, I strolled through the crowded streets, and found myself finally before the headquarters of the local Military Command. Several hundred persons had collected around the building. I was told they expected to be informed momentarily of the final decision which would mean either war or peace. When an acquaintance of mine, a first lieutenant of the Home Defense, happened to leave the building, I hailed him. He turned around, recognized me, and said:

"Go put on your uniform; it's war!"

Next morning, proclamations calling for the mobilization of several army corps covered the walls of the capital. Among those listed was the XIII Territorial Army Corps of Croatia and Slavonia. As I have explained, the military organization of Austria-Hungary included, in addition to the Regular Austro-Hungarian Army, the Austrian Home Defense, the Hungarian Home Defense, and the so-called People's Mobilization. All persons who had completed their military service in the Regular Army or in the Home Defense groups were (for fifteen years after completion of service) to rejoin their units in the event of war. The People's Mobilization called up the reservists from 36 to 50. Those under 42 became part of fighting units, while the remainder formed the so-called Stage Troops. Officers to command People's Mobilization regiments and battalions were chosen from the active or retired officers of the Home Defense; People's Mobilization companies were led by reserve officers of the Home Defense considered capable. I was assigned to the 25th Regiment of the People's Mobilization and given command of the 3rd Company.

The mobilization order required everyone to report to the place of his assignment within 24 hours. I reported on July 27. Before settling down in the barracks, I went to see Stephen

Radić. I found him in the bookstore operated by his wife, Maria.

I asked Radić how he thought the war would end.

"My dear friend," he exclaimed. "I am not a prophet. But I suppose you want to know my wish. In that case, listen well. The only chance for the Croats lies in a total defeat of Austria-Hungary without, however, causing its dissolution. A victory of the Dual Monarchy, allied with Kaiser Wilhelm's Germany, would have catastrophic results for all the peoples within its frame except Germans and Magyars. On the other hand, the crumbling of the Hapsburg Empire would spell disaster for all of them, Germans and Hungarians included."

The significance of these words became clear to me after Hitler seized power in Germany and flung Central Europe's door open to war and, ultimately, to Bolshevism. Thirty years after Radić forecast the serious and irreparable consequences of a dissolution of the Austro-Hungarian Empire, his analysis was echoed by the British statesman, Sir Winston Churchill.

As a simple soldier, I directed myself to the assembly grounds, a large yard framed by the new buildings of the Faculty of Medicine of the University of Zagreb. Several thousand men, answering the call of the People's Mobilization, had already gathered there in civilian clothes; a few Home Defense officers could be seen in uniform. Lieutenant-Colonel Bolto Pintar took command of the regiment. I had no way of knowing why his superiors had considered him second-rate and assigned him to the People's Mobilization. But in time I could not help noticing his bravery and courage and I came to admire him as a most gallant officer. In the course of the war, he rose to the rank of general.

The distribution of the men took place simply. The regimental adjutant, standing on a chair in the midst of the crowd, called out the names of the districts dividing the country. When their district was called, the appropriate men stepped forward and were directed to one of three different corners. Thus a battalion was formed in each corner. I formed the first of them, replacing its still-absent commander. It took me an hour to do so.

Provisions for the men had not yet been supplied, so Colonel Pintar ordered the distribution of silver coins that had been brought in two bags, a half-florin for each man. No account was kept of the money, and I was convinced that an innate sense of honesty prevented the men from asking twice for their pay.

After three days, while the battalions of the Stage Troops were being formed, the supply officer reported for duty, the field kitchen at last began to prepare meals, and the handing out of silver coins ceased. The men were uniformed and given Manlicher rifles, while the Stage Troops were supplied with Werndel rifles of the single-shot breech-loading variety.

The Regular Army and Home Defense units left Zagreb in the first days of the mobilization: our regiment stayed another three weeks. We moved by railway to Bosnia on August 20, and camped on the left bank of the Drina River near its junction with the Sava. After a few days a Magyar regiment took over our position, and we moved to another spot along the Bosut River, on the left bank of the Sava. In the encounter with the Serbs which ensued, I received my baptism of fire. The commander of our regiment showed his fearlessness on this occasion for the first time. When we first heard the enemy's bullets whistle past our ears, I instantly ordered my company to get to the ground, and did likewise. Colonel Pintar meanwhile stood calm and erect in the field, surveying the enemy across the river through his spyglass. After the firing ceased, I indicated my astonishment at his taking such risks, contrary to all military rules. He said quietly:

"My dear Maček, what does it matter? If your fate is to be killed, it will happen whether you stand up or lie down. If it is decided otherwise, you can plant yourself right in front of a gun's mouth and go unscathed. You can't escape your destiny. If you don't die here, you will die in bed some day."

Observing him later in various battles, I had to admit that fate seemed to vindicate his words. He emerged from the war alive, though taken prisoner on the Russian front after having fired his last revolver bullet, but died a few months after the signing of the peace from the effects of a common cold. I have tried to adopt his fatalism in some measure, though without success, to this day.

I have no intention of describing the strategy Austrian General Potiorek was then employing nor of giving myself credit for displays of courage. Let me but say that I participated in the bloody battle near the localities of Pećinci and Popinci, in which we destroyed a whole Serbian division which had crossed the Sava. Victorious, we pursued the foe across the river into Serbia and advanced with more or less severe skirmishes to the Kolubara River. While passing through this territory, I received a minor leg wound and was sent from my regiment to a hospital at Novi Sad at the end of November.

Shortly afterward, the Serbs pierced the Austrian lines, forcing them to withdraw across the Sava into Croatia and beyond the Drina into Bosnia. Subsequently all the People's Mobilization regiments were abolished, and officers as well as soldiers integrated into the Home Defense units. The Stage Troops of the People's Mobilization alone remained in existence.

My wound soon healed, enabling me to return to a formation of the Home Defense Reserve Battalion in Zagreb before Christmas 1914. There, a decoration was conferred on me for "courage in the face of the enemy," followed by promotion to the rank of a first lieutenant.

I had no great desire to go back to the front. Pleading failing eyesight (I suffered from a natural astigmatism), I succeded in being declared medically unfit for front line service.

At the beginning of 1915, the Russian Army conquered part of Austrian Galicia, forced its way through the Carpathian mountains and threatened Budapest. The alarmed authorities hastened to fortify the city. Fatigue-companies were formed of refugees from Galicia to build the fortifications. Instead of Magyar officers who could not understand Slavic languages, Croatian officers were placed in command of these companies. I was one of them. My company, consisting of Poles and Ukrainians, constructed fortifications around Budapest for a month, before being transferred to Pola in Istria to erect fortifications around this Adriatic port. We were there two months when Italy declared war on Austria-Hungary at the end of May 1915. The civilian population for 20 miles around Pola was promptly evacuated. Since it was harvest time, my company had to abandon the fortifications and bring in the harvest.

Now began the most pleasant time of the war for me. The harvest was followed by the vintage, after which we plowed the arable land for the next sowing. I changed from a soldier into a farmer. All the men in the company were peasants and carried out their tasks with pleasure. No efforts were necessary to maintain discipline. This idyll lasted until the autumn of 1916, when, armed with rifles and building tools, we were sent by way of Zagreb, Sarajevo, Kotor, Cetinje, the Lake of Scutari and Scutari to Albania, with orders to construct a road between Lezh and Tirana.

I recall my stay in Albania, from the autumn of 1916 to the spring of 1917, as a rather unpleasant time. In addition to roadbuilding, we had to perform the duties of occupation troops. These were not too difficult. The criminal idea of starting guerilla warfare, in which the principal victims are the aged, the children and the helpless, had not occurred to anyone at that time. When the Austrians occupied the country, all the leading Albanian personalities either left the country or were taken prisoner. Thus the country itself was quite peaceful.

I could ride my horse, with an official gun in its holster as my only weapon, several miles from our camp.

But heavy rains, with hardly an interruption from October 15 to March 15, made our life in army tents unbearable. As direct communications with Austria-Hungary did not exist, we lacked fresh food. The population turned down our worthless Austrian paper money and refused to sell us anything but tobacco. When the military authorities tried to requisition supplies, the Albanians hid their cattle in the mountains. The company's only food consisted of canned meat and dried beans, which in time provoked scurvy, as well as many cases of malaria and typhus. The officers managed to fare somewhat better. They were authorized to purchase weekly rations of salt, sugar, coffee and rum at the military store which they traded to the Albanians for fresh eggs and sometimes even a chicken. Coffee and rum were the most appreciated items. An Albanian peasant brought me a whole lamb for Easter in exchange for half a pint of rum.

Bad food, in addition to unhygienic living quarters, finally caused a real epidemic in my company. Transporting the sick men to the nearest hospital at Scutari, over almost impassable roads, then became my main task. After six months, the company had shrunk from 250 men to a mere ten. I seized the occasion to send these ten to the hospital as well, in order to get myself home.

My stay in Albania did, however, give me an opportunity to observe with great interest the primitive way of life of the local peasants. Agriculture in any sense of the word had no meaning for them. They cultivated corn only, and even that in a very primitive manner. The Mathi River, in summer only 30 or 40 yards wide, swells enormously with the first autumn rains, eventually becoming a mile wide. In spring it falls back again, leaving a deep sediment of fertile mire. The peasant turns this mire with an old-fashioned wooden plough, then plants his corn.Thereupon he leaves everything to providence.

He does not bother about it all summer. In the fall, he is lucky if every third or fourth plant furnishes an undersized ear of corn, to be gathered before the Mathi rises again. The people subsist chiefly on meat and dairy products; keeping cattle is their main occupation.

The Albanian has something that modern people lack most: time. He is never in a hurry. His usual means of transportation is a small horse, furnished with a wooden pack-saddle, which can carry a weight of nearly 300 pounds for miles. An odd little cart is also used for bringing grain to distant mills. It consists of a box on two wooden wheels (a foot thick and two yards in diameter), which will hold 100 pounds of corn or flour, topped by the driver—all pulled by a pair of bisons. The peasant drives his animals by alternating verbal encouragement with the whip, an excellent method as long as the sultry heat does not induce the bisons to make for the first inviting water pool. If so, they bathe at leisure, cooling themselves thoroughly, and no power on earth can make them move before they are ready to go on their own accord. I often watched this take three or four hours. During these forced halts, the driver remains sitting on his cart, calmly smoking a pipe. He has no choice but to await the complaisance of his animals. The Albanian does not know nervousness: time means nothing to him. What he cannot do today he easily postpones until tomorrow.

At present, Albania is under the Communist yoke. But I doubt whether those modern "progressives" have significantly altered the soul of the Albanian peasant. He feels happiest when left in peace. I further venture to say that the economic conditions of Albania are apt to change only when this people, persecuted and oppressed for centuries, is allowed to control its own destiny by choosing its own democratic leaders.

Once my company dissolved, I was anxious to leave Albania as quickly as possible. I told my superiors in Zagreb that my eyesight had improved and that I wished to join a war formation again. This request was promptly granted, and June 1917 found me in Zagreb, attached to a reserve battalion of the Home Defense Regiment.

Before continuing with my life as a soldier, I must add a few lines on the political atmosphere of the time. In the spring of 1915, the Austrian Parliament in Vienna, the Hungarian Parliament in Budapest, and the Croatian *Sabor* in Zagreb were convoked. They remained in session until the end of the war (that is, until the dissolution of the Hapsburg Empire). While on leave, I never missed an opportunity to see Stephen Radić and discuss the political situation with him. Moreover, I read with attention, though sometimes belatedly, the speeches he was making in the Croatian *Sabor*. Though this body was not empowered to make foreign policy decisions, Radić did not hesitate to treat foreign policy. He seized every chance to lash out at Prussia and at Kaiser Wilhelm. On one occasion he expressed his hope that the German Emperor would end as a prisoner on Sakhalin Island.

When the old Emperor of Austria-Hungary, Franz Josef, died in the autumn of 1916, his great-nephew Karl succeeded him on the throne. When I returned from Albania a few months later, Radić was optimistic. He hoped the new ruler would conclude a separate peace with the allies and transform the Dual Monarchy into a confederation of free national states. But it soon became clear that the well-intentioned Karl was too weak to liberate himself from Wilhelm's influence and to resist the chauvinism of the Magyar aristocracy and the middle classes (the Magyar peasant at this time carried even less weight in public affairs than the Croatian). Therefore, Radić thought it necessary to deliver another speech in the *Sabor*. After enumerating the countless benefits the Croats had reaped in the service of the Emperor and the reasons which bound them to the Hapsburg dynasty, he insisted once again on his own loyalty and that of all the Croats to the dynasty. But he concluded as follows:

"And yet, should this loyalty demand that the Croats

and all other Slavs accept the Germans and the Magyars as their rulers, then I am the first to shout: 'Down with the Hapsburgs!' "

This speech, apparently, was Radić's farewell to his vanishing ideal—Danubian Confederation.

After two months devoted to military drill in Zagreb, I went in the fall of 1917 with the first transport to the Russian front in Southeast Galicia. When we reached our destination, the war with Russia was practically over. Peace was signed, and our division ordered to the Italian front in the South Tyrol at the beginning of 1918. I was promoted to captain and given command of the 3rd Battalion of the 26th Karlovac Home Defense Regiment. We participated in the unsuccessful offensive near Assiago, after which we were withdrawn from the front for reestablishment at Pergine. There I saw, for the first and last time, the Emperor Karl as he reviewed our division.

In September 1918, we found ourselves once more at the front, holding a defensive position between Monte Asolone and Ponte Pertica. Then, in October, came the general breakdown. It may be of some interest to learn how it was manifested in our regiment.

The Croatian Home Defense Division was composed of two brigades, one forming the first line, the other posted in reserve about 12 miles in the rear. The two changed positions every three weeks. In October, the Osijek brigade occupied the first line, while the Zagreb brigade, consisting of the Zagreb and Karlovac regiments, stayed in reserve. We passed our time in reserve inspecting our equipment and weapons. A few hours daily were devoted to drill. On October 28, my battalion drilled on the village pasture as usual. At 11 A.M. I took their salute and sent the men to their quarters. Strolling toward the officers' mess, I sat down on a bench outside to wait for lunch. I had been there only a few minutes when the officer on duty approached me in haste to report that the soldiers refused to eat their lunch. I immediately went to their quarters, where complete disorder reigned. In the midst of the tumult, I could hear the men shout that on this sort of food nobody could fight, followed by other remarks in the same vein. I tried to reason with the excited soldiers, assuring them that fresh food transports would soon arrive. In the end, I succeeded in calming them; they ate their lunch.

On returning to the officers' mess, I reported the incident to the regimental commander, Lieutenant-Colonel Toša Malešević. He told me of similar occurrences in two other battalions. He had already communicated the news to the division command, together with a request to send better food immediately; otherwise he could guarantee nothing.

After lunch, I went to my room to rest, but to my great surprise I found my orderly, Joža, tying up my personal belongings into neat parcels. I asked him why, and got the imperturbable answer:

"But, captain, we are going home!"

With some common but effective Croatian curses, I reasserted my authority and ordered him to untie everything and prepare my bed. Shrugging his shoulders, he complied:

"Well, you are the one who commands, I the one who must obey."

I had to lie down for appearance's sake, to maintain my authority, but after ten minutes I got up, belted my saber and went to inspect the quarters of my men again: There, a new wonder greeted me. The tents had been pulled down and the equipment was packed for moving. I summoned the sergeants of the different companies, but none of them answered. Then I noticed that the insignia of all the non-commissioned officers had vanished. Recognizing my men perfectly, nevertheless, I asked one of them:

"What is the meaning of all this?"

No reply! The man went on with his work without ever looking at me. I studied the familiar faces, one after another.

Here was the sergeant of the 9th Company, there a fieldleader of the 12th; they all acted as if I were not present. I left this strange company to its own reflections and went to report to Colonel Malešević. I found him sitting helplessly in his chair, smoking one cigarette after another. As telephone communications had been cut, he had sent the commander of the 1st Battalion, Major Wels, to division headquarters by car. There remained nothing to do but patiently await his return with new orders.

In my quarters, Joža was again packing my things. I gave vent to my displeasure, but he parried smoothly:

"Sir, you are certainly a reasonable man. I am sure you do not want to stay alone among the Italians when we are all going home."

With a shrug of my shoulders I turned away and left him alone.

By this time, our regiment had divided itself into two opposite camps: one including 20 officers, their orderlies and the administrative personnel—150 men in all—and the other numbering all the rest. As evening drew near, the officers assembled in the mess hall. It was useless to try to intervene: therefore, we watched further developments with resignation. From time to time, we sent one or two orderlies or clerks into the other camp to find out what was happening. Thus we learned that the regiment was determined to go "straight home." At dusk, the sound of bugles told us that the men were gathering, and not long afterward the whole regiment advanced with regular steps on the road to the north. The soldiers marched in columns of four with two battalions in the lead, followed by the wagons and the third battalion. When the first men reached the officers' mess, the regiment came to a halt. I sat facing the door when it opened and two soldiers, in full field equipment, entered and saluted. Addressing themselves to me, the two envoys said politely:

"Sir, the regiment asks to be taken home."

I remained silent and pointed to the regimental commander seated opposite me. They repeated the same words to him and got a sharp rebuke in return. The commander violently criticized their conduct, citing the paragraphs of the military regulations which dealt with insubordination and exerting pressure on superiors with the use of arms. At this both of them saluted, turned on their heels and left the room. Ten minutes later they were back, this time without equipment or weapons of any kind. Again one of them told the commander:

"Sir, the regiment *commands* to be led home!"

The lieutenant-colonel jumped up and began to shout. I remember distinctly his tragicomic declaration:

"I am the only one who commands here!"

When he had finished, the men left again. The commander, realizing his mistake too late, presently asked me to go outside and try to induce the rebels to change their minds. I enjoyed a reputation as the most popular officer of the regiment. Besides, my own battalion stood at the head of the column. Unarmed, I climbed on a milestone and began to talk to the men. I tried hard to convince them of the impossibility of carrying out their plans—explaining that we were too far away from our homeland, surrounded on all sides by regiments of Germans and Magyars. This rebellion, I said would bring about the dissolution of the regiment, which would then be incorporated into German and Magyar units. My speech met with some approval and my battalion set about going back to its quarters. But the soldiers of the second battalion, who had not heard me or were unwilling to accept my reasoning, fixed their bayonets and forced my men to keep their ranks. With apparent unanimity, the long column of the rebellious regiment began to move forward again and proceeded on its way home. Leaving me stranded in the middle of the road, the column of four split in half and the men marched two by two around me on each side, as if I had been a statue. Two battalions passed by and then came the wagons. I stepped to the side of the road and watched. At last the wagon carrying my private belongings and Joža came in sight. I shouted to the driver to stop and turn the wagon into the nearby yard of the officers' mess, which he did.

The rest of the regiment moved slowly into the distance, and I returned to the commander to tell him that I had failed in my mission. There was much discussion that evening until we finally parted for the night. Coming to my rooms, all my things greeted me from their familiar places where Joža had again returned them. I had hardly fallen asleep, when I was suddenly awakened. Somebody was knocking on the window with a saber. Jumping out of bed, I recognized the commander. Now quite desperate, he suggested that I pursue the men! Perhaps they would cool off en route and be more apt to listen to reason. In the company of one of the more courageous lieutenants I left on horseback to overtake the deserters. The road soon wound steeply uphill, which slowed us down considerably. Some time after daybreak we reached a lonely house on a mountain pass. From its inhabitants we learned that our regiment had stopped there two hours before; the soldiers had drawn water from the well and then moved on. We could merely retrace our path and admit failure, for it did not look as if the men had cooled off. Since there was no hurry, we fed the tired horses and granted them a few hours' rest. Wrapped in warm blankets, we, too, soon fell asleep.

The next morning, on the way back, what had happened became apparent to us. The whole Austro-Hungarian Army had broken down, and our regiment was just one of many which had abandoned their posts. The road was thronged with hundreds and hundreds of deserters from all sorts of formations and places—men on foot, horseback or wagons going in the same direction as our regiment. At our quarters, we heard that Major Wels had returned from headquarters and brought an order for us to cross the Alps and swiftly reach the Tyrolean borough of Predazzo, where the regiment awaited us.

A certain General Munich, just arrived from Zagreb, met us there with the news that the Croatian *Sabor* had proclaimed all ties with Hungary severed. He could not tell what would follow; as a soldier he thought it no concern of his. But, he added, it was our duty as officers to lead the men home as quickly as possible.

Our runaway regiment had meanwhile been completely "bolshevized"; the regiment, the battalions and the companies each had their respective commissars. When my battalion assembled before me at the call of a bugle I told them what was happening in Zagreb, that the war had ended, and that our only problem consisted in getting home as soon as possible. I said that, if they wished me to lead them there, they would have to observe the same discipline as on the first day of war. Otherwise they could do as they pleased, for all I cared. I would find an easier way home without them. They accepted my proposition eagerly and promised to maintain strict discipline. To show they meant it, they at once gave me an example of their goodwill by forming ranks, exercising and presenting arms under my command, then marched past in files. The next day we undertook the journey toward our homeland; we first struck north across a second Alpine pass. Two other commanders had re-established order in their respective battalions in the same manner as I had.

I later discovered that the revolt had been planned in advance and precisely executed. The ringleaders were former non-commissioned officers who had voluntarily surrendered on the Russian front. Upon being exchanged and returned home, they were demoted and sent to the front as common soldiers.

We covered about 25 miles a day, advancing chiefly by night when the roads were less blocked by the remnants of the Austro-Hungarian Army hurrying homeward in utter confusion.

In order to keep up our supplies, we took what we could in the way of wagons and horses from the deserters of other smaller regiments. At one point we also confiscated the provisions stored in a military depot, loading our wagons with plenty of rice and flour. In addition, I requisitioned from the elder of every village we passed a sufficient quantity of beef, as well as hay for the horses. I countered protests and demands for payment with the words:

"I have no money to pay, but here is a certificate for executed requisition." They could do little but give in.

On the other side of the Alps we descended into the valley of the Drava. When we reached the source of the river, Lieutenant-Colonel Malešević left us and headed for Budapest to join his family. His place as commander was taken by the senior Captain, Ivan Murković. Traversing the length of the Geissler Valley we marched into Kranjska Gora in Slovenia on November 18. There a few arguments with the local National Committee finally won us railway transportation from nearby Jesenice to Karlovac. We arrived home on November 20. Our soldiers, safely back from the Italian front, stopped at the barracks just long enough to deposit their rifles, then left for their homes without asking permission from anyone. The first days of December found me reunited with my old parents in Zagreb. My military career was over.

CHAPTER VI

Birth of Yugoslavia

*P*EOPLES AND PROVINCES are not to be bartered away from sovereignty to sovereignty as if they were chattels and pawns in a game, even the great game, now forever discredited, of the balance of power." With these words, contained in his message to the Senate on January 22, 1917, the President of the United States, the great idealist Woodrow Wilson, emphasized the one policy that promised to assure the lasting peace so much desired at the end of World War I.

Unfortunately, before Wilson entered the scene, the diplomats of Tsarist Russia, France, Britain and Italy had arranged a secret pact, called the "London Treaty." This pact, when applied, divided Croatia and Slovenia between Italy and Serbia "as if they were chattels and pawns in a game."

The position of the so-called Yugoslav Committee, which had been formed in exile, was a difficult one from the start. Its leading personalities, the famous sculptor Ivan Meštrović, Ante Trumbić and Frane Supilo, were all Croats from Dalmatia. Contrary to the opinion of Stephen Radić, this committee had since the outbreak of the war favored the dissolution of the Hapsburg Empire and the union of all the South Slav provinces of the Dual Monarchy with the Kingdom of Serbia. This view also prevailed among a large part of the Croatian

76

intelligentsia. Nobody bothered to inquire about the views of the broad masses of the people.

The members of the Yugoslav Committee, however, were determined to reserve a distinct identity for the different peoples entering the union. This view met with the forceful opposition of the Serbian Royal Government, headed by the shrewd and experienced statesman, Nikola Pašić. Annexation of territory from the Hapsburg monarchy struck Pašić as a natural Serbian war aim. Since in this matter he was strongly supported by Tsarist Russia, he refused even to talk with the members of the Yugoslav Committee. Only when the March 1917 Revolution had overthrown Tsarism did Pašić adopt a more conciliatory attitude, as a result of pressure from the British Foreign Secretary, Sir Edward Grey. Pašić summoned the representatives of the Yugoslav Committee to a conference on Corfu Island, then the seat of the Serbian Government-in-exile, and after a month of strenuous deliberations, the so-called Corfu Declaration was signed on July 22, 1917.

This declaration could in no way be acceptable to the Croats, as it deprived Croatia and Slavonia of even those fragments of sovereignty which the country had preserved under the Magyars. Nevertheless, Pašić went further and declared a short time later that he had been forced to this declaration "by circumstances," and that he "had signed it only to show a more agreeable face."

The Croato-Serbian Coalition, which then held a majority in the Croatian *Sabor,* set about preparing the ground for the unification with Serbia of all South Slav lands which had belonged to the Hapsburg Empire. Svetozar Pribičević, an energetic Serb from Croatia, became the leader of the Serbo-Croatian Coalition. His politics revealed considerable caution. The Croato-Serbian Coalition did not reveal any desire for change until the Hapsburg Monarchy was doomed. It did not act, for example, when the Croatian and Slovenian members of the Austrian Parliament, under the leadership of the

Slovene, Antun Korošec, and the Croat, Matko Laginja, proposed in Vienna the unification of all lands occupied by Slovenes, Croats and Serbs in a sovereign state under the Hapsburg Dynasty. But when the Dual Monarchy had collapsed, and delegates had assembled in Zagreb on October 6, 1918 to found the National Council of the Slovenes, Croats and Serbs, then the Croato-Serbian Coalition joined in the movement. Svetozar Pribičević quickly assumed the leadership of this National Council.

Three weeks later, on October 29, the Croatian *Sabor* announced the rupture of all state relations with Hungary and Austria. Dalmatia, Croatia and Slavonia, together with Medjumurje and Rijeka, were proclaimed one independent state. It was announced that, on a basis of national unity, the Serbs, Croats and Slovenes would combine their ethnic territories to form a common state, without regard to territorial or national boundaries. Zagreb was delirious with enthusiasm. People, especially the younger ones, realized but a single thing: liberation from Austro-Magyar oppression was theirs. They did not as yet perceive the trap concealed in the phrase *national unity without regard to territorial or national boundaries.*

The peasants remained skeptical and were reserved from the start. I had noticed this even during our retreat from Italy, when I informed the soldiers about Croatia's separation from Hungary. Several privates, peasants in ordinary life, came to me for more details. One of them asked me: "Do you think, captain, that things will be better from now on? Won't the Serbs oppress us now?" I could not answer him; the words of the French philosopher Montesquieu came to my mind: "I much prefer to talk with a peasant; he is not learned enough to be able to arrive at a wrong conclusion."

Soon I found out on my own that this illiterate peasant had reasoned correctly. Immediately after the proclamation of the independent state of Dalmatia, Croatia and Slavonia, including Medjumurje and Rijeka, the new state had joined a kind of federation, formed by all the South Slav provinces of the former Hapsburg Empire, under the name of the "State of the Slovenes, Croats and Serbs." The supreme power was exercised by the National Council, presided over by the leader of the Slovenian Populist Party, Antun Korošec. Its two vice-presidents were Svetozar Pribičević and a Croat, Ante Pavelić.*

The State of the Slovenes, Croats and Serbs opened negotiations with the Kingdom of Serbia as an equal partner, and at the end of these negotiations Korošec and Trumbić signed a joint declaration in Geneva with Serbian Premier Pašić. It was formally agreed by both parties that the Serbian Government and the National Council would exercise full authority over their respective territories until a new and common constitution was voted. Four days had hardly passed after the signing of this pledge when the Serbian Government notified Korošec and Trumbić that it rejected the Geneva Declaration.

Meanwhile, the energetic Pribičević in Zagreb lost no time in promoting the unconditional union of all the South Slav provinces with Serbia in a single, centralized state called "the State of the Serbs, Croats and Slovenes." This project was successfully carried in the National Council of Zagreb on November 24 and officially proclaimed as a fact by Regent Alexander of Serbia in Belgrade on December 1, 1918.

Stephen Radić made a final attempt to deflect the members of the National Council from this decision by proposing his own motion, conceived in the spirit of the Geneva Declaration. It obtained a single vote, that of Dragutin Hrvoj, a *Sabor* member belonging to the Croatian Party of Rights.

Following this event, Radić left the National Council and carried his struggle for Croatia's freedom to the peasants. With growing misgivings they had watched these important changes take place and, a few weeks later, they had begun to assert their pronounced dissatisfaction.

At that time I sold my lawyer's office at Sveti Ivan Zelina,

* Not to be confused with the Ante Pavlic of Ustasa notoriety.

thus acquiring a certain sum of disposable money, and settled in Zagreb so as to be able to assist Radić in his work. While talking to people in the capital, I could not fail to observe that the enthusiasm of October 29 had notably cooled off after six weeks. Zagreb still seemed stirred by an enthusiastic current but this was artificially created in the streets by students who for the most part were Serbs from Croatia or Croats from Dalmatia. They were encouraged by sailors of the former Austro-Hungarian Navy, brought expressly for this purpose to Zagreb by the National Council. All sorts of demonstrations were organized daily, which by evening would take a menacing and even terroristic turn; few people still dared to state their views openly.

In the villages the situation was quite different. The peasant with his acute instincts sensed danger immediately. He felt, that, after shaking off Magyar domination, the Croats were inevitably sliding downward again, to succumb this time to Serbian hegemony. The peasants, who had shed the most blood in the war, came to regard, rightly or wrongly, emperors and kings as personally responsible for such wars, and thus had come to favor the establishment of a republic. Suddenly the peasantry, having just been freed from one dynasty, was being forced into the service of another—and one, to boot, which it considered inferior to the first.

In all the villages of Croatia and Slavonia, a spiritual revolt broke out, and the cheers that could be heard had but one meaning: "Long live the Republic!" Men, women and children alike participated in these demonstrations. A clever official tried to silence them by sending Serbian Army units to the Croatian villages. The soldiers started to beat the peasants with their gun-butts, shouting coarsely: "Here, take King Peter's greetings!" To the cries of "Long live the Republic" was promptly added: "Down with King Peter."

Relatively few educated professionals had belonged to the Croatian Peasant Party before the war. Now, many young men who had just finished their academic studies joined us, among them August Košutić, Juraj Krnjević, Ivan Pernar, Josip Torbar and Žiga Šol. We were kept busy from morning to night meeting the demands of the people who wanted to hear Radić speak at public assemblies, or else send a representative to explain the aims of the Party.

Meanwhile, a "Temporary National Assembly" had been set up in Belgrade. Although it purported to represent all the territories of the State of the Serbs, Croats and Slovenes, this was not an elected assembly. Nevertheless, representatives of all the prewar parties from each province were invited. Thus, credentials as deputies were issued to Stephen Radić, Dragutin Kovačević, a member of the *Sabor,* Josip Predavec, an agronomic engineer, and myself. We refused, however, to participate in this assembly. Instead, Radić summoned delegates from every corner of Croatia and Slavonia to a general meeting of the party in Zagreb at the beginning of February, 1919. Here was formulated a demand for the creation of a Neutral Peasant Republic of Croatia; the intention was to submit this resolve to the Peace Conference in Paris. Printed forms were distributed in the villages in order to collect signatures, and within six weeks 260,000 people had signed.

The death of Ante Radić on February 10, 1919 was a heavy blow to the party. And, about a month after the death of his brother, Stephen Radić was arrested. For a while he was held at the police-station, then transferred to the prison of the Court of Zagreb, under the direct vigilance of the police force. The duty of sending the memorandum to the Paris Peace Conference fell on me.

Not knowing the French language, I needed the help of a young priest from the Archbishopric of Zagreb, Ljudevit Kežman. Radić had drafted the memorandum himself and then sent it piece by piece to his wife Maria through a friendly policeman. Maria Radić had collected the pieces, assembled them and, with the aid of her daughter Mira (later Mrs. August Košutić), copied it. Josip Predavec and I signed it, while Kežman took it on himself to find a way to send it to the Peace Conference. We could expect no support whatsoever from the French Military Mission in Zagreb—the Quai d'Orsay had sided openly with the Serbian regime. Kežman established contact, therefore, with the Italian Military Mission at Ljubljana. The Italians agreed not only to send the memorandum and the list of signatories to Paris, but also to help Predavec and Kežman travel personally to the Peace Conference.

Our preparations were prematurely discovered by the government. Both Predavec and Kežman were arrested, the former in Ljubljana, the latter at the Zagreb railway station. The memorandum and signatures, meanwhile, passed the frontier safely in the hands of an Italian officer. The next morning, I, too, was arrested.

Predavec, who had been imprisoned at Maribor, managed at the investigation to justify his presence in Ljubljana by mentioning his attendance at an agricultural congress there. Since nothing could be proved against him, he was released, though restricted to his native village of Dugo Selo. I never learned where the list of signatures finally ended, because when I was released from prison months later, it was immaterial.

Kežman and I were kept in the military jail for investigation, then, after fourteen days, transferred to the prison of the Court of Zagreb. The proceeding against us, indictment for high treason, was based on the Serbian Criminal Law. The proceedings appeared to be conducted fairly. Since we did not yet rank as important political personalities, we were able to maintain contact with the outside world without much hindrance. The investigation was terminated after one hearing, and the choice lay then between indictment and dismissal of the charges.

The criminal code then used required the police to place an arrested suspect at the immediate disposal of the court.

The investigating judge could then order either his release or further detention. If the latter, the investigating judge compiled a summary of the case taking into account all the recommendations made—both by the public prosecutor and the defense. This investigation often lasted several months, sometimes a year. Upon its completion, the public prosecutor would prepare an indictment, on the basis of which the defendant would be tried by the Court Senate, composed of five qualified judges. Should the public prosecutor fail to indict within eight days after the end of the investigation, the suspect would be immediately set free.

At the time we committed our crime, the State of the Serbs, Croats and Slovenes had not yet been formally recognized: thus, no conscientious court could have found reason to detain us. To elude this natural result, the investigation documents regarding us were sent to the Military Court, on the pretext that this court alone had competence in our case. While the documents lay quietly in the Military Court, Kežman and I continued to inhabit a prison cell of the Court of Zagreb. By extraordinary chance, Radić was confined in the same prison, and even occupied the same floor. Thanks to the indulgence of the prison guards and the policemen, we frequently joined him to discuss the latest events. Once again I had the opportunity to admire his rare intellect and political ability.

Each morning Radić received a pile of Croatian, Serbian, German and French newspapers. His sight was so bad that he could not recognize a man standing two feet away from him, and to read the paper, he had to hold it a few inches from his eyes. Nevertheless, he managed to go through all his papers; he believed that books ought to be read, newspapers only looked over. He always passed the pile of them on to us afterwards. We found all the news and articles of some importance marked with a red pencil and often commented on in the margin.

We had spent more than five months in prison, when the

Military Court at last decided it had no jurisdiction in our case. The Court of Zagreb finally freed Kežman and me, though not Radić. We recovered our freedom on paper only, for they transferred us first to the police prison, less comfortable than the one we had left, then to the District Office of Zagreb for further confinement ordered by the police.

The District Office was the administrative and police center for the villages surrounding the Croatian capital. As soon as we arrived there, I knew our stay would not be too terrible. Two rooms, one larger than the other, led into a small corridor, where a toilet and wash-basin, provided with running water, had been installed. (In the prison of the Court of Zagreb, water for drinking and washing was kept in the same bucket, while the obligatory urinal stood in a corner for personal needs.) In the larger of the two rooms were lodged about 30 peasants from the nearby village of Markuševac, to be detained for two or three days for political offenses or for causing forest damage. The smaller room had been reserved for Dr. Kežman and me. Our supervisor was the District Office janitor, a former gendarme, Djuro Hruškar. Like all the common people, he declared himself sympathetic to our cause. He never locked the door of our room, the doors in the corridor, or even the main entrance to the building. There were no beds in our cell, but we laid out bedding of our own on the wooden bunks, which made them quite acceptable.

Furnished with booklets, pamphlets and leaflets from the Radić book store, I started to train the peasant prisoners in the adjoining room and soon had them formed into an organization. Once back home again, these peasants did all they could to contribute to its expansion. It was the custom to jail peasants who had been sentenced by police magistrates during the winter months, when their farms required least attention. It so happened that peasants from practically every village in the Zagreb District served short terms in this prison while I was there, which enabled me to organize the entire district within the shelter of a dry room, without the wearisome walks through mud and snow.

Janitor Hruškar became very dear to me, from the time, a few days after my arrival, when he helped me call on my sick mother, whom I had not seen in many months. All he did was accompany me in the evening to my parents' house. After this first visit, he said casually: "I guess you don't need me any more now; I'm sure you know your way there and back alone." From then on, I went regularly by myself. Of course, my visits were somewhat prolonged and, when I would return to prison, I had to knock on the main door and Hruškar had to come down to open it. After several days he had had enough. "I have to get up early in the morning," he said, "and I can't sit up to wait for you. Here is a key to the prison; I am sure you will be able to get in by yourself."

Hruškar also allowed Kežman and me to go for daily walks, although, in order not to be seen by some official, we had to await the end of the usual office hours. Our walks remained restricted to the area around the District Office Building, situated at the time on the city's outskirts.

These easy arrangements were to last a month and a half. Then, one day, Hruškar came and announced with a sad face that he had been discharged as our guard, and that peasants would not be interned in this prison any more. Another room, once reserved for women but long unoccupied, was being prepared to accommodate new prisoners who were expected. All of us would be placed under police guard.

That evening, we heard the announced prisoners being brought in. Shortly afterward, a key turned, and the door of our small corridor was locked securely. When all was quiet, I left the room on tiptoe; through a loop-hole in the door which separated our corridor from the upper stairs, I saw a heavily armed policeman posted on the outer side of it. Next I went to inspect the room abandoned by the peasants. To my surprise, Ivo Stožir, Judge of the Court of Zagreb, and Viktor Benković, a high official from the Municipality of Zagreb, greeted me there. They had been arrested for conspiracy to organize a strike against the devaluation of the crown, which had reduced wages to a fearfully low level. Six post-office employees were being held in the "women's" room for the same reason.

The new order in the prison was not unbearable. Every morning and afternoon, we ten prisoners would descend into the small yard for the habitual promenade. The police did everything to prevent contact between us and the outside world, but this was difficult: the same building not only housed a number of offices, which were constantly invaded by the public in need of legal certificates and so on; it also served as residence for many officials who had private apartments in it. My only great disappointment was that my visits to my sick mother had become impossible. The family cook, nevertheless, brought me meals from home twice a day. Moreover, it did not take me long to contrive a plan to make the visits to my mother possible again.

The policemen who examined clothes, underwear and other articles sent to prisoners usually did a very superficial job, unless an inspector forced them to be more thorough. Thus, a strong steel file and a solid rope were smuggled to me, undetected. I now possessed the necessary tools to execute my plan. The inspector made his last rounds at 9 P.M. to make certain we were all in our cells. He then left, locking the door behind him. In the corridor, halfway between our cells and the "women's" room, a policeman stood watch. A second was posted in the yard. The window of my cell overlooked the deserted fields, where no guard had been placed. After the inspector had gone, I began to file on the iron bar of the window. The noise it provoked threatened to give me away, for the guard was bound to hear this grating sound sooner or later. But Benković obligingly came to my rescue. He seated himself close to the door and began to sing in an agreeable and sonorous voice, accompanying himself with his guitar. For two hours on each of two evenings he sang one tune after another in waltz time to the great enjoyment of the policeman outside, while I filed away on the iron bar to the harmonious and regular rhythm of the bass notes produced by the guitar. At the end of the second evening, the bar gave way under the file and could be pulled out. The opening thus obtained was big enough to let me through. During the day, I put the bar back in its proper place and fastened it with wire. A bag of apples conveniently hid the telltale marks. Every second or third night I could now, by means of the rope, reach the deserted fields below. On returning from my visits, I climbed back into my cell as I had left it. This was relatively easy for me; I was only 40 and in my younger days I had taken great pleasure in athletics. For six weeks, I continued to see my mother completely unhampered.

The government in Belgrade changed, and a Croat from Istria, Matko Laginja, was named *Ban* of Croatia. As a result, those accused of organizing the strike were released without delay; the police guards were relieved, and Djuro Hruškar reinstalled as supervisor. Stephen Radić obtained his liberty a short time later, and finally, on March 1, 1920, Kežman and I were also set free.

At the beginning of 1920, when the few intellectual members of the Peasant Party (Radić, Predavec, Kežman, Pernar and others) were imprisoned, the peasant members of the party's central committee called a secret meeting at the village of Stupnik, near Zagreb. They dismissed the two vice-presidents of the party, Tomo Jalžabetić (peasant) and Benjamin Šuperina (lawyer), for their laxity, and replaced them with Josip Predavec and myself, whom they considered not only younger, but more active and, above all, more intransigent politically.

As soon as we had recovered our freedom, we took up our former political activities with greater animation than ever. The popularity of the party had so grown that small meetings became impossible; large public assemblies had to be organized to satisfy crowds which sometimes numbered tens of thousands of people. Radić spoke only at three such assemblies during March, because after the third one, held in a suburb of Sisak on March 21, he was rearrested. The new arrest only strengthened the movement. Radić had to face the court immediately and, since the government had meanwhile replaced all the former judges with more docile ones, it was obvious that he would be condemned. I acted as his defense counsel and as such could visit him in prison.

On April 11, I summoned the public to an assembly in Zagreb. About 20,000 people heeded the call. But that morning *Ban* Laginja forbade us to proceed further, on the pretext that the meeting would endanger public safety. I went to see him personally to try to change his mind, but he repeated that he would not permit the meeting to take place either in Zagreb or its immediate vicinity, and would use military force to disperse it if necessary. Finally, he consented to the holding of the meeting at Podsused, some six miles from the capital. After I had announced the *Ban's* decision to the gathered people, the whole crowd together made the two-hour march to Podsused.

Radić was convicted and sentenced to two and a half years in jail, and this conviction poured fresh fuel on the smoldering fire. Insurrection was in the air throughout Croatia. The first provocation was apt to start a riot. At this point the very primitive Serbian military organization issued an order that all animals which might be mobilized in a military emergency, such as horses and oxen, had to be branded. Everywhere, the people reacted with instant revolt; gendarmes were disarmed, railroad tracks damaged, and in Sveti Ivan Zelina the overzealous district chief was assassinated. The Army then moved into action. Local battles were fought here and there, as the peasants still possessed the arms brought back from the front. But the Army soon succeeded in scattering the improvised peasant opposition. Mass arrests followed, to the extent that I feared a second, more serious insurrection. It took revocation of the order to brand animals and the announcement at the end of August of elections for a constituent assembly to quiet the people. The thought of the coming elections—to be held on November 28, 1920—had a miraculously soothing effect on everybody.

The electoral law, devised by a temporary assembly, was just. The suffrage was extended to all men over 21 years of age. The deputies were chosen by counties, with one seat for every 30,000 inhabitants; this law contained one peculiarity, though. A fourth of the proposed list of candidates had to show an academic education; these were called the "qualified" candidates. This requirement had been added to prevent the constituent assembly from being dominated by the peasants, who were regarded as too much to the left. Of course, this was nonsense, because the peasants are the least tempted to become leftists: long political experience has taught me that it is the educated, or semi-educated people, who are most apt to become extremists either of the left or of the right. But this stipulation in the electoral law compelled us to nominate several men with an academic background whose political views were far removed from the peasant ideology, and who later proved troublesome when the party fell victim to persecution.

The elections for the constituent assembly were honestly conducted, and the government did nothing to stop pre-electoral agitation. As far as I know, no complaints were made, except in the Vojvodina and in various districts of Serbia.

The Croatian Peasant Patry nominated candidates only on the territory of Croatia and Slavonia. The party did not yet have organizations in Dalmatia, Bosnia and Hercegovina. In competition with six other political parties from Croatia, our party obtained an absolute majority. I was elected, for the first time, as a "qualified" candidate, supported by approximately 85% of all votes cast. On the very day of the election, Radić was released; his case, pending at the court of appeals, was simply "abolished."

Although the State of the Serbs, Croats and Slovenes had been recognized in the Peace Treaty of Versailles, the people themselves refused to do so. The question of whether the elected deputies would form part of the constituent assembly had been raised before the elections. To this, the unanimous answer, from all parts of the country, was that the elected deputies were not to join it. Many among them had been obliged to promise solemnly beforehand they they would renouce the right to go to Belgrade.

The elected candidates of the Croatian Peasant Party gathered in Zagreb on December 7, 1920, proclaimed themselves "the Croatian National Representation" and formally refused to participate in the constituent assembly. Their decision was made known the following day at a large public meeting in which the peasants, for the first time, had been joined in great numbers by Croats of the middle classes. It was estimated that 100,000 persons were present. I thought the estimate exaggerated. Because of my usually more moderate estimates of such crowds President Radić liked to call me a "defeatist." Later, when we would report to him on various activities, he asked me: "How many people were present at your gathering?" If I replied that there had been 3,000, he would be sure to retort: "When you say 3,000, it must have been 10,000." Generally, the opposition papers the next day published an estimate somewhere between our two guesses.

Our party's strongest opposition in Croatia was the Democratic Party, with the Serbian politician Ljuba Davidović as its president. In Croatia, however, the true leader of this party was Svetozar Pribičević. All the Serbs from Croatia, as well as a considerable number of Croatian intelligentsia, belonged to it. They were known as "Orjunaši," after their fighting organization "Orjuna" (Organization of Yugoslav National-

BIRTH OF YUGOSLAVIA 91

ists). Because of their terroristic acts, they gained a bad reputation.

While we devoted our time to developing the Croatian Peasant Party's numerous organizations, the constituent assembly in Belgrade voted the new constitution on June 28, 1921. For approval, this constitution had to obtain a qualified majority, according to a particular agreement concluded in exile during the war. Pašić interpreted this to mean "at least one more than half" of all elected members, whether present or not. To avert the danger of failure, Pašić promised the Moslem members from Bosnia and Hercegovina, for the most part large landowners, that the agrarian reform, then affecting them, would be modified. Thus, he secured 18 additional votes and the constitution was accepted by a scant majority. After the ancient Orthodox calendar, June 28 was St. Vitus' Day and the constitution became known, after it, as *Vidovdanski Ustav*. (St. Vitus' Day is a Serbian national holiday in memory of the battle of Kosovo between Serbs and Turks in 1389.)

The newly voted constitution could be called quite liberal, although unacceptable to the Croats. There was in it a marked trend toward centralization, which eliminated the historic provinces of Croatia, Slavonia and Dalmatia, Bosnia and Hercegovina, and Montenegro. The country was divided into 33 departments, and local authority was negligible; local affairs were strictly supervised by the central government in Belgrade. Croatia and Slavonia were divided into four districts, Dalmatia into two, while Bosnia and Hercegovina formed six. The *Ban* of Croatia and Slavonia, reduced in 1919 to a simple executor of orders from the central power, made way for a royal governor whose chief duty was to liquidate the remains of Croatia by transferring authority in all matters to ministries in Belgrade. Thus, Croatia, a nation for a thousand years, had been wiped from the map, but continued to live on, ineffaceable, in the souls of its people, the Croats.

CHAPTER VII

Early Struggles With Belgrade

$\mathcal{F}$OR TWO YEARS, I had given myself wholly to politics, living on the proceeds of the sale of my law practice at Sveti Ivan Zelina. When this source began to dry up, I opened a new practice in Zagreb, and henceforth divided my time between politics and law. After a long illness, my mother passed away on February 5, 1922; my father and I went on living together in the same house.

After voting the St. Vitus Constitution, the Constituent Assembly had proclaimed itself the National Assembly and remained in session to prepare new laws. When it dissolved, just before Christmas 1922, new elections were announced for the spring of 1923. This time, the Croatian Peasant Party put forth candidates not only in Upper Croatia and Slavonia but in Dalmatia, Bosnia and Hercegovina as well. Campaigning scarcely proved necessary, since the peasantry of Dalmatia, as well as the Catholic peasants of Bosnia and Hercegovina, spontaneously joined our party. They selected candidates from among themselves and sent them to Zagreb to be confirmed by President Radić. The local leaders understood that the large masses of the population would vote for only those candidates approved by the President. When I said that in Bosnia and Hercegovina the Catholic peasants joined our party, this meant that the Orthodox peasants clung to the Serbian political parties, while the Moslems backed their own Yugoslav Moslem Organization. Our party won 73 seats at this election, but we again decided to abstain from the National Assembly.

The electorate had sent to the Assembly in largest numbers members of the following parties:

The Serbian National Radical Party led by Nikola Pašić;
The Yugoslav Democratic Party headed by Ljuba Davidović;
The Slovenian Populist Party (clerical) of Antun Korošec;
The Yugoslav Moslem Organization of Mehmed Spaho; and
The Serbian Agrarian Alliance, whose leader was Joca Jovanović.

Particularly interesting, from the viewpoint of the Croatian Peasant Party, were the Slovenian Populist Party of Dr. Korošec, a Catholic priest, and the Yugoslav Moslem Organization headed by Dr. Spaho.

Although the overwhelming majority of the Slovenes, including Korošec himself, clearly opposed a centralized state, Korošec and his party strove to avoid sharp conflicts with Belgrade. Instead he saw to it that either he or one of his men was in the cabinet, no matter who headed it. When I had occasion to make his acquaintance more closely in 1924, I told Dr. Korošec that the Croats condemned this opportunistic attitude. He answered me to this effect:

"I understand and respect the Croats. The territory of Croatia and Slavonia was recognized under the Austro-Hungarian Monarchy as a political nation, and succeeded in preserving its autonomy to a considerable extent. The Croats, therefore, have lost so much to the new state that their unyielding opposition to it is most understandable. But you should understand us, too. We lost nothing—on the contrary, we have achieved noteworthy gains under the new order. Under Austria-Hungary, we Slovenes did not have our own high schools and a Slovenian university seemed a utopian dream. The Croats had their own schools from first grade through university, Croatian was the official language on Croatian territories. In the Slovenian provinces, German had been imposed. In the new State, the Slovenes received all they had previously lacked, high schools and a university to boot. As long as my party is represented in the government, Belgrade will allow us to administer Slovenia according to our own wishes. Although I realize that this centralizing system cannot maintain itself very long, I consider it wise to profit from the circumstances as they exist and to obtain a few favors in the bargain."

Another factor motivating Dr. Korošec was his opinion that only a union of all Serbs, Croats, and Slovenes possessed enough strength to liberate the half million Slovenes (and a considerable number of Croats) in Gorica, the Trieste area, Istria and a part of Carniola fallen to Italy through the Treaty of Rapallo.

The Yugoslav Moslem Organization of Mehmed Spaho also avoided conflict with the governing circles of Serbia, but for different reasons. Serbia had suffered through four centuries under the Turkish yoke. The deep hatred that the Serbs had cultivated for all things Turkish did not abate after they achieved independence. This hatred extended to all Moslems, whom they quite simply identified as "Turks," although the Moslem population in Bosnia and Hercegovina had ancient roots in these provinces. When Belgrade after the war achieved mastery over Bosnia and Hercegovina, the Moslems logically began to fear Serb persecution, and joined the ranks of the powerful Moslem Organization for self-defense. They named their organization "Yugoslav," regardless of the fact that in the Belgrade Parliament in 1924, all the deputies of the Moslem Party insisted on their Croatian nationality, with the single exception of Dr. Spaho himself, who declared himself a Yugoslav.

Despite their national feelings for Croatia, however, the members of the Yugoslav Moslem Organization also pursued a policy of opportunism and participated in nearly all the interwar governments.

Opportunism failed both these groups, however, for a short period after the elections of 1923. Because of the abstention of the Croatian Peasant Party, Pašić's Radicals had a clear majority in Parliament. He formed a one-party cabinet and thus forced the Slovenian Populist Party and the Yugoslav Moslem Organization into the opposition.

This opposition soon made overtures to the Croatian Peasant Party, in the hope of persuading us to enter the National Assembly and thus to undermine Pašić's position. The wily Pašić himself, however, communicated at once with President Radić through the Royal Governor in Zagreb, Dr. Ernest Čimić, and Radić sent Juraj Krnjević and myself to Belgrade for informal talks with the Prime Minister in an effort to find some *modus vivendi* between Croats and Serbs. Čimić introduced us to Ljuba Jovanović, the Minister of Education, who in turn brought us face to face with Nikola Pašić, whom I had never met before. I soon realized that we were dealing with a man who would not abandon his reserve easily. I had heard too many anecdotes, perhaps some of them fictitious, about his ways of political maneuver to be deceived by his acting the senile old gentleman (which he did, by the way, with great skill). He pretended ignorance and surprise at the most obvious facts. After two hours of meaningless talk, neither I nor Krnjević had succeeded in extracting a coherent sentence from him, let alone a concrete proposition. Finally, I decided it was useless to prolong this sterile interview and rose to take my leave, uttering a few polite banalities. Immediately Minister Jovanović interrupted me:

"Gentlemen, I take it that our real conversation has not yet begun and certainly it is not yet finished; therefore we will meet again in the afternoon."

In the afternoon we felt we were confronted by an entirely different man. Pašić not only could and did analyze the precise political situation in all its detail; but he let us know he was fully aware of our main objective. We held that the St. Vitus

Constitution should not be applied on the territory of Croatia, Slavonia and Dalmatia, because this would mean that Croatia would be divided into six artificial departments and thus lose its national identity. Provided Croatia was governed from Zagreb, the Party would even accept a Royal Governor as representative of the Belgrade Government. Pašić appeared willing to comply with our demands if we continued to abstain from the National Assembly, thus preserving his government; he said he would send a delegation to Zagreb empowered to conclude a formal pact with the Croatian Peasant Party. Satisfied, we soon left Belgrade.

We had hardly returned to Zagreb, when Pašić's delegates, Marko Gjuričić, Marko Trifković and Voja Janjić, all cabinet members, arrived. Radić, Predavec, Košutić, Krnjević and I received them on behalf of our party. After many hours of discussions, we made no progress. Then I began to speak in blunt terms:

"Gentlemen," I said, "we are at war, though both of us desire nothing more sincerely than peace. To make this peace a reality, the cessation of all hostile activities is necessary. First of all, partial or complete dismemberment of Croatia must stop at once. Moreover, the regime must immediately and unequivocally put an end to the persecution of Croats, in particular of the Croatian Peasant Party."

These proposals were unanimously approved by those present, and we proceeded to draft them as a protocol, which became known as the Marko Protocol, after the first name of two of the Serbian delegates.

Pašić, whose aim had been to put the Constitution into effect during his term, found it extremely difficult to arrest the progressing dismemberment of Croatia, for such a course flew in the face of his larger program. The Croatian Peasant Party respected his desire to keep the Protocol secret until both parties felt free to publish it. Thus the agreement remained an empty text, predestined for premature death. Our party kept its pledge by not entering the National Assembly, which it had had no intention of doing in any case. But Pašić did not keep his part of the bargain. The territorial dissection of Croatia took its course, and the persecution of the Peasant Party did not relent for a moment. Gendarmes dispersed all our public meetings of any size. Therefore, on July 14, Bastille Day, Radić held a special meeting in Zagreb attended mainly by bourgeoisie, intellectuals, and a number of news reporters. He peppered his speech with sharp criticisms, aimed not only at Pašić's government but at the King, and gave the press the text of the Marko Protocol. As soon as the meeting ended, Radić left Croatia and travelled through Hungary and Austria to London.

The British Government, however, turned a deaf ear to Radić's solicitations, and so with his wife Maria he returned to Vienna at the beginning of 1924.

I decided to go and see him there, although I could not obtain either a passport or a visa. I decided to cross the border illegally. At the end of February I passed through the town of Varaždin and the Prekomurje region in the company of Dr. Krnjević. Aided by a trustworthy peasant who had offered us his service, we crossed the Austrian border without incident. In Radkersburg we boarded a train to Vienna. Some minutes later, the Austrian frontier-police asked for our passports, and, as we had none, brought us before the immigration officer of Spielfeld. He said he did not care whether we had the necessary papers or not, but that we did have to pay the official tax for our entry permit. After we had paid 100 dinars—about two dollars—he gave us each a small piece of paper permitting us to go to Vienna and stay there 14 days, at the same time certifying that we had paid the official entry tax.

In Vienna, Radić informed us that his mission in London had failed and instructed us to establish contact with the parliamentary opposition in Belgrade and to try somehow to make an internal political issue out of our cause. Meanwhile he would "take a hop" to Moscow in the hope of finding better comprehension of our problem there than in the West. After a short stay, Krnjević and I returned to Zagreb by the same route. I asked my friend Predavec, vice-president of our party, to go to Belgrade and contact Ljuba Davidović of the Yugoslav Democratic Party, the most influential opposition leader. Our overtures were welcomed by the opposition. Davidović declared himself ready to collaborate reasonably with the Croats with a view toward a legal revision of the St. Vitus Constitution, and a similar revision was desired by the Slovenian Populist Party and the Yugoslav Moslem Organization.

At this point I married for the second time. My first wife had divorced me during the war, when I was at the front. Now the girl of my choice was 22 years younger than myself. Her mother, the widow of a poor workingman, had four other children, all younger than my Mary. At the time I married Mary, only the two youngest children were not yet provided for. Mary's formal education had been limited to elementary school, but she had been endowed by nature with a bright and open mind. At the age of 12 she had become a salesgirl in the Radić book-store, where she read many a useful book, acquiring thus a general knowledge comparable to that of any girl who had graduated from gymnasium. I had known her at this young age and met her again as a clerk at our party organ *Dom,* when I returned from the front. She had grown into a pretty and sensitive blonde who belonged with all her soul to the Croatian Peasant movement. In 1919, when President Radić, his wife Maria and all the educated leaders of the Party were arrested, she occupied herself (at 18) with the Party's numerous organizations, communicating with dozens of peasants who came daily to seek her advice about all kinds of problems and giving them useful suggestions. We were married on March 10, 1924. A fortnight later, on March 23, I had to go to Belgrade as the head of the Croatian Peasant Party's delegation to the National Assembly. My young wife stayed behind to nurse my nearly 80-year old father.

Though warmly welcomed by the opposition, we were unable to take part in the debates of the Assembly, nor were we authorized to vote, because our credentials had to be certified first. Of course, the Radicals deliberately dragged out this certification, aware that our active participation would end their majority and bring the fall of their government. This was true even after Svetozar Pribičević, resenting Davidović's collaboration with the Croatian Peasant Party, split away from the Democratic Party with 20 other deputies to found the Independent Democratic Party. The united opposition still had more than the combined forces of Pašić and Pribičević. When we had finally been sworn in, Pašić resigned, and parliament was recessed until a new government could be formed.

I returned to Zagreb and did not bother to follow the maneuvers in Belgrade for more than six weeks. One Sunday in July, I received a sudden invitation from Davidović to come to Belgrade immediately. I caught the first evening train and arrived next morning. I learned that Davidović had formed a coalition cabinet including his own Democrats, the Slovenian Populist Party, the Yugoslav Moslem Organization, and one Radical, Nastas Petrović, who had claimed the most important ministry in the Balkans, the Ministry of the Interior, which controlled the police.

Davidović told me that he had formed this government on the express assumption that the Croats would support him. If not, he would have to resign before he had even started to govern. In return for our support, I asked him for the same guarantees we had asked from the Radicals in the Marko Protocol the previous year, namely, that the division of Croatia as foreseen in the St. Vitus Constitution would not be pursued any longer, and that all persecution of the Croatian Peasant Party would stop. Davidović consented and advised me to discuss further details with Minister of the Interior Petrović, who was the King's man in the government. (Alexander could not rely on Davidović, Korošec, or Spaho.) Nastas Petrović showed himself a faithful partner toward us. He restored the partly liquidated executive administration in Zagreb, appointing Gavro Gojković as Acting Royal Governor and several department heads as well. The Croatian Peasant Party was given full freedom for its political activities. But King Alexander and the Serbian military circles did not approve of this policy of the government and began creating difficulties for it. At first, the King convinced Davidović that the Croats should actually join the government instead of merely supporting it. With the agreement of our national deputies, I therefore designated four persons, including myself, to enter the cabinet. But the expected reshuffling of the government did not occur; Davidović soon notified me that the King strongly objected to our joining it on the ground that we were well-known republicans. I retorted that we had never asked to enter Davidović's government, that our sole aim had been to maintain him in power, and that we would stick to this without the slightest ambition to join in the central administration.

News then reached me that Radić was back from Moscow, which he had visited in the company of his son-in-law, August Košutić. Following his escape from Croatia in July 1923, a warrant had been issued warning the frontier-police to arrest Radić as soon as he tried to enter Yugoslavia.

I made Nastas Petrović aware of this and told him to cancel the warrant. He gave me his promise, though he considered it of no importance since Radić, a national deputy, enjoyed parliamentary immunity. When I learned that Radić had arrived in Vienna, I lost no time and caught the first train leaving Belgrade in order to join him there. My first question, of course, was on the success of his Moscow visit. Had he accomplished anything? "Nothing," Radić replied. "The Communists do not want allies, only servants."

After giving Radić the facts about the political situation at home, I begged him to wait a while in Vienna, until I had arranged the repeal of the warrant for his arrest or, if that were impossible, until I had time to bring about a cabinet crisis. Radić refused to hear of it. Impatient to reach Zagreb, he insisted on taking the train that same evening. If he were arrested, he said, we could always overthrow the cabinet afterward. At last, yielding to my entreaties, he postponed his departure until the next morning when we could cross the border in broad daylight instead of tricky darkness.

The following day, I found myself on the way back, together with Radić, his daughter Mira and her husband Košutić. When we neared the border, the Košutićs settled in another compartment, leaving me with Radić. The police had already been notified of our passage by its Vienna agents. The train stopped, and policemen appeared almost immediately in the doorway to demand our passports. For some time the officer examined my passport minutely, then handed it back to me with visible disappointment. Then he turned to Radić who, lacking a Yugoslav passport, produced a certificate of identity issued by the London police which had been stamped all over with the visas of various European countries. It was folded three times forming an octavo; across the last page was a huge stamp of the Soviet Union in Cyrillic characters. The fact that Yugoslavia had no diplomatic relations with the Soviet Union should have been suspicious, but, fortunately, the Serbs also use Cyrillic letters and the official must have thought he was looking at a special visa from Belgrade. He bowed courteously to Radić and left. We continued our trip undisturbed for about two hours. Then another policeman appeared in our compartment asking for Radić's passport—apparently the first official's mistake had been discovered. By now, however, the train had covered a considerable distance on Yugoslav territory, and Radić insisted with success that he did not need a passport to travel in his own country.

In the months following his return, Radić was extremely active. He convened great mass assemblies which irked Court circles, and thus tended to embarrass Davidović—the most conspicuous of them at Varaždin and Vrpolje. Later Nastas Petrović, who continued friendly to me after having left the government, told me that King Alexander had urged him to arrest Radić following the Vrpolje assembly. Petrović said he replied: "Your Majesty, your advisers may be fools, but I for one am not!" The King's attitude left little doubt that he desired the fall of the Davidović Government.

According to the law, the National Assembly re-convened regularly on October 20 to elect its presiding officers (a president, two vice-presidents and secretaries), and its several committees. Before the 1924 meeting, we were determined to use every legal means to defeat the Radical opposition, the trusted ally of the Court and military circles—first of all by excluding them from the Assembly's roster of presiding officers. I was to be nominated for president, and a Davidović Democrat and a Slovenian Populist for vice-presidents. At first Davidović seemed to agree, but in the end he feared an open fight against the Royal Court. He insisted that I leave the presidency to Ljuba Jovanović, confidential spokesman for the King; I was to become first vice-president and Msgr. Hohnjec of Korošec's Slovenian Party second vice-president. But our complaisance contributed nothing to the improvement of relations with the King. How strained they were was revealed in the following:

The practice was to introduce the newly elected officers of the Assembly to the King at a specially arranged audience. Eight days passed after Ljuba Jovanović announced this audience to the Court without any sign of a formal invitation to us. Hohnjec and I took the hint and left Belgrade. Jovanović could go to the audience alone; he had been a daily guest at the Court anyhow.

The Davidović Government was doomed. After its rapid fall, the King nominated a new government composed of

EARLY STRUGGLES WITH BELGRADE 103

Radicals and Independent Democrats (the Pašić-Pribičević government), dissolved Parliament, and instructed the new government to hold elections. Great confusion then ensued. According to the law, the so-called Committee of State supervised elections. It consisted of six presidents of Cassation Courts and the president and two vice-presidents of the former Assembly. As Ljuba Jovanović chanced to fall ill, I automatically assumed his place as Acting President of the Committee; Msgr. Hohnjec, equally disliked by Alexander and his government, became my deputy. The Committee of State had a free hand in the application of electoral law. It could determine the number of mandates to fall to the different electoral districts, nominate the electoral commissions in those districts, designate local election boards in some thousand communities across the country, appoint their chairmen and so on.

On Christmas eve the government applied an extraordinary law, called the *Obznana,* against our party which it declared to be Communist on the basis of Radić's trip to Moscow. Predavec, the Košutić brothers, Krnjević and I were arrested on January 2, 1925. Radić could not be found that day and the police seized him a few days later. We refused to answer the questioning of the police, invoking our parliamentary immunity, which we maintained remained in force until the new elections had been held. We were arraigned before the Court of Zagreb, where the public prosecutor accused us of Communist propaganda and demanded a legal indictment. The ordinary guards were replaced by policemen faithful to the Pašić-Pribičević regime. But all these efforts came to naught. The judges, granted independence by the Constitution, decided that the charges against us lacked sufficient basis to warrant arrest. The Court of Appeals confirmed this judgment and set the date of our release for January 14. A separate trial had been arranged for Radić, and he was detained in the prison of the Court of Zagreb. In spite of the two judicial decisions, we were not set free either, but arraigned under a law which authorized the police to confine vagrants, prostitutes and persons without profession to "an assigned place of residence." The police did not specify into which of the three categories we had presumably been classified. The "place of residence" clause was also used strangely. Although the text of the law made it clear that such a place would be a community or a village, we were confined to a room in the police barracks in Zagreb.

If our arrest was illegal, at least we could not complain about our treatment. The five of us shared a room about 45 by 15 feet. Large windows fronted on a sunny yard. Meals were brought from our homes, and relatives and friends were allowed to visit in the presence of one or two police officers. Two days before our transfer to the new prison, on January 13, my daughter was born. I got my first look at her when, as a baby of three weeks, she was brought to me in jail on a visit.

It is interesting to note the special manner in which legality was mixed with obvious breaking of the law in Yugoslavia in those days. As long as legal procedures were compatible with the interests of the regime they were observed with painstaking thoroughness; but if, on the other hand, the law was considered harmful to government interests, it was bypassed in a downright shameless way. I was still a vice-president of the National Assembly and thus a member of the Committee of State. As such, even in prison I received my full salary of 10,500 Dinars ($300) a month, plus a thousand cigarettes for "representation" purposes. In this strange manner I was encouraged to "represent" the National Assembly in my capacity as a prisoner, before my friends and visitors. Still another aspect of this episode was just as ridiculous. During my imprisonment Ljuba Jovanović recovered. He resumed as president of the Committee of State by radically changing all the former election regulations which had been published in the *Official Gazette*. He also replaced the members of the various electoral commissions. These changes were made public anew in the

Official Gazette over the signatures of all the Committee of State members, including myself. I had no opportunity to deny my consent or my printed signature. We hoped that this state of affairs would end with the elections; once we were elected deputies again (we did not doubt this for a second, nor did our adversaries), we would recover our freedom.

Although the popular vote for the Croatian Peasant Party increased considerably, the Pašić-Pribičević coalition succeeded in reducing the number of our deputies from 73 to 65 by combining their lists in various districts. Nevertheless, the coalition fell short of a majority by two or three seats. The coalition's problem now became one of simple arithmetic. If the six of us (Radić, Predavec, S. Košutić, A. Košutić, Krnjević and I) were barred from the Assembly, the coalition would have its majority. The simplest solution was to keep us in prison.

In our absence, the Assembly considered credentials, pronouncing ours void and suspending those of the rest of our party—to be judged by a special parliamentary examination as to culpability with regard to Communism. This measure was approved by a majority of two votes. But Nikola Pašić, a shrewd old politician, did not want to go to extremes. He had told Trumbić, who acted as Radić's lawyer: "I know that Radić is no more a Communist than I am. He saved Croatia from the growing Communist influence in 1919-1920. But sentimentality has no place in politics, and I will not shrink from using effective means to gain my ends." At the same time Pašić approached Radić through the investigating judge. They finally reached an agreement, which was announced in Parliament by Pavle Radić, nephew of the Party President. In it the Croatian Peasant Party recognized the Dynasty and the St. Vitus Constitution as facts, without, however, renouncing its determination to struggle, employing all legal means, for revision of the latter. The suspended deputies of the Party, though not us six, were now seated. Shortly afterward, on July 25,

1925, Pašić removed the Democrats, including Pribičević, from the government, replaced them with four members of the Croatian Peasant Party, and released us from prison. Since then our party has never been accused of Communism, by Pašić or anyone else. Several months later, Radić himself entered the government as Minister of Education.

My seat in Parliament having been voided, I was excluded from its sessions for two years and therefore could not personally follow the numerous disputes which succeeded one another during the life of this unnatural coalition between the Serbian Radical Party and the Croatian Peasant Party. It broke up in the middle of 1926, and our party was again in opposition. The St. Vitus Constitution at last came into force, and the 1000 year old Kingdoms of Croatia, Slavonia, and Dalmatia were divided into six departments. The very thing had happened against which we had struggled so fiercely.

On October 24, 1926, my son was born and named Andrej after his great-grandfather.

CHAPTER VIII

The Murder of Stephen Radić

WITH THE ST. VITUS Constitution in force, our party was obliged to concentrate its strength on the four Croato-Slavonian and two Dalmatian departments, while working in the Bosnian and Hercegovinian departments through coalition with the Bosnian Moslems. By the time elections for the department assemblies took place, the Croatian Peasant Party was already in the opposition, although the Bosnian Moslems were still in the Belgrade Government. But the important thing was that the Croatian Peasant Party succeeded in dominating the departments of Osijek, Zagreb, Karlovac, Split and Dubrovnik, while the Bosnian Moslems, in coalition with our party, won in all the Bosnian and Hercegovinian districts.

I was then elected chairman of the Assembly of the Zagreb Department, which consisted of 80 deputies, 70 of them from our party. The ten in opposition included four members of the Croatian Union (the remaining former Croat adherents of the Croato-Serbian Coalition and the Mile Starčević group), three of Svetozar Pribičević's Independent Democrats, two Communists and one Frankist. All 10 oppositionists had been elected in Zagreb, Varaždin, Sisak and Križevci. The city of Zagreb, with eleven deputies, had chosen the two Communists, the last of their party to assume public office before World War II.

With a seven-eighths majority in the Zagreb Assembly, my position as chairman presented few major difficulties. The real problem was that our "autonomy" and field of action were very limited. About all we could do was order road repairs and assign a few physicians to those extremely poor sections where the population, before then, could hardly afford to see a doctor, much less call one to their homes. In this manner I served as chairman from the spring to the fall of 1927.

Meanwhile, the Belgrade Government had plunged from one crisis to another until Parliament was dissolved in June and new elections were announced for the fall. I was elected again by a great majority to represent my old district of Bjelovar in the National Assembly. Since the law did not permit anyone to be simultaneously a member of both the National Assembly and the Department Assembly, I had to resign from the Zagreb District Assembly, relinquishing its chairmanship as well.

A week after my election to the Belgrade Parliament on September 11, 1927, I received the heaviest blow in my life. For September 18 marked the death, at the age of 26, of my unforgettable wife, Mary. I was suddenly forced to face the future as a widower with a daughter of two-and-a-half years and a ten-month-old son, not to speak of my father, already past 80. I began to consider seriously the thought of abandoning politics altogether and devoting myself to my children. After much persuasion on the part of President Radić I finally gave up this idea. My late wife's younger sister, a girl of 19, assumed the care of my children and my father. When Parliament was in session, I would alternately spend three days in Belgrade and one in Zagreb, thus passing most of my nights for some seven months on the train between the two cities.

In the Parliament that emerged from the autumn elections of 1927, the Radicals under the leadership of Velja Vukičević (Pašić had died the previous year) formed a coalition government with Davidović's Democrats, Korošec's Slovenes and Spaho's Bosnian Moslems. In this manner, the Croatian Peasant Party found itself in opposition along with the Independent Democrats of Pribičević and the Serbian Agrarians led by Joca Jovanović. Then developed what few, least of all the Radicals, had ever expected, and that was the formation of an alliance between Stephen Radić and his most implacable antagonist for nine long years, Pribičević. The dynamic Pribičević was known for attacking his enemies without mercy and pursuing his goals with unabating energy; the same qualities now made him a partner of undivided loyalty. To us, he seemed to have transformed himself from a Saul into a Paul; for, after having been an extreme centralist, violently opposed to Croatian demands, he now wholeheartedly supported the newly-formed coalition and, above all, the Croatian cause. His main concern was the preservation of Yugoslavia, still called "the Kingdom of the Serbs, Croats and Slovenes," on which he looked, not without reason, as his own child. But his political sagacity compelled him to recognize the necessity of acknowledging the Croats and all other historical provinces on a level of parity with the former Kingdom of Serbia. In the existing Parliament this was not possible. We had only two choices—either to start a revolution or to encourage a passive resistance among the people and at the same time try to stop the action of the Parliament designed to establish centralism. Hence, once it was formed, the Peasant-Democrat Coalition became an unceasing source of trouble for the government. The Coalition began to practice systematic obstructionism in the National Assembly, aided by the quite liberal order of procedure. Countless motions were made at every session, all labelled "urgent," in order to gain precedence over the regular parliamentary business. The Coalition thus in effect suspended the Assembly's ordinary tasks indefinitely. The general atmosphere of Parliament soon became fraught with tension; and threats like "It can't go on this way much longer" and "Blood will have to be spilled" were uttered by certain Radicals. And, indeed, catastrophe came soon enough.

On Saturday, June 16, 1928, I went to spend three days in Zagreb. On Tuesday, I left again for Belgrade which I reached the following morning, June 20. From the station I went straight to the National Assembly. I found Stephen Radić in the party's club-room, surrounded by our party's deputies who were greatly agitated. They despairingly tried to persuade him to abstain from attending the parliamentary session that day, because they had heard rumors of a planned attempt on his life. Despite their entreaties, Radić said: "If it were just a question of missing today's session, I would listen to you. But suppose they are really determined to do it and fail today? They will only postpone it until tomorrow or the day after. That means I would have to stay away permanently—which I certainly won't do. Besides, they can perhaps kill me, but that will never enable them to destroy our ideology which, after winning all Croatia, has already penetrated far beyond her boundaries." Seeing there was no restraining him, a Montenegrin deputy of our party, Dr. Sekula Drljević, asked him to promise not to say anything during the session, so as to avoid any plausible pretext for an incident. Radić gave his promise and kept it.

I no longer remember who was speaking in Parliament that day, nor what he was talking about, though I clearly recall the several challenging interruptions of a rather provocative nature coming from the Radical benches. Ivan Pernar of our party ultimately turned around and voiced his indignation, countering their attack. But the turmoil gradually subsided, and the scheduled debate at last came to an end. At that moment Puniša Račić, a Radical deputy, got to his feet and, betraying an unusual excitement, asked for permission to speak. Dr. Ninko Perić, president of the Assembly, told him that it was too late, that the debate had obviously come to a close. Thereupon Puniša Račić sank back in his seat, apparently relieved that his opportunity to speak had passed. Noticing this, Perić promptly volunteered: "In case you consider yourself personally offended by someone in some way, you may speak on a point of personal privilege." Puniša Račić rose again and began to speak from his bench. But Ninko Perić quickly pointed toward the tribune and added: "Will you come over here, please, I am sure we shall hear you better." The Tribune was situated precisely in front of the benches occupied by the members of the Peasant-Democrat Coalition. On the first of these were seated from left to right Ivan Pernar, Ivan Grandja, Stephen Radić and Svetozar Pribičević. Because president Perić gave Puniša Račić the floor after he himself had already concluded the debate, and because he directed him to take his stand right in front of our benches, I am inclined to believe in Ninko Perić's tacit complicity in the doubtless premeditated plot.

No sooner had Puniša Račić reached the tribune than he pulled a gun from his pocket and shouted: "Anyone who dares to get between me and Pernar shall meet his death!" At the same instant, Ninko Perić announced from his chair, "The session is adjourned," then got up and ran from the hall. The Minister of Justice, Vujčić, who sat close to the tribune, jumped up and seized Račić's right hand, but Račić hurled him back and simultaneously fired at Pernar a few feet away. Without a sound Pernar fell to the floor. I was sitting exactly two rows behind him, the one between us being empty. Moved by the instinct for self-preservation, I rushed forward to the left, in front of the Radicals, where I watched the rest of this outrageous performance. After the first shot, Gjuro Basariček, whose place had been at the stenographers' table near the tribune, dashed at Puniša Račić trying to grab his hand, but Račić, faster, aimed sideways at his right shoulder, not half a foot from the gun, and killed him instantly. Then, with a swift turn Račić pointed the deadly weapon at Radić. The latter's left-hand neighbor, Grandja, intervened and was trying to push our President under the bench, when he received the third shot into his left arm. Instinctively he withdrew it, and a fourth shot, closely following the third, hit Radić in the abdomen. The leader's nephew, Pavle Radić, had been standing outside the hall when he heard the first shot. Alarmed, he came running to his uncle's side and, screening him from Puniša Račić received the fifth ball, shot into his back and piercing his heart. Those nearer the scene told me later that Račić had said to Pavle Radić when he noticed him: "You're just the one I was waiting for!" After the fifth shot, Račić leapt down from the tribune and strode rapidly toward the door and out of the Assembly Hall.

An ambulance rushed Pernar, Grandja and Stephen Radić to the hospital. The chief surgeon, Dr. Kostić, decribed Pernar's condition as very serious. The bullet had gone clear through his arm, then pierced the breastbone and lodged close to the heart. An immediate operation would present too great a risk and would therefore only be undertaken if absolutely ncessary. Grandja's wound was not found dangerous. The surgeon operated immediately on Stephen Radić and, when it was all over, said he was confident that things would turn out well.

That same afternoon, Dr. Gottlieb, a famous surgeon from Zagreb arrived by plane to examine Radić. Later he told me rather pessimistically that the operation did not look satisfactory to him, but that all we could do now was hope for the best and trust in God.

The bodies of Pavle Radić and Gjuro Basariček were transported to Zagreb and buried in the arcade of Mirogoj, the city's central cemetery. Meanwhile, Stephen Radić, Pernar and Grandja remained in the Belgrade hospital.

The deputies of the Croatian Peasant Party and the Independent Democratic Party decided, in the wake of the assassination, to leave the National Assembly without any intention of returning. I went to see Radić at the hospital the evening of the shooting. He was lying in bed quite motionless, with his eyes closed. When I had finished expressing my sympathy, he spoke: "Listen, after what happened in Parliament today, we shall want to have little or nothing to do with them any more. Maybe we will just settle for common foreign-affairs and common defense, maybe not even that much. It will depend on the circumstances, and you are clever enough, I have no need to teach you. I merely beg you to abide by the peaceful methods of struggle which I have always used." I replied that I was sure he would soon make all the major decisions himself, but that now it was imperative for him to relax and to avoid any form of excitement.

Indeed, Radić's condition seemed gradually to improve. After a fortnight, all three, Radić, Pernar, and Grandja, had recovered sufficiently for the doctors to permit them to travel to Zagreb. When they reached the Croatian capital on July 7 at 4 P.M., tens of thousands of people waiting at the station broke into frenzied acclamations. Radić appeared to have regained some of his strength, for after having stepped off the train with my help, he resolutely refused further assistance and walked alone through the station to the waiting car. His condition proved satisfactory in the days that followed, when he presided over several meetings held in his apartment.

While Radić had been lying in the Belgrade hospital, Svetozar Pribičević had had a few interviews with King Alexander, who had tried by various maneuvers to separate Pribičević from Radić and the Croatian Peasant Party. His efforts were in vain, however; Pribičević followed Radić almost immediately to Zagreb, although his own family was living in Belgrade.

On Sunday, July 22, August Košutić, the President's son-in-law, telephoned me to come to the Radić house after lunch. On my arrival, a small party of intimate friends and close relations had gathered on the veranda, all set for a celebration.

I was told that Radić's last bandage had been removed that day, and that this event marked his complete recovery. In the midst of this gay party, Radić himself happily picked up his beloved *tamburica* (a sort of guitar) to play some of his favorite tunes. But he soon complained of what he called "rheumatic pains" in his arms and legs.

It had been decided that Radić should spend his convalescence at the Spa of Varaždin and that Vice-president Predavec should go there two days after this party to make the necessary arrangements. On July 24, I brought my own children and my sister-in-law to Vrbovsko in Gorski Kotar, where on their doctor's advice they were supposed to profit by a few weeks of the healthy mountain air. A few days after my return to Zagreb, I learned that the President had not yet left for the spa and was bedridden with a high fever. He was, therefore, unable to participate in the meeting of the deputies of the Peasant-Democrat Coalition that took place on August 1 in Zagreb. This meeting was held to protest the convocation of another parliamentary session in Belgrade, in spite of the recent events there. Before the meeting opened, Dr. Klepac, the District Health Officer, called the most important party leaders into a separate room and told them the unanimous opinion of the medical consultants: namely, that Radić's illness would be of long duration and that a total recovery, enabling him to resume his political tasks, appeared questionable. The meaning of the doctor's words was only too clear.

Vice-President Predavec communicated the doctors' prognosis to the full meeting and proposed that I be nominated Acting President of the party during the absence of the convalescing Radić. The proposal was accepted unanimously without debate. Svetozar Pribičević acted as chairman of the meeting itself. The meeting's resolutions made the following points:

1. The rump National Assembly, convoked for August 1, 1928, has no right to vote any decisions affecting the whole of

the country. All such decisions, particularly those on financial engagements, are forthwith declared void in all parts of the former Austro-Hungarian territories represented henceforth by the Coalition, among which Croatia plays a special part.

2. The Coalition emphasized that the Kingdoms of Croatia and of Montenegro, as well as all other historically defined entities in the National Council, did not, in forming the common State of the Serbs, Croats and Slovenes with Serbia, surrender their separate existence in favor of any other country, but solely for the benefit of the common state. In view of the fact that the Act of December 1, 1918 and the Constitution of 1921 had served to impose the hegemony of the former Kingdom of Serbia on all the other lands having joined the common state, we declare that the organization of the state, as it had existed up to now, must be considered null after the recent tragic event and that, with the utmost determination, we shall continue our struggle for a new and better organization of the state, in order to secure complete equality for all the above mentioned lands. Other decisions will be taken when the president, Stephen Radić, assumes his post again.

3. The Peasant-Democrat Coalition invites all political parties and groups of the former Austro-Hungarian territories to participate in the fight for equality. We expect the peasants of Serbia to support us in their own interest, inasmuch as a victory in accordance with the principles previously outlined constitutes the only guarantee strong enough to save our common state.

The character of Svetozar Pribičević was revealed strikingly at this meeting. For under his chairmanship the Coalition condemned the Act of December 1, 1918, and the Constitution of 1921, in both of which he had been instrumental, and called for an uncompromising campaign against the organization of the state which he had molded. Pribičević might thus be cited as one of the outstanding examples of a statesman who not only perceived his former mistake, but had the courage to publicly avow it and take the consequences and risks which such a reversal implied.*

The condition of president Radić grew worse from day to day. I went to see my children at regular intervals, thus spending half of my time at Vrbovsko and the rest in Zagreb. When, on August 8, I returned from the mountains again to Zagreb, I found Radić in an advanced stage of death agony. A last faint hope was set on a heart specialist from Vienna, for Radić was unfortunately a victim of diabetes and his wound had provoked a sepsis that directly threatened his heart. Without the complicating factor of diabetes, the septic wound would not necessarily have proved fatal. Too agitated to hear the verdict of the doctors' consilium, I went out for a walk to collect myself. When I returned at 8 P.M., Msgr. Kerdić, the priest of St. Blaise parish, was administering the last sacraments. At 9 P.M., the heart of Stephen Radić had stopped beating, the heart whose every beat since early youth had been a testimony of undivided love for the Croatian peasantry.

The funeral of our President was held a few days later, on Sunday, August 12. The preceding day, a solemn memorial meeting took place in the historic Croatian Sabor Hall, at which I alone spoke on behalf of the departed leader. I stressed the principal ideas to which he had devoted his life. Some

* Ante Trumbic of the Croatian Union and Ante Pavelic of Frank's party also attended these meetings and voted for these decisions, though they were the two Croatian deputies elected outside our party in 1927. After the Belgrade assassination, they came to join the deputies' club of the Croatian Peasant Party, and by the end of December both of them had entered the ranks of the Party. Pavelic withdrew from it two weeks later, when King Alexander had proclaimed his dictatorship, and went into exile to pursue policies of his own. He joined, and soon became the leader, of the extreme nationalist *Ustasha* movement which advocated a complete destruction of Yugoslavia and which was sponsored first by the Hungarian and later by Mussolini's Italian government. Trumbic, however, remained a member of the Croatian Peasant Party and was one of my most valued collaborators until his death in 1938.

fragmentary quotations may suffice to convey the general sense of what I said:

"Even before Radić there were patriots who loved our country, who also loved their people, but they loved them only as a whole, perhaps only as a symbol. Stephen Radić's love for his people was born out of a simple love for his fellow man, particularly the one of humble class, most abused and oppressed. His people were, first and foremost, the millions of abused and oppressed individual peasants to whom he became attached in a very special way. . . .

"The Croatian peasantry constitutes not a mere class, but a nation which desires to be recognized as such. . . .

"The right of the Croatian peasant people to govern themselves engenders the logical need for the right to have their own free state of Croatia. . . .

"Stephen Radić strove hard for this free state of Croatia, governed by the Croatian peasantry, where oppressed individuals and, even more, oppressed national groups would be nonexistent. With this ultimate aim before him, Stephen Radić became, even at the start of his political life, a champion of complete parity between the Serbs and the Croats in Croatia. . . .

"It is obvious that the conception of a free Croatia excludes any form of commonwealth which tends to limit her own freedom to the advantage of any other member of this commonwealth, except the commonwealth itself. Croatia will however not forsake the privilege of self-government that is due an equal partner in a common state, not even in favor of the common state itself. The latter is created by the interested parties to guarantee their liberty, not to curtail it. . . .

"Stephen Radić was a convinced pacifist who believed that everlasting peace among peoples was well within the realm of the possible, and who did not lose his faith even at the trying moment when the deadly bullet struck his own body. . . .

"Of course, as a pacifist whose scope embraced the entire world, he could not conceivably be an imperialist, nor a man disposed to tolerate imperialism anywhere, near or far. Stephen Radić, therefore, resolutely attacked the imperialistic and hegemonic politics pursued by the Serbian ruling class, until he fell a casualty of that struggle, bequeathing us a legacy of fight against that imperialism, but willing us also his faith in ultimate victory, the salvation not only of Croatia, but of all the Southern Slavs. . . ."

Without the least exaggeration, it can be asserted that about 300,000 people from all parts of Croatia accompanied Stephen Radić to his final resting-place. Several speeches were made to do him honor, and when I spoke in my turn, I emphasized that his Serbian adversaries must have killed him because they were afraid the Serbian peasantry would not hesitate to adopt Radić's tenets as the Croats had done. I closed with the thought that, whenever a blow was directed at the Croatian people, Stephen Radić exposed his own breast to receive it, just as he had offered his shoulders to carry the weight of the cross intended for his people. When the next day, August 13, 1928, I was chosen to succeed Radić at the meeting of the Croatian National Representation, I felt that this cross had fallen on my shoulders.

CHAPTER IX

At The Head Of The Croatian Peasant Party

*M*Y ELECTION as President of the Croatian Peasant Party was quite orderly. While some intellectuals among the Party's deputies were inclined to favor vice-president Josip Predavec as Radić's successor (he was, indeed, more active and eclipsed me when it came to fighting the Party's foes), all the peasant deputies were my staunch supporters. As these formed the great majority, Predavec thought it wise to nominate me at the plenary meeting which at once elected me unanimously.

My new position was most difficult. The June 20 shooting in the Belgrade Parliament and the ensuing death of Radić had plunged all Croatia into indescribable agitation, and an armed revolt was believed imminent. The news of the Belgrade murders caused violent riots in Zagreb with many casualties. During the time Radić lay ill, a Croatian youth killed a journalist from Belgrade in broad daylight in Zagreb; he said he had done so because somebody had told him of "this journalist's coming to the Croatian capital for a renewed attempt on the life of the Croatian peasant leader."

For nine years, the Belgrade regime had celebrated "National Union Day" on December 1 with the simple formality of a church visit by civil and military officials, thus allowing it to pass unnoticed by the public at large. In 1928, however, the regime unwisely planned a special celebration, more solemn than any that had preceded it, to mark the tenth anniversary of the State's existence. All secondary-school students were ordered to participate, together with the civil and military servants. This order provoked a storm of protest. The students not only refused to participate but organized violent demonstrations in the streets of Zagreb. When the army generals drove up in front of the city's Catholic Cathedral, three young students unfurled three black flags on its towers. The police quickly intervened and succeeded in getting hold of two of the flags. The third, pinned to one of the tower's ornaments, remained out of their reach; firemen were summoned to bring it down. The generals, meanwhile, moved on to the Orthodox Church, too impatient to wait for the firemen. In the streets, exasperated crowds continued their demonstrations, with workers and bourgeoisie joining the enraged students. In the end, many people were wounded, and a boy of 18 died.

I did everything in my power to prevent an open revolt, which threatened not only in Zagreb but throughout Croatia. I did so not merely because of Radić's wishes and my own pacific tendencies, but because it would have been utter folly to let the political struggle stray onto a field where we would necessarily prove the weaker.

As one avenue of peaceful struggle, the Croatian Peasant Party attempted to interest the Western democracies in the hopeless political situation of Yugoslavia. One opportunity was furnished at the 25th session of the International Interparliamentary Union, held in Berlin on August 21, 1928, for the purpose of promoting the parliamentary system and the spirit of brotherhood and peaceful coexistence among the various nations. Our party leaders sent a telegram to the president of this Union, who happened to be the president of the German Reichstag. We formally protested the attendance of the Belgrade delegation and denied it the right to represent Croatia;

AT THE HEAD OF THE CROATIAN PEASANT PARTY 121

we declared that delegation unqualified to collaborate with other nations for the furthering of the parliamentary system and true democracy, and unfit to promote international peace and brotherhood. We expressed the hope that the representatives of all the civilized countries at the conference would condemn the terrible assassinations in the Belgrade Parliament as a direct attack against the very institution of parliamentarism. Our own delegates, general secretary Juraj Krnjević and Ivan Pernar, went to Berlin. But even Pernar's story of the bullet still lodged near his heart failed to impress anyone at the conference. Not a soul bothered to consider our protest.

This was only one of many cases in which the other nations failed to intervene. Such consistent non-intervention and abstention from resolving the internal conflicts of various states finally brought about the Second World War.

While the rump Assembly in Belgrade was proceeding without Croatian representatives, Pribičević and I kept up our vigilant struggle against Belgrade's hegemony. As the Serbs from Croatia also began to resent this hegemony, we tried to tighten the connection between them and the Croats. The parties of both became quite active, calling joint mass meetings in Sisak, Pakrac and Gospić where Croats and the Serbs are strongly intermixed.

Belgrade was headed more and more for dictatorship, and a prolonged crisis resulted in the fall of the government at the end of December. On January 3, 1929, the Chancery of the Royal Court sent telegrams inviting Pribičević and myself to a consultation with King Alexander. We deliberated a while before deciding to accept it. We reached Belgrade on January 4. That morning, I was given audience by the King; Pribičević's turn came in the afternoon.

My interview lasted scarcely half an hour, although it was my first conversation with Alexander. I introduced myself with the customary greeting, conveying the thought that I placed myself at his disposal. In return, he offered me a seat and asked me without preliminaries to explain the exact nature of the Croats' dissatisfaction with the regime. He wanted to know if there was any possibility of securing their collaboration with a view to achieving a more harmonious state. I gave him a detailed account of all the grievances the Croats had been harboring against the regime since 1918. I emphasized that the core of the trouble was that State policy was not only being decided without the Croats but was actually aimed to harm them; for it certainly had proved detrimental to their rights and interests. The principal fault rested with those in Serbia who considered Yugoslavia as an enlarged Serbia rather than as a new multinational state. (Officially, Yugoslavia was still the Kingdom of the Serbs, Croats and Slovenes.) I then quoted the historic advice of the old Magyar statesman, Francis Deak, to the Emperor Franz Josef: "If a vest is buttoned the wrong way, the only thing to do is to unbutton it and button it again the right way." To consolidate Yugoslavia, it would be necessary to go back to 1918 and start all over, this time with the true representatives of the Croats taken into account. The King had listened in silence to what I had to say, scribbling a few notes in his agenda. When I was finished he "graciously" dismissed me.

After the audience, I went to lunch with Pribičević and his family at their home and stayed there to await his return from the afternoon audience. He returned visibly shaken and angry with the King, and told me that he had found himself in immediate conflict with Alexander. He had reproached him with total incomprehension of the political situation, pointing out that the King had been able to spare "no more than twenty minutes" to talk to me, the representative of all the Croats, while spending hours at interviews with relatively obscure personalities from Serbia. In answer to Pribičević's remonstrances, the King had rolled up the sleeve of his uniform and pointed to his veins with the bland remark: "I cannot possibly deny my own blood." Pribičević thereupon had challenged him: "You will have to decide whether you want to be King of the Serbs alone or of the Croats as well. Should the second be your choice, then come to Zagreb to solve the Croatian question on the spot." After this, Pribičević told me, he had turned on his heels and left the King's office without another word, slamming the door hard behind him.

After my conversation with Pribičević, I crossed the Sava by boat, bound for Zemun. There, I visited my friend, Sekula Drljević, intending to continue by train to Zagreb that evening. An hour before I was to leave, however, the Chancery of the Royal Court reached me by telephone and invited me to a new audience with the King the following morning.

At this second audience, on January 5, Alexander asked me to expound my conception of a reorganized Yugoslavia. I complied readily enough. I said that the very existence of Yugoslavia depended on its being founded on a truly federal basis that would keep intact the seven federal unities, within their historical boundaries as they had existed in 1918: (1) Slovenia, (2) Croatia, Slavonia and Dalmatia, (3) Bosnia and Hercegovina, (4) Montenegro, (5) Serbia, (6) Vojvodina (southeastern part of Hungary), and (7) Macedonia. All of these should have their separate governments and parliaments for their autonomous affairs. A central government and parliament would assume authority over all common affairs, linking the different unities together in their relations to foreign countries as one representative state. To the King's remark about possible divergences between the laws of the different unities, I replied that I did not believe in the probability of such conflicts, since all autonomous laws would be subject to approval by the common king. Alexander had no comment on my last words, but, nevertheless, thanked me for the "valuable information," adding determinedly: "Be assured that I have been properly convinced that things cannot go on in this way:

I shall take them into my own hands and am confident I can succeed in putting an end to all conflicts." With this vague intimation, he granted me leave.

When I reached the car, however, one of his footmen came running after me and said that the King wanted me to return for a moment. As I entered his office again, I found him standing two feet from the door. I guessed immediately that he was about to tell me something, but could not bring himself to do so. I looked at him expectantly for a few seconds, but then he merely said: "I just wanted to tell you that I don't need your services any longer at present. You are free to journey back to Zagreb."

"Your Majesty, that was exactly my intention, and I shall, indeed, take the first available boat to Zemun and from there the next train to Zagreb."

"Very well!" the King said. After a pause he added that he would consult with Professor Slobodan Jovanović, a noted specialist on constitutional science, about the formal organization of the State according to the basic outlines of my proposal.

"This seems to me a secondary measure of minor importance," I remarked. "Bismarck unified Germany in 1871 without violating the boundaries of the particular German States, even leaving them under the rule of their local dynasties. He left it to the scholars to settle the question of whether the united Germany would be called a federation, confederation or some other name. In spite of this apparent neglect, almost the whole world had to unite to defeat a Reich organized in this way."

This talk was the last we had together. As soon as I had informed Pribičević about it, I crossed over to Zemun. There I learned from some friends about preliminary arrangements for a proclamation of the dictatorship. And, when I reached Zagreb the next morning, the early editions of the newspapers had already published the King's Manifesto proclaiming his dictatorship and nominating a new government with General Peter Živković as Premier. Under this dictatorship, the King

AT THE HEAD OF THE CROATIAN PEASANT PARTY 125

intended to mold the Serbian, Croatian and Slovenian nations, which long ago had developed a strong national consciousness, into a new unified Yugoslav nation. Henceforth the state was called officially "Kingdom of Yugoslavia."

It appears fitting to say a few words about the meaning of the word "nation," since the American conception of it differs somewhat from the European. For where an American uses "nation" to mean a territory under the authority of a central government, the European uses "state." To the European, the word "nation" means rather a "people" who are bound usually by a historically defined language, culture and institutions and always by the very consciousness of belonging together regardless of whether they have their own government, are subject to foreign domination or even divided among several foreign states. Of course, the definitions of "nation" and "state" coincide frequently in Europe, but not in all cases. For example, until the end of the First World War only two states existed within the Hapsburg Empire: Austria and Hungary. Nevertheless, with Austria were grouped several peoples with fully developed national consciousness—Czechs, Slovenes, Poles and Ukrainians. The Germans of Austria, likewise, looked upon themselves as a part of the German nation. Similarly, the Slovaks, Rumanians, Ukrainians, and Serbs under the Hungarian state could not accept the Hungarian nation as their own, being too deeply aware of their own nationalities as Slovaks, Rumanians, Ukrainians and Serbs. The Croats within the Hungarian state had won recognition as a political nation through the agreement of 1868, while the Croats within the Austrian state (in Dalmatia and Istria) in turn had never lost their distinction as Croats.

The national consciousness of practically all these peoples of the Dual Monarchy was ignored after the First World War. An exception was made for the Poles from Austria-Hungary who joined with the Poles from Germany and Russia to become the postwar Poland. The Croats and Slovenes were amalgamated with the Kingdom of Serbia into a centralized state. The ensuing conflicts between Croats and Serbs have already been described. Now to make it worse, King Alexander came forward with the peculiar idea of extinguishing with a single decree the thousand-year old national consciousness of the Croats and Slovenes, and producing by magic a new "Yugoslav nation." Of course, this was utter nonsense; as one of our wittier party members put it: "Nobody has ever been able to create a baby with a decree—yet King Alexander fancies he can create a nation that way!"

The first step of the dictatorship was to reinforce the Draconian law already in existence for the defense of the State; the second step was the formation in Belgrade of a special Central Court for the defense of the State with final jurisdiction. All political parties were ordered to dissolve. Pribičević and I, as well as other important political leaders, were placed under strict police surveillance. Three plain-clothes policemen were ordered to watch me and my house constantly and to question all my visitors. I was followed closely wherever I went. Meanwhile, the dictatorship attempted to present itself to the outside world as the form of state that genuinely expressed the desire of the people. The regime faked numerous congratulatory telegrams and organized pilgrimages to the Monarch from all parts of the country.

Through these measures, the dictatorship succeeded in detaching a few lukewarm followers from Pribičević. With the exception of a Croat and two Serbs of no consequence, his loss consisted mainly of Slovenes. They had abandoned him not only because they preferred to submit to the dictatorship, but because his new federal policies were not at all to their liking. Political life among the Slovenes was dominated by two distinct groups, the Clericals and the Liberals. To offset the indisputable predominance of the first, led by Msgr. Korošec, the Liberals had joined Pribičević. But when Pribičević renounced centralism and entered the coalition with the Croats, his centralist-imbued Slovene friends found themselves in a dangerous position. During one of the countless debates in Zagreb, Pribičević told one of them who had voiced dissatisfaction with the new state of affairs: "My friend, we can't go on playing the gendarme in Slovenia forever. Korošec has the majority; that's a fact we won't change."

In the middle of April 1929, the editor in chief of the daily newspaper *Novosti,* Toni Schlegel, was murdered not far from his apartment, shot in the back with a revolver. The paper had been favorably inclined toward the dictatorship. The next day, all the important members of the Peasant-Democrat Coalition were summoned to the police station for a special investigation. It soon became obvious that we could not have had anything to do with the killing, and so the affair went no further than this first hearing. Later that fall, numerous members of the former Croatian Party of Right, the "Frankists," were arrested in connection with the assassination of Toni Schlegel. They were cross-examined and cruelly tortured in the hope of extracting confessions. Some of those obtained in this manner were true, some false.

In May, Pribičević decided to go to Belgrade in the hope of establishing contact with some rebellious Serbian politicians who opposed Alexander's totalitarian government. Janko Bedeković, chief of the Zagreb police, joined him just when he was about to board the train. Bedeković tried to dissuade him from going to Belgrade with the covert warning that the trip could prove fatal. Pribičević paid no heed to this threat and went anyhow. But when he stepped off the train in Belgrade, he was arrested and conducted under police guard to his old home, where his family was still living, and held there as a virtual prisoner. Two days later, the police ordered him to the solitary village of Brus in central Serbia for a prolonged strict confinement. He spent two years either at Brus or in the hospital of Belgrade, before he was given a passport permitting him to go to Karlove Vary in Czechoslovakia to undergo medical treatment. The passport was probably due to the repeated intervention of Thomas Garrigue Masaryk, President of the Czechoslovak Republic. Pribičević remained in exile, at first for some time in Czechoslovakia, then in Paris, and finally again in Czechoslovakia. He died in Prague of lung cancer on September 15, 1936. He had tried to fight King Alexander's totalitarian regime in exile, but in vain; for the Czechs and the French, doubtless proud of their democracies, saw no paradox between their own political institutions and the support they were simultaneously lending a dictator in the Balkans. (At this writing we are watching history repeat itself; the Western democracies again do not find it incompatible with their own ideals to keep a Communist dictator in the saddle.)

The Croatian Peasant Party was compelled to take recourse in small secret gatherings, though I still received a great number of adherents daily from all over Croatia. In giving them directions on how to proceed at such clandestine meetings, I tried to maintain the spirit of opposition which the regime itself had unwittingly aroused throughout the nation.

In September 1929, secretary general Krnjević and vice-president August Košutić of our party went into exile with my formal approval to make the public opinion of democratic Europe aware of the realities of Alexander's dictatorial regime, and to win European onlookers to the support of the political aims of the Croats. Without a passport, Krnjević passed through Hungary to Switzerland, where he lived until the autumn of 1939, the year of my agreement with Prince Paul. Košutić sailed in a small boat from the Croatian coast to Italy, went on to Germany where he remained until Hitler's rise to power, and from there to Austria. He finally returned home from Austria in January 1937, because I needed his help.

Soon after the departure of Košutić and Krnjević from Yugoslavia, King Alexander abolished the departments into which the country had been thitherto divided and split it into nine *banovinas* of which only two, Savska and Primorska, had

AT THE HEAD OF THE CROATIAN PEASANT PARTY 129

a clear Croatian majority. Dravska *banovina* was entirely Slovene, while the remaining six were gerrymandered so as to yield sure Serbian majorities.

During the celebration of National Union Day on December 1, 1929, several bombs exploded with minor detonations. No property was damaged and no persons were hurt, but a group of the young members of our party were arrested. The police learned that they had prepared to sabotage a train scheduled to convey a group of pilgrims loyal to the regime. The police also discovered that I often gave financial aid to the University Organization of the Croatian Peasant Party, most of whose members had taken part in this plot; therefore, I, too, was arrested on December 22. After a preliminary hearing I was transferred, together with 24 other defendants, to the Court for the Defense of the State in Belgrade on the night of January 4-5, 1930. The regime hoped to have me condemned to several years of penal servitude and thus to eliminate me from politics.

According to existing laws, during the period of inquiry an accused man could talk to his lawyer only in the presence of the examining magistrate, but once the indictment had been drawn he could see his lawyer alone. After my transfer to the court of inquiry in Belgrade, the King ordered that the law be revised so that forthwith an accused could not consult his lawyer privately even after the indictment had been submitted. Yugoslav jurists called this the *Lex Maček,* as it had obviously been introduced to affect me.

The prison in Belgrade was filled with all kinds of political prisoners; most were Communists. There were no beds, and the prisoners had to sleep on the floor, covering themselves with whatever they had chanced to bring with them. The prison was overcrowded, and several men had to share each cell. I found myself separated from the rest of the political offenders and locked in with two Italian citizens accused as spies. One was a navy captain of advanced age and Croatian origins, though he considered himself an Italian; his name was Frane Šoljan. The other, his first mate, appeared to be a genuine Italian from Sicily. They had spent the last eleven months in prison. The captain, who spoke Croatian in the unmistakable dialect of his native island of Hvar, had a tidy sum of money which procured him various privileges from the guards. I profited from this simply by being cooped up in the same narrow cell. The very first day, he told me that to secure the goodwill of the gendarmes I had to give them small sums of money from time to time. The tactful way was to ask them to get me a package of cigarettes or a bottle of wine, then let them keep the change, something between 10 and 50 dinars. Through this simple device I found it possible to talk occasionally with other prisoners, including my co-defendants.

After about four months of inquiry the trial began on April 24, 1930. Some hundred lawyers, mostly from Croatia but several from Serbia, had volunteered to conduct my defense. Seven judges presided at the court—three Croats, three Serbs and a Slovene. The presence of so many lawyers annoyed the court, which declared at the start that it would permit no more than seven in my behalf, since it was not disposed to appreciate such a "demonstration." The first Foreign Minister of Yugoslavia, Ante Trumbić, attacked this decision "with indignation" and stated that nothing indicated a demonstration, though one might call it a "manifestation." At any rate, I picked my seven counsellors, and each of my co-defendants picked two or three, until about fifty lawyers were acknowledged. The remainder were asked to leave. When this had been settled and the indictment read, all the defendants were led back to their cells. In the subsequent weeks they had to face the judges one by one. In this manner none of them could take part in the proceedings before his turn had come, making it impossible to hear the testimony of the other defendants. I was relegated to the last place and did not leave my cell during the

AT THE HEAD OF THE CROATIAN PEASANT PARTY 131

trial for a month. The utmost care was taken to keep me in ignorance about the course of the trial. My Italian companions had been condemned to five and two years imprisonment respectively and were at once transferred elsewhere, leaving me alone in the cell. Newspapers were not allowed to reach me from outside, for fear that they would divulge the details of previous testimony. Useless precaution! To my surprise, the prison sergeant brought me the *Politika,* a Belgrade paper, every evening after the first day of the trial, when he had entered my cell with an official air, thrown the paper hidden in a large envelope on my table and announced in a casual tone: "A letter for you!" Thanks to the regular reports in the *Politika* I was always well informed about the latest developments at the court. When I tried to express my gratitude to this Serbian guard in the form of a sum of money, I discovered that I should not have judged him by his fellows. He categorically refused the offer and explained with finality: "It is my firm conviction that you are an honest man. How good it would be if all our politicians were like you! I know that, instead of sitting here in this cell, you could have become a minister in the government if you had only wanted to, but you are here, and I respect you for it." I received many compliments before and after this one, yet none lifted my spirits as high as the simple words spoken by this Serbian gendarme.

During my imprisonment in Belgrade, a different conversation I had with another gendarme served to characterize life in the former Serbia and, to some extent, in the new Yugoslavia. The man, well past middle age, kept watch over me during my daily airing in the prison yard. Sometimes he would sit down with me on a hard bench for a friendly chat. "Ah, brother," he began on one occasion, "I am in this service for forty years and have lived through a lot of things worth remembering. I shall never forget one time when I was young and keeping watch in this same yard. Right over there, in that cell, the late

Pašić was wasting away, and not like you—you have it well—but chains on his hands and chains on his feet. One morning, my captain appeared with two other men and asked me where Pašić was. When I pointed to the cell over there, the captain ordered: 'Unlock the door and take off his chains!' As soon as I had done so, two of them lifted him slowly by placing his arms around their shoulders and half carried, half dragged him out of sight. For goodness' sake! I thought. What's going to happen to him now? Would he have to face a firing squad? Good Lord, have mercy on his soul. When I took up the paper the next morning after duty, the first thing I saw was that Pašić had become Prime Minister. Thank God, I never had done anything to breed his ill will! You see, that is why I prefer to stay on friendly terms with the likes of you."

I was finally summoned to stand trial and thenceforth spent my days with the others in the Justice Hall. I again shared my cell with two other prisoners, which I preferred to remaining alone all the time. The entire trial lasted six weeks. Influenced by the liberal-mindedness of the chairman, the former Radical deputy and Minister of Justice, Jovan Subotić, the court had taken an impartial attitude. On June 14, about half the defendants were condemned to penal servitude, their terms ranging from one to fifteen years, while the other half, including myself, were acquitted. The verdict was final and set me free at once.

The regime had not yet succeeded in corrupting the judges, even though the law granting independence to the courts had been previously declared void. The judges selected for this trial had already reached the top of their profession and could not, therefore, be bought with promises of promotion or other compensations; the pension awaiting them was fixed and could not be altered by anybody or anything. Chairman Subotić and three other judges were, indeed, pensioned after the trial, while one of the younger magistrates was reduced to a lower rank.

On the evening of my liberation, I was sitting with my

counselors and a few friends at dinner in a garden restaurant at Zemun. Hardly an hour had passed when the police arrived, forced the guests to leave and arrested several of my former legal advisers. The Serbs among them were treated with particular severity; condemned to thirty days in prison, they had to spend them, day and night, on the bare concrete floor. The policemen did not lay hands on my person, but ordered me to take the first train for Zagreb, which I did at dawn the next morning.

During my imprisonment, the regime managed to undermine the good faith of several of the Croatian Peasant Party's national deputies. Disheartened by my detention, they bowed to the dictatorship. Four entered the dictatorial government as ministers. I emphasized their case in my plea to the court by comparing the Croatian masses with a forest after the passage of a heavy storm. Branches had necessarily been broken, but, once no longer attached to the tree that gave them life, they would dry up, even if they might, for a short time, adorn ministerial seats. When I regained my liberty, I soon found that my prophesy had been accurate. The turncoats had no followers and shortly afterward were themselves anxious to retire from public life.

While my trial was going on in Belgrade, Josip Predavec was facing a court in Zagreb. He had not been accused of any political crime, but was being prosecuted as the president of the Agrarian Cooperative Bank. This bank had been declared bankrupt, as the result of a campaign previously launched against it by the dictatorial regime, which suspected it of lending financial support to our party. The persecution was so thorough that even the director of the First Croatian Bank, who tried to rescue the Agrarian Cooperative Bank, was summoned to Belgrade and advised to keep his hands off. Since the regime controlled the Yugoslav National Bank, it was in a position to deny all credits to the First Croatian Bank and thereby threaten its very existence. Under such pressures the bankruptcy of the Agrarian Cooperative Bank could not be avoided. Predavec was condemned to two-and-a-half years of penal servitude and began his term in the penitentiary of Lepoglava.

The Predavec conviction also showed how the dictatorship corrupted the judiciary in Croatia. The examining magistrate, who had come to the conclusion that Predavec was not responsible for the bankruptcy of the Agrarian Cooperative Bank, had submitted a formal demand to the senate to countermand the trial and free Predavec. In reply, the chairman of the Court of Zagreb took the case out of the hands of this scrupulous judge and nominated a senate which he was sure would find Predavec guilty.

One final note on the Cooperative Bank: In 1931, August Košutić, who had gone into exile in September 1929, visited the United States and was denounced by Yugoslav officials there as an embezzler of several million dinars from the Agrarian Cooperative Bank. Of course, the American authorities eventually concluded that the whole story had been invented by the Yugoslav government.

My stay in prison had aggravated a derangement of the bile from which I had been suffering. I found it necessary to undergo medical treatment at Karlove Vary in October 1930. To procure a passport I sent a personal letter to Premier Petar Živković. He immediately ordered the Zagreb police by telephone to issue one in my name. I believe the regime hoped that I would remain in exile, where I would prove less of a danger. On my way to Karlove Vary I stopped in Vienna and met with Krnjević and Košutić; and from Karlove Vary one day, I went to Prague for a long talk with my old friend Milan Hodža, a Czechoslovak minister. He sympathized with the problems of Croatia, but told me frankly that King Alexander's regime enjoyed the unequivocal support of the so-called Entente and that nothing effective could be undertaken against the dictatorship from the outside.

AT THE HEAD OF THE CROATIAN PEASANT PARTY 135

From day to day that dictatorship became more and more ruthless in its weapons against adversaries. On February 19, 1931, a university professor, Dr. Milan Šufflay, was ambushed and killed in the heart of Zagreb. Public opinion attributed the crime to agents of the city police, and this opinion was confirmed at a trial much later. Professor Šufflay, a follower of the Croatian Party of Right, was a man of vast learning, high ethics and refined culture. He had been an old friend of mine, our friendship dating back to our high school days. Fluent in most of the important European languages, he had helped me greatly by translating essential foreign news for me.

August Košutić succeeded in rousing public opinion outside Yugoslavia to manifest its indignation at the odious murder of Professor Šufflay. He composed a formal protest that was signed by various prominent figures of European culture, among them, Albert Einstein and Heinrich Mann. Unfortunately, this righteous appeal did not affect the conscience of the Western democracies.

The trial of the group of Frankists arrested for the killing of the journalist Schlegel in 1929 and other terroristic activities took place in Zagreb in the spring of 1931. The counsel for the defense, of which I formed part, brought proof in court that Schlegel had been shot by two men who had successfully escaped to Italy. But the corrupted court brushed our evidence aside and sentenced most of the accused to long prison terms and two young men to death. Both, Hranilović and Soldin, were hanged soon after. The year before, a peasant lad, Rosić, had also been hanged for having attacked and killed a village mayor on a country road. The mayor, who had been elected as a member of the Croatian Peasant Party, had then joined the dictatorship. On the other hand, Puniša Račić, who killed three Croatian national deputies at an open session of Parliament, got away with twenty years of penal servitude, as did a man named Pejnović who murdered Karla Brkljačić, one of the most popular Croatian deputies, in broad daylight. I do not wish to give any impression of vindictiveness; opposed to capital punishment on principle, I never wished to see anyone receive the death penalty, not even Račić or Pejnović. I merely wish to show the double standard of justice King Alexander's regime applied—lenient to its own supporters, extreme toward those of the opposition.

On September 3, 1931, the regime proclaimed the "end of the dictatorship" and a new constitution. The latter was a figleaf to cover the bare-faced totalitarian system. It aimed to create an obedient, submissive parliament. The new electoral law required that each party ticket obtain a minimum of 60 signatures in every county of the State. Yugoslavia was nationally heterogeneous and its Parties were national, so that only the regime could be sure of collecting 60 signatures in every district, or at least of having them forged by its policemen. Thus Premier Živković was the only one who could present a list of candidates. Although the regime had not succeeded in collecting more than 15 per cent of the vote in the Croatian villages, the government had the effrontery to declare that its candidates had received an overwhelming majority.

Although on the paternal side I was two generations, and on the maternal side three generations, removed from my peasant ancestors, I had still felt since early youth a peculiar yearning to become a farmer. At the beginning of 1932, I bought a farm from a Czech family, situated near the small village of Kupinec, about twenty miles south of Zagreb. The property had been neglected and the soil was not of the best. But with the help of my brother-in-law, Ivan Čavlek (I was soon afterward condemned to three years of penal servitude), I transformed it into what may be called, under the circumstances, a model farm. Stock-breeding and raising pigs were its principal aims. When living in Zagreb, I used to go to Kupinec on every free day. At Christmas, Easter or during the school vacations, the whole family moved there. The days at Kupinec brought a wonderful change not only to me but, above all, to my children, who had the opportunity to swim, ride horseback, skate, and enjoy many other invigorating outdoor activities. The children became used to real farm work. My daughter Agnes, when she was fifteen years old, could milk six to seven cows an hour with her own hands. My son Andrej intently checked the food for the animals, examined the quality of the milk and followed up the daily increase in the weight of the hogs. This happy life has long since receded into the irrevocable past, leaving us only memories to treasure. The Communist regime in Yugoslavia ultimately confiscated my farm in Kupinec, and today, I have learned, it is again completely neglected. My daughter, meanwhile, had been married to a college professor in the United States and my son, who obtained his Ph.D in physical chemistry, is working as a research scientist. Both have lost all ties with our dear Croatian village.

On July 6, 1932, my younger brother Paul died. Paul was a quiet man with artistic and scholarly inclinations. At the time of his death he was the principal of a Zagreb gymnasium. While his passing affected everybody in our family, it was an especially heavy blow for my father who was over 86 and of failing health.

From 1931 on, my activity was limited to receiving and talking to people from all parts of Croatia who poured in on me daily, and to giving interviews to foreign journalists who occasionally dropped in. At such interviews I inevitably expressed sharp criticism of the dictatorship without worrying about what might happen to me. Nevertheless, Pribičević's followers reproached me, as head of the Peasant-Democrat Coalition, for being too slack in fighting King Alexander's dictatorship. Stirred by these reproaches, I convoked a meeting of the principal leaders of both parties in Zagreb on November 7, 1932. The time was not propitious and the situation hardly inspired confidence, for I feared that the Democrats might sway in the direction of "unitarism" again without Pribičević himself at hand.

The Croatian Peasant Party was represented by myself, Trumbić, Predavec and Jure Šutej. Mile Budak of the Croatian Party of Right attended at my invitation. The Independent Democrats were represented by Većeslav Vilder and Hinko Krizman, both Croats with a Yugoslav orientation, and by three Serbs, Dušan Bošković, Dušan Kecmanović (an Orthodox priest) and Sava Kosanović.

Our meeting took a smooth course at first. We all agreed to combine forces for the destruction of the dictatorship. But I could not suppress a faint uneasiness when the question of how to replace it was about to be raised. In the evening the meeting was adjourned, and all of us accepted an invitation to dinner with Josip Trbuha, the parish priest of Saint John's in Zagreb. During the meal, Trumbić severely criticized the rule of Alexander and concluded: "We, the Croats and Serbs from Croatia, Bosnia and Vojvodina, must stand together at any price and adapt our relations with 'those across the Drina' to the degree of reasonableness they are capable of showing." I was pleasantly surprised when I observed that not only the Croats but Sava Kosanović, the Serb from Croatia, Dušan Kecmanović, the Serb from Bosnia, and Dušan Bošković, the Serb from Vojvodina, applauded these words warmly. When the dinner party broke up, it was past midnight. Before we left, I told everybody that the meeting would be resumed at 4 o'clock the next afternoon, and when Trumbić and I separated, I asked him to prepare a resolution composed in the spirit of his speech and bring it to me at noon the next day. Trumbić was at the time a gentleman of about 70, but despite his advanced age he conscientiously brought me the draft resolution a half hour early. We reviewed it together and gave it final form. At the meeting, held this time in the apartment of Većeslav Vilder, the resolution was read to those present and unanimously accepted and signed. The text of the resolution follows:

(1) Subscribing to the principles of democracy we consider the sovereignty of the people the foundation on which the organization of the State must rest and the people themselves the sole and unique source of all political sovereignty and of all public power.

(2) The peasantry, viewed as a collective concept, is the depository of the national culture and the basis of economic life, upholds the social structure as well as its standard of moral values, and represents the majority of the nation; it should form the cornerstone in the organization of our national life.

(3) We must point out that Serbian hegemony, imposed from the start on Croatia and all the other lands on this side of the Sava, the Drina and the Danube, has acted destructively through its obvious incapacity to govern, its tyranny and its use of immoral means. It has monopolized all the powers of the State and destroyed our moral values and our progressive institutions as well as our traditions. It has not respected the material possessions of the people and even robbed it of its spiritual peace. This state of misrule reached its peak when the absolutist regime was introduced on January 6, 1929, reinforcing this hegemony with fatal consequences and, worst of all, abolishing civil and political freedom.

(4) Considering these disastrous experiences, we have arrived at the inevitable conclusion that we must go back to the starting-point of 1918 in response to the pressing need to conduct a decisive and organized battle against that hegemony, in order to free our lands from it and deprive it of power and influence by eliminating its representatives.

(5) Only by carrying out the program previously laid down can the new organization of the common State be undertaken. Without entering into details at this time, the principal basic ideas underlying such an organization may be summarized as follows:

The commonwealth, as we conceive it, must be an association of interests, founded with the free consent of each member, ruling out domination of one or more over the others, and thereby giving each the right to safeguard its particular interests on its own territory, or to administer, in concert with the others, the joint affairs of general concern, on the strength of mutual agreement. Thus will progress be assured in respect to the moral development, as well as to the gradual improvement of material conditions, among the Serbs, Croats and Slovenes. The individual interests of minorities speaking a foreign language shall be specifically guaranteed.

Because of the Draconian criminal law, we decided not to give this resolution excessive publicity, but merely to send a copy to each of the leading personalities of the Peasant-Democrat Coalition and to the leaders of the Serbian opposition parties. Nevertheless, a few days later, the regime-controlled papers published the resolution with fierce attacks. They thus gave it a wide publicity which, because of the strict censorship, would have been impossible for us to attempt. The government's obvious efforts to incite Serbian public opinion against us failed lamentably. The Serbs themselves were rather inclined to view this resolution as a bold act by those who openly dared to oppose Alexander—which they admired—rather than as a blow directed at Serbia. They even enjoyed reading the resolution.

It is interesting to note that Mile Budak, representative of the Croatian Party of Right, whose leader Ante Pavelić was an exile in Italy and enjoyed the hospitality of Mussolini's Fascist regime, had also signed the resolution. Budak's signature apparently remained a thorn in the flesh of Pavelić and his hosts.

Earlier, in the summer of 1932, an adherent of the dictatorship had assaulted Budak during the lunch hours in one of Zagreb's most crowded streets, hitting him on the head with a club and wounding him grievously. Budak, unlike Professor Šufflay, was physically strong and managed to pull a gun from his pocket and send a bullet after his aggressor. He missed,

AT THE HEAD OF THE CROATIAN PEASANT PARTY 141

while the latter fled. Alarmed by the shot, the crowd instinctively chased the culprit, who was caught a few minutes later by passers-by and surrendered to police. He eventually was tried and given a three-year prison sentence. Budak was hospitalized for three weeks. After he was discharged, he seemed to have recovered entirely and paid no attention to the unfortunate incident.

But when the resolution was made public several months later, Pavelić's adherents spread news in Zagreb that Budak's life was in danger and that he intended to leave Croatia for an indefinite stay in exile. I do not know whether Budak actually feared for his life or whether he had been ordered by Pavelić to join him in Italy; it is certain, though, that the Frankists wished to remove their representative from the sphere of my influence, and they succeeded. He left the country in possession of a regular passport.

By and by, the regime abandoned its campaign against our resolution, and most likely there would have been no aftermath if foreign newsmen had not come to seek interviews with me. I made diverse statements to them in which I dealt unsparingly with the dictatorship, and this had a more stinging effect on the Royal Government than the resolution ever could have provoked. Quite unexpectedly, after an especially outspoken declaration to a reporter from the French daily *Le Petit Parisien*, the regime decided to arrest me.

CHAPTER X

Prison

$\mathcal{I}$ WAS ARRESTED at 8 P.M., on January 31, 1933. The Chief of the Zagreb Police was Stanoje Mihaldžić, who six years later was to be my colleague in the Government of Dragiša Cvetković. When I was brought in to face him, he began to excuse himself for troubling me—he had been ordered to examine me about a few matters. I advised him with a smile to drop the formalities and tell me where I was to go. I retained no illusions about the regime and, therefore, had no doubt that some sort of confinement was coming. For a second, Mihaldžić was taken aback; then he replied flatly that I had to go to Čajniće. On my request he produced a map and together we searched for the exact location of my forced abode. After we had found it, I proposed that we start drafting the protocol. He confronted me with a text of our Resolution of November 7, 1932 and inquired whether I had composed and signed it. I told him truthfully that the Resolution was the joint work of all the undersigned; I had taken the initiative in signing it and the rest had followed suit. This was all the Chief wanted to know, for he ceased asking questions and contented himself with repeating in an official manner that I would be confined at Čajniće for an indeterminate period. Unofficially he informed me that I was to leave that very night via Belgrade, Užice and Višegrad. I had two hours left, and Mihaldžić telephoned my house to give my family and friends an opportunity to part with me.

Three police officials escorted me to Belgrade. Upon our arrival on the morning of February 1, they were relieved by three Belgrade plainclothesmen, who took me to Ustiprača, a little station on the Belgrade-Sarajevo line not far from Višegrad. We reached it toward evening the same day. The Chief of the Sarajevo Police, Musakadić, had two cars waiting for us. He and I sat in the back of the first one, an agent of the Sarajevo Police sat next to our driver, and the Belgrade policeman followed in the second car. On the road Musakadić said to me: "Although we can easily make Čajniće tonight, I think it advisable to stop at Goražde, eight miles away, and to spend the night at one of the hotels there. Tomorrow morning, we can continue to Čajniće by daylight with the gracious help of Allah." (Musakadić was of Moslem faith.)

At Goražde, the Police Chief ordered dinner for the two of us in a separate room. During the night, a pair of police agents were posted outside my door. The next morning, we drove from Goražde to Čajniće, and Musakadić delivered me to Tomek, the county Chief, who had been given charge of me. Tomek, a man of Czech origin, showed at once a deliberate circumspection in his manner toward me, in which I could detect a strange apprehension that my restraint under his control might turn out to be to his own disadvantage.

Čajniće was known in Eastern Bosnia as a fashionable summer mountain resort, situated about 3000 feet above sea-level and frequented by Sarajevo's wealthy society. Tomek assigned me a very nice room on the second floor of a summer tourist home. The house had its own restaurant where I ate my meals. The owner of the boarding-house was an Orthodox Serb named Vaso Dumandžić. His wife, however, was a Croat and a Catholic, the only Catholic—apart from County Chief Tomek and his family—amid a population divided between Moslems and Orthodox. Practically all the inhabitants of Čajniće, whether

Serbs or Moslems, treated me at first with friendly benevolence. Under the Austro-Hungarian Monarchy, half a battalion of infantry had been garrisoned at Čajniće, for whom a small Catholic chapel had been built in addition to the two Moslem mosques and the beautiful Orthodox church. The parish priest of Višegrad, Father Roje, arrived the following Sunday to celebrate Mass and afterward paid me a visit. His parish was of unusual dimensions, embracing the three bishoprics of Sarajevo, Mostar and Skoplje—a wide area with as much as a hundred miles between its members, which forced him to travel perpetually from one chapel to another.

The second Croat to call on me was Jure Šutej of our party. He had come to Čajniće under the pretext of legal business in the town. Upon my entering the restaurant for breakfast one morning, Vaso Dumandžić whispered into my ear that Šutej had come a short time before and that my police guard had refused him entrance. A short time later, the County Office janitor brought an invitation from the District Chief to come and see him. When I got there, I found Šutej waiting in the company of Tomek and a Belgrade Police agent. We were allowed to converse for half an hour in their presence. Needless to say, we could not discuss the things that principally animated our minds.

However insignificant this incident seemed, it proved ruinous for Tomek, who was ordered by telegram to leave Čajniće a few days later. I had become accustomed to spending my evenings in his company, usually joined by several local citizens who sat with us around our regular table in the restaurant. These friendly and quite harmless gatherings came to an end when, one morning, I was confronted with a new County Chief named Živković who told me that Tomek had been recalled. The consequences soon made themselves felt. Quite suddenly nobody dared enter the inn any more. Men who had treated me till then with sincere cordiality disappeared into their shops or houses at the very sight of me in the street. My host Vaso

explained that the new County Chief had fined two or three
of them a hundred dinars for having exchanged greetings with
me. The citizens of this small resort town naturally considered
such greetings too expensive. Živković always displayed punc-
tilious courtesy toward me; his drastic measures were aimed to
prevent me from making contacts among the population, principally with persons of political significance. His efforts were
successful; the only man in the whole borough who openly
(indeed, with a sort of supreme indifference) sought my company and shared my table, was a young Orthodox priest named
Vlado Sokolović. His name reminded me of Mehmed Pasha
Sokolović, the famous Grand Vizir of Suleiman the Magnificent. The Grand Vizir, a native of Čajniće, had nominated his
half-brother Makarije head of the restored Serbian Orthodox
Patriarchate in 1557.

Toward the end of February, I was summoned to the County
Office for a hearing before a specially-designated examining
magistrate from the Court for the Defense of the State. Apart
from some questions concerning the composition of our Resolution of November 7, 1932 (the cause of my confinement),
and my interviews with the foreign press (rigid censorship had
suppressed their publication in the country), the interrogation
hardly resembled a hearing on a specific offense; it rather
seemed a sounding of my political views. My replies openly
expressed my position. As a result of this hearing, Musakadić
arrived on March 10 with a warrant to take me to the Ustiprača station and there to surrender me to the Belgrade Police.
When I asked what the Belgrade Police intended to do, he said
that he knew no more than I did.

On March 11, we traveled from Čajniće to Ustiprača; then
Belgrade police agents took me by train to the Serbian capital.
At the Belgrade station, Job, the examining magistrate, entered
my carriage and informed me that the Court for Defense of
the State had ordered another hearing and issued a warrant
for keeping me under arrest until then. He drove me in a

police car to the notorious Glavnjača prison, where I was locked in the wing assigned to prisoners of the Court of Belgrade. The President of that Court, Filipović, had a bright, clean cell with a new bed ready for me. Upon entering it, I silently noted the progress made since 1930, for Filipović now found it necessary to tell me that he had nothing to do with my case and that I must consider myself merely his "guest." In fact, he behaved very civilly throughout my stay. After hours each day he visited me, saw whether my wishes had been complied with, heard my complaints and, after a gendarme had brought coffee, engaged in friendly conversation.

Otherwise, I was completely isolated from the world. The only human being I could speak to was Sreten, the "Sergeant No. 1" and a well-known figure in Belgrade. Each of Yugoslavia's thousands of gendarmes wore his particular number; the "Sergeant No. 1" occupied the post of Commandant of the Prison. Sreten enjoyed a reputation as a rough character, and I was prepared to expect inconsiderate treatment. But I must confess that he gave me no reason for complaint at any time and, strange as it may seem, plainly indulged in feelings of commiseration. I devoted the better part of my time in prison to reading, and when I grew too tired, I would stretch out on my bed, while he paced the floor in the corridor. Sometimes, when he discovered through the small window in the door that I had ceased reading, he would enter my cell and talk with me for an hour or two about whatever came to mind. He would pour forth countless questions on science, geography, history, astronomy and even politics, then listen attentively to my words; one would have to be a living encyclopedia to answer all his questions. He would never sit down, persistently declining my offer of a seat with the excuse that he was used to standing; nor would he accept a cigarette. He was annoyed when I refused to have my feet washed by a young criminal prisoner who brought water each day from the well in the courtyard. For my meals, he invariably called in a waiter from a neighboring restaurant with the day's menu; I underlined the foods I preferred and was sure to get my choice. Contrary to custom, I was left in possession of my money and small personal effects such as my rings, which enabled me to pay my running expenses.

But the isolation was so complete that I was not even taken to the court house for questioning. The examining magistrate came to the prison for my hearings, which took place in Sreten's adjacent room. At the end of a month's inquiry, the bill of indictment was submitted to the Court. The only charge brought against me was that of being the principal author of the Resolution of November 7, 1932; the more outspoken interviews had been omitted from the bill. The moment I learned the composition of the Court Senate, I knew that my conviction was already decided, and that the court proceedings would be merely empty formality.

This time I had a single counsellor to defend me. (The law had been revised after my first trial, so as to admit only one defense attorney before the Court for the Defense of the State.) Dr. Milan Kostić, a Serb from Croatia and Independent Democratic deputy, acted as my counsel. All the signatories of the Resolution, with the exception of Mile Budak who was in exile, traveled to Belgrade to be at the immediate disposal of the examining magistrate. In a fine spirit of solidarity they demanded to stand trial "en bloc" by my side. Their demands, however, were not heeded. During the trial I was asked, among other things, where the Resolution had been drawn up. When I declined to answer it, deputy Većeslav Vilder, seated among the throng of spectators, got up and stated calmly: "In my apartment, Mr. Chairman!" After this frank statement, all the signatories of the Resolution were banished from Belgrade by the police.

The plea in my own defense was very brief. I said, in essence, that the Croatian nation must obtain her liberty at all costs, either within the boundaries of the Yugoslav State or without.

As everyone could deduce from past trials, my colleagues and I had endeavored to solve the Croatian problem within the limits of the State. Should the Court judge such activities to be criminal, let it condemn them.

The next day, April 30, I was sentenced to three years of rigid confinement at Mitrovica, with the privilege of *custodia honesta*.* When I returned to my cell, sergeant Sreten was already standing there waiting to hear the news. "How much?" he eagerly inquired. I lifted three fingers in answer, whereupon he asked: "Three months?" When I said it was three years, his eyes brimmed with tears: "They have no souls, they can't have souls!"

Since on May 1 most of the police were out trying to guard against possible Communist demonstrations, my transfer to the penitentiary was postponed until May 2.

Two Belgrade police agents escorted me to Mitrovica, which we reached during the night. I was temporarily housed there in the court cell until, at 6 A.M., I was transferred to the prison itself.

The place struck me at first sight as not unpleasant, considering its purpose. A little door in the 20-foot stone-wall around it opened on to a lovely orchard. I was stunned by the enchanting beauty suddenly revealed to my eyes. Around me the fruit-trees stood in full bloom, shimmering in snowy whiteness under the radiant light of the morning sun. The orchard covered about two acres of land. In the center of it rose a one-storey structure, the former prison hospital, which at the time held a host of political prisoners in its four rooms. All

---

* Prisoners granted the *custodia honesta* did not have to serve their terms in the penitentiary three miles outside the town of Mitrovica and were not subject to the discipline established at the discretion of its director. They were detained in a special prison located in the center of the town where the rules were laid down by the Chief of the Court of Mitrovica. They were relieved of work, wore their own clothes, and could smoke and order their meals from outside. Moreover, the law said, they were entitled to receive visitors "more often."

but one of these were spacious. Among the prisoners at the time were Dean Škrbec, parish priest from Kranj, Janez Brodar, national deputy of the Slovenian Populist Party, and twenty of their Slovene compatriots; Ivan Pernar and Djuro Kemfelja, two of my Croatian colleagues; a Serbian lawyer and a Serbian professor; as well as some young men from Croatia and the naval captain Frane Šoljan, my cell-mate of 1930.

Prison rules were not strict at all, and inmates were on the whole treated leniently. The roms were unlocked at 7 A.M. and locked again at 9 P.M. All prisoners were allowed to stroll at leisure in the orchard and could enter one another's rooms as often as they liked. Friends flocked in for visits at all times. They simply announced themselves to the Commandant of the Prison Guard, who would send one of his men to look for the wanted prisoner and then permit them to talk to him in one of the guard rooms across the street quite freely, without close watch. The majority of the detained received their lunch and dinner from a restaurant, for 300 dinars a month. Food portions were generous, so that they could be shared with those less able to pay for them. Hence, everyone could abstain from the unwholesome prison food.

Shortly after my arrival, however, things changed for the worse. The old Commandant of the Guard was replaced by a younger man with ambitions. The right to visit prisoners was reserved to family members alone, who had to limit their conversation to twenty minutes in the study of the President of the Court. Except for two hours in the morning and one hour in the afternoon, the prisoners stayed locked in their cells. It was against the rules to keep money of our own, and a special judge was expressly placed in charge of keeping accounts for each of the inmates. If one wanted to buy something, he had to specify the article on a slip of paper and send it in the morning to the President of the Court, who after brief scrutiny would instruct the judge to appropriate the necessary amount. Cigarettes topped the items most in demand. Apart from reading, endless card games took up the larger part of our leisure hours. In the absence of money, we played for cigarettes.

Although we did our utmost to kill time, it seemed to drag on unbearably, so much so that I formed the habit of measuring it in units of three weeks. This was the interval between the much longed-for Fridays on which my sister-in-law would bring my children from Zagreb for a visit. Despite express orders from the Ministry of Justice prescribing a maximum of twenty minutes for interviews, the President of the Court, Stjepan Rogulja, let us talk together for two hours, one in the morning and one in the afternoon. He was well aware that my family had to travel for seven hours from Zagreb to Mitrovica in order to see me and that it would be cruel to restrict the meeting to twenty short minutes controlled by a stop-watch. We, too, had to see each other in his study. But he would remain seated at his desk at one end of the large room throughout the interview, thus allowing us as much privacy as possible around a table at the opposite end. We could broach any subject without being disturbed and even availed ourselves of an old trick employed by prisoners for exchanging secret notes, which he indulgently pretended not to notice. After he gave us permission to smoke, my sister-in-law produced a book of matches from her bag, in which a tiny piece of paper containing a message and a few questions had been hidden. The matches were left casually on the table during our conversation, and when we separated, I slipped them inconspicuously into my own pocket. During lunch, I was able to read the note and jot down my answers containing political advice as a rule. I hid my reply in the same way, and the matches finally were carried away by my sister-in-law after our second meeting in the afternoon.

In mid-July I learned from the newspapers that my Acting Representative, Josip Predavec, the Vice-president of the Croatian Peasant Party, had been ambushed and assassinated.

The murder of Predavec made the party's position most

difficult. Košutić and Krnjević were in exile. Pernar and I were in prison. None of the representatives of the party were left in Zagreb. Once again, my sister-in-law bore a message in a match book to our Party members. In it I instructed them to follow the direction of the old and experienced politician, Ante Trumbić, even though he had joined the Peasant Party fairly recently.

In the fall of 1933, I received the painful news that my father, already in his eighty-eighth year, was suffering from pneumonia. According to the existing ordinance, a prisoner could apply for a temporary release not exceeding a fortnight in case of serious illness or death in his family. When I submitted an application to this end, the Ministry of Justice rejected it. On December 22, President Rogulja handed me a telegram which announced the death of my father. Although I made no further effort to obtain a leave, Rogulja himself asked the Ministry of Justice to let me attend my father's funeral. A positive reply arrived the next day. I was supposed to take the train on the 23rd at 7 P.M., but my departure was delayed until midnight. Neither I nor the President of the Court understood the reason for the delay. But upon my arrival at Zagreb on December 24, its cause became clear. The Zagreb Police had previously informed my family that I was not to follow the hearse from our house, but would join the funeral procession later at the Mirogoj Cemetery for the burial ceremony. They had deferred my departure from Mitrovica in order to prevent my arrival at Zagreb before my father's body had reached the cemetery. The purpose was to avoid at all cost the much-feared mass protests they could expect if I appeared in person in the crowded streets of the city.

Although it was Christmas Eve, thousands of people accompanied my father on his last journey. When the ceremonies were over I was taken to my house, from which all but my family and close relatives were barred by the ubiquitous police.

My leave of absence expired at the end of three days, and so the day after Christmas I was scheduled to go back. An hour before my train pulled out, an official of the Zagreb Police, Dragi Jovanović (he was later Police Minister in the Government formed by General Nedić during the German occupation of Serbia) came to see me and suggested that I make a written request, "only a few words," for an extension of my leave. He would vouch for it, he assured me, that I would on no account have to return to Mitrovica again. I emphatically declined his offer and started on my trip back to prison punctually that very evening.

The leaders of the regime had begun to realize that my arrest had failed to solve their problems. On the contrary, the resistance of the Croats, far from diminishing, had increased; it was a quiet, pervasive and constant resistance. King Alexander reluctantly made up his mind to re-establish contact with me, and chose Ivan Šubašić as an intermediary.

I had met Šubašić for the first time in 1921, at the wedding of Stephen Radić's eldest daughter. Radić's new son-in-law, Josip Vandekar, contracted tuberculosis soon afterward and had to abandon the city for the lovely mountain town of Vrbovsko. There he spent a year as the guest of Šubašić, who had his legal practice in the town. I saw both of them occasionally when business took me to Vrbovsko, enjoyed myself in their company and maintained friendly relations with Šubašić after Vandekar's death. In 1928, when our physician prescribed a stay in the mountains for my children, Šubašić found them a suitable boarding-house. Mrs. Šubašić and my sister-in-law were of the same age and felt drawn to each other; a close friendship sprang up from this mutual sympathy between our families. When Šubašić's daughter was born, I had the pleasure of being her godfather. Šubašić also escorted me to Karlove Vary in 1930, carrying a loaded gun in his pocket to parry a possible attempt on my life. His devotion to me was most sincere. In 1933, when my trial was about to begin, he came to Belgrade on his own initiative and tried to get me out of prison and have the court case dismissed. He had been a Yugoslav volunteer in the first world war which made it easy for him to obtain an audience with King Alexander. When I learned of his efforts, I urged him through my counsel to relinquish the part of Tosca. (Tosca, the young heroine of Puccini's opera, surrendered herself to the tyrant to save her lover's life. A vain sacrifice, because the tyrant, once his wish had been fulfilled, shot the maiden's lover all the same.) After receiving my message, Šubašić had left Belgrade without delay and had severed all ties with the King for more than a year.

Now, at the beginning of June 1934, the Monarch instructed Šubašić to prepare the ground for a compromise with me. The latter paid me two visits at Mitrovica, during the first of which we entertained ourselves in the presence of President Rogulja. We did not touch on politics throughout the interview. Šubašić thereupon went back and reported to Alexander that we had avoided mentioning politics because the ordinance issued by the Minister of Justice made it impossible for him to see me in private.

Meanwhile, I had fallen ill. The consequences of an oral sepsis had weakened my heart to such an extent that the director of a Zagreb hospital, Dr. Lujo Thaller, who had been called in, demanded my immediate transfer to a hospital. Since Dr. Thaller was devoted to the regime, he effected my transfer to the Hospital of the Catholic Nuns of Zagreb on July 15, 1934.

Several days prior to my removal there, Šubašić arrived with authorization to talk with me confidentially. On doctor's orders, I had to stay in bed all day long. To secure the necessary privacy, my bed was pushed into the shady orchard, and Šubašić was left alone with me. He conveyed a message from the King, who asked me merely to make a formal declaration that I was not against the Yugoslav State. I replied that that fact had been proven by all my political activities, but that

I could definitely not acquiesce in the present organization of the State and would abide by my earlier statements, made in the course of the inquiry before my last trial and at the trial itself. Šubašić appeared unsatisfied with this categorical answer and pointed out to me the precarious, even dangerous situation in which I stood at this moment. We at last agreed that he should tell the King of my determination to refrain from political negotiations so long as I remained imprisoned.

A few days later, I lay in the hospital where prison discipline had to be somewhat relaxed. I had been given a very comfortable single room, outside which a police agent guarded my door. A special permit from Zagreb Police Chief Mihaldžić was required of anyone wishing to call on me. No person was allowed to enter my room without being accompanied by a police agent. But Dr. Thaller succeeded in preventing the agents from following the doctors and nuns into the room on their regular rounds. Mihaldžić had also kindly issued permanent permits for my children and my sister-in-law to visit me whenever they wished. Through the intermediary of doctors and nuns, I was able to maintain close contact with my friends who were denied access to my sickroom.

A few days before King Alexander's fateful visit to France, Šubašić communicated to me his last message: "Tell Dr. Maček," the monarch said emphatically, "that I shall free him as soon as I return from France. But then I shall deal with him in person."

Death disengaged Alexander from his promise on October 9, 1934, when he fell victim in Marseilles to Croatian and Macedonian extremists. The day after the King's assassination, Dr. Thaller tried to persuade me to send a letter of condolence to the royal family. I told him that since I was opposed on principle to terrorist acts of any kind, I sympathized sincerely with the widowed Queen and the dead Monarch's children; but I could not and would not send a formal letter of condolence, which in the present situation could be wrongly interpreted from a political viewpoint. Yet, Dr. Thaller transmitted such a statement without my knowledge to the Royal Government in Belgrade. The latter, however, showed sufficient prudence not to take Dr. Thaller's message as an official one and dispatched a special delegate to my bedside to record my words of condolence in protocol. I confirmed to him the contents of my previous conversation with Dr. Thaller, but pointed out that I had never authorized him to convey its contents to the Royal Government. My condolence, therefore, did not figure among the published list of testimonies of sympathy, written either spontaneously or under pressure. Dr. Thaller later told me that his sole intention in sending the message had been to expedite my liberation. As I knew his personal integrity, I did not doubt his good intentions.

After the death of Alexander, I stayed another two-and-a-half months in the hospital. The new King, Peter II, was still a child of twelve, which meant that a Regency would serve until he came of age. The late King had appointed its members by testament. The dignities and tasks of first Regent, naturally, were to fall on Alexander's cousin, Prince Paul, who would be assisted by Radenko Stanković and Ivo Perović. Three alternates were designated in the case of death or abdication. No Slovene had been included in the Regency, even as an alternate; and Ivo Perović, who was ostensibly to represent the Croats, was himself born in the small Albanian colony of Arbanasi, near Zadar in Dalmatia.

The Regency did not assume power without an incident. The Government, whose Premier was Nikola Uzunović, was probably unaware of the existence of the royal testament; it nominated a rival Regency with Uzunović himself at its head. Prince Paul, who was in possession of the testament, asked the Premier to an audience. Anticipating resistance on the part of Uzunović, he also summoned the Commandant of the Royal Guard, General Pera Živković. Prince Paul handed the document to the Premier and demanded that he take cognizance of Alexander's last will. When Uzunović finished reading it, he was about to slip it into his pocket with the brief remark that the Royal Government would make a decision regarding the matter. He had not reckoned with General Živković, who started to thump on the floor with his sword and roared: "What decision? A testament is a testament and must be respected without argument." Uzunović saw no other way out but to accept the fact. This was probably one reason why certain "Great Serbian" groups thoroughly disliked Prince Paul.

On December 22, I read in the paper of the formation of a new cabinet with Bogoljub Jeftić as Premier. The same evening, Stanoje Mihaldžić phoned me with the confidential news that I was about to be granted an amnesty and that he hoped to confirm this officially in the course of the night. An hour had hardly elapsed when a police official came to announce my newly-gained freedom. The news spread incredibly quickly all over Zagreb, and when I reached my home, numerous friends thronged in my apartment, hall, and stairway to receive me. I celebrated a joyful Christmas, surrounded by my loved ones, although my father's absence cast a shadow on our common happiness. Without our "grand-dad," Christmas had lost some of its brightness.

Decency required that I thank Prince Paul for the amnesty. I telegraphed: "Thanking Your Highness for my regained freedom, I hope and I believe that your act is the first sign of a new and more correct approach to the Croatian problem." The government never published that telegram and when some non-regime papers (no opposition press existed) planned to print it, the censors forbade it.

A month after my liberation I married for the third time. My sister-in-law Josipa, who after the cruel loss of my wife took charge of my children and nursed my father until his death, had agreed to become my companion for life. It stands to reason that it was not romantic love that moved us to take the decisive step. A much deeper feeling bound us strongly together—her immense love for my children, whose mother had been her own sister. Despite the great difference in age, our married life has always been harmonious. Together we shared many a happy day before the German and Italian occupation. During the occupation, she endured, with me and the children, the distressing existence of a long internment under enemy forces and now stands by me, day in and day out, to make the best of an often wearisome life in exile.

CHAPTER XI

The Boom of the Party

*I*MMEDIATELY AFTER the Orthodox Christmas (January 7), rumors began to circulate about impending parliamentary elections. These rumors were soon confirmed by the newly-named Premier, Bogoljub Jeftić, in a statement about me to a French correspondent. Jeftić said that I was in very ill health and, in any case, incapable of exerting notable influence on the broad masses of the people—the proof of which would soon be revealed to the public eye. Since the impossible electoral law had only been slightly altered since 1931, however, I saw no choice but to abstain again from the elections.

At the beginning of February, 1935, Dragoljub Jovanović, a left-wing member of the Serbian Agrarian Party,* transmitted to me the Serbian Opposition's request to participate in the elections. I would be the top nominee on a united list representing our party as well as the Serbian Opposition. This proposal was a delicate one, for the attitude of the Croatian masses to such cooperation could not be foreseen. After

* Jovanovic remained on good terms with the Croats even after the bloodshed in the Belgrade Parliament in 1928. In 1932 he published a pamphlet entitled *What We Must Pay for Our Quarrel with the Croats.* The pamphlet argued that the Serbs, in their effort to oppress the Croats, had lost their own freedom and now had to live under a dictatorship. As a result of that pamphlet Jovanovic was sent to prison for a year.

After the Second World War Jovanovic joined Tito's movement, but clashed with him only a year later, opposing the forced collectivization of the peasants. He was promptly expelled from the Communist Parliament and sentenced to nine years at hard labor. He served this sentence almost in full, i.e. over eight years. He lives retired in Belgrade.

THE BOOM OF THE PARTY 159

Radić's assassination, many people believed that relations between the Croats and Serbia had been permanently broken. I could not give Jovanović a definite reply, though I promised to think about his proposal and to reply within a few days to the letter from Ljuba Davidović that he had brought me.

Jovanović had scarcely left Zagreb when the "Official Gazette" published an ukase announcing the elections. I had to decide quickly, and had no one to consult. Košutić and Krnjević were in exile, Predavec was dead and Trumbić was under the influence of Zagreb intellectuals ill-disposed toward any collaboration with Serbian parties. I thought of calling together a few dozen peasant representatives from the provinces, but it was already too late. The decision, therefore, rested solely with me.

I had heard of a theory in some occult science which invests man with three different personalities, respectively physical, mental and astral. When he is asleep, he somehow acquires the faculty of sudden insight into what formerly seemed inextricable problems. God only knows whether there is any truth in this theory, but I must admit that I have often found myself unable to solve an obstinate problem in the evening, suddenly seeing the right solution clear as crystal the next morning. This time was no exception. Lying in bed I weighed the pros and cons with little success, yet in the morning I had not the slightest doubt that we had to participate in the elections. We could not hope to obtain the absolute majority which would automatically give us three-fifths of the total seats. The Government was used to gerrymandering and would have no scruples about falsifying the results of the polls in many provinces. But this fact did not overshadow the opportunity to demonstrate publicly the substantial size of the opposition. I decided to accept the offer of the Serbian Opposition and, to this end, sent a special messenger to Davidović.

The strict censorship forbade the press to print news about the various opposition movements, and the papers therefore ignored the fact that the Opposition I was chosen to lead had entered the elections until the very day the Court accepted our list. Notwithstanding the censorship, the news of my candidacy spread swiftly and reached the most remote Croatian villages.

Apart from the Croatian Peasant Party and its ally, the Independent Democratic Party, the Opposition list was composed of the Democratic Party of Ljuba Davidović, the Serbian Agrarian Alliance of Joca Jovanović and the Yugoslav Moslem Organization of Mehmed Spaho. The Serbian Radical Party's formal head was the octogenarian Aca Stanojević, though the Party was actually led by Miša Trifunović. The Radicals, as well as the Slovenian Populist Party of Korošec, did not join the united Opposition but proclaimed their abstention. The reasons for this were disclosed to me later. The two parties had been promised that after the elections Jeftić's Party would relinquish its sole power and form a new government in coalition with them. Korošec's abstention put our Opposition in a difficult situation in Slovenia, since his major local antagonists, the Slovene Liberals, had endorsed the dictatorship at its very birth. Hence it was up to me to collect for our list the required sixty signatures in each Slovenian district. In the districts bordering on Croatia this was not difficult, since they included many old sympathizers of ours. It seemed more difficult to procure the required sixty signatures in Central and Western Slovenia. Yet, it turned out to be much easier than I had thought. I sent some Party members from Zagreb to the peasant districts of Slovenia to put up their candidacies and, more important still, to gather the required signatures. Though the candidates had no chance of being elected, my collaborators undertook the task with cheerful readiness, and thus we were able to present the prescribed number of signatures in Slovenia.

At the time I decided to enter the elections, the Zagreb bourgeoisie, which had always displayed extreme nationalist tendencies, manifested a distinct unwillingness to make common cause with the Serbs. In the villages, where there were similar tendencies, I nevertheless enjoyed unwavering confidence; I soon witnessed an unreserved readiness to prepare for the impending electoral battle.

The beginning of this battle was a bloody clash between peasants and gendarmes at the village of Sibinj; nine peasants died and many others were wounded. Obviously, the regime had tried to intimidate the people, in order to undermine the recruiting efforts of the Opposition. But the bloody encounters spurred the peasants to fight more fiercely than ever.

At Zagreb the Frankists and their sympathizers, indisposed to join the campaign, rallied around Ante Trumbić. He called on me, intent on convincing me that the Croats had made a serious mistake. But, after hearing the reasons for my conduct, Trumbić reversed his opinion and offered both to stand for election himself and to go to Belgrade and compose our official list of candidates to be submitted for Court approval. The latter task was important as well as delicate, because the list was liable to be declared void on the strength of the slightest formal error, and the regime could be expected to avail itself of any opportunity to rule us out.

It is interesting that, in addition to the Frankists, Svetozar Pribičević also favored abstention, though for different reasons, of course. He feared that the regime had done such a good job of intimidating the population that the election could only convince the outside world of the Opposition's impotence. The exiled leader of the Independent Democratic Party expressed this fear to me in a letter. Later, when the results of the polls were published, even though they had been tampered with at our expense he sent me enthusiastic congratulations in another letter that began: *Kapu dolje pred Hrvatima!* ("Hats off to the Croats!")

After Trumbić had deserted the camp of abstainers, everybody rushed into the electoral battle. Trumbić himself was a candidate to represent his native city of Split, as well as the

District of Imotski in Dalmatia. Moreover, he ran as a candidate for deputy representative in Zagreb, where one of the four candidates was Ivan Peštaj, the unforgettable leader of the Croatian workers.

The people of each district proposed their own nominees; as a rule I did not interfere. In the districts where the nomination was contested, I was called upon to play the role of arbitrator, whose decision people respected in every case. Foreseeing their own failure to agree, some districts asked me to designate their candidates. In several cases I suggested younger, educated members of the Party, who were accepted at once and without comment.

Fearing that the government might try to use force to falsify the election, I instructed the people to take preliminary measures for their defense, to set up a force of their own strong enough to repel attempted violence and, if possible, thwart the regime's plans to infringe on their rights. Several officials favorably disposed toward the Opposition had revealed to me that, by government order, various District Chiefs were already busy "arranging" false electoral returns to be substituted for the genuine totals.

The date for the elections had been fixed for May 5, 1935. The voting was open: Every voter was obliged to state his preference orally to the electoral commission. Nevertheless, in the villages abstention was practically nonexistent, and even in the cities about 70% of the voters used their privilege. In the Croatian section of Yugoslavia, the Government obtained most of its votes from citizens dependent on it—government officials, certain industrialists, merchants, bankers, etc. Independent voters almost unanimously supported the Opposition. Falsification of results met with but moderate success in the Croatian parts of the country. One case is known to me, where the chairman of the electoral commission in the Sveti Ivan Zelina Disrict was assaulted by gendarmes on his way to the District Office and robbed of the electoral protocol. Later it

THE BOOM OF THE PARTY 163

was returned to him with forged figures. An analogous attempt was made by gendarmes in the city of Sisak; but there the chairman was accompanied by a peasant detachment, which defended him in an ensuing battle against the gendarmes in front of the District Office. One peasant retrieved the protocol from the gendarme who had seized it, and received a bayonet wound. Despite this, the brave man first ran to the Court Magistrate to deliver the document, smeared with blood, and only then went to see a doctor for medical treatment.

In Serbia, there was less enthusiasm and a lack of efficient organization, and in the terrorized provinces of Vojvodina and Macedonia, the regime pushed its fraudulent methods to an extreme. As the Cyrillic alphabet was used to draw up the protocols in Vojvodina, many of its inhabitants who had voted for the Opposition list, especially the Germans and Magyars, could not verify results given in the unfamiliar script. The commission made good use of this advantage. A similar situation developed in certain other sections of the country.

Despite all this the Government list of Bogoljub Jeftić obtained 1,746,982 votes and my Opposition list 1,076,346 votes. In the Croatian part of Yugoslavia, *i.e.*, Croatia, Slavonia, Dalmatia, Bosnia and Hercegovina, Jeftić received 520,144 votes and the Opposition 797,197. The voters of Zagreb, despite the many state officials and businessmen whose existence depended on the regime, cast 31,260 votes for the Opposition list and 10,356 for the Government candidates. The strength of the Opposition rested on the small businessmen, the workers and the great majority of lower state employees who had supported us although most of their superiors voted for the Government. The 1935 elections again confirmed that it was mainly the poor people who carried the burden of the struggle for national freedom and justice.

The peculiar electoral law ruled that the Government list, since it had "obtained the majority," automatically received three-fifths of all seats; only the remaining two-fifths were allotted to either Government or Opposition by respecting the majority in each instance. Thus, in the District of Klanjec, for example, the Government candidate was seated, though he had received only 208 votes against the 6,693 cast for his rival representing the Opposition. Similar rulings were applied in many other Croatian districts. The regime justified this arbitrary law with the contention that it was conceived after the "British model"; in fact, it was a typical Balkan dictatorial model. It would have been useless for our insignificant number of deputies to sit in such a rigged Parliament, so we decided to abstain, contenting ourselves with the clear display of our strength that the voting had provided.

On the evening of June 20, 1935, six weeks after the elections, Marko Kostrenčić, Ban of Savska Banovina, reached me with the news that the Jeftić Government had resigned and that I was invited to Belgrade for a consultation with Prince Paul. The next morning found me on my way to Belgrade where I arrived at 2 P.M., In spite of the obvious cordiality displayed by the Prince Regent, I was immediately aware that my consultation was a mere formality. The newspapers confirmed my impression the next day, announcing what had obviously been a carefully-prepared alliance. Milan Stojadinović was to be named Premier in a new government composed of the Serbian Radicals* and the Slovenian Clericals of Korošec (both of which had abstained from the elections), as well as the Yugoslav Moslem Organization of Mehmed Spaho. The three parties continued to be separate political bodies, but proclaimed an external unity under the name of Yugoslav Radical Union. Stojadinović himself claimed the Ministry of Foreign Affairs, while Korošec obtained the Police Ministry, a most important one in the Balkans.

After the audience with Prince Paul, I held a lengthy con-

* Soon, however, a part of the Radicals, under the leadership of Aca Stanojevic joined the opposition.

ference with Ljubomir Davidović and Joca Jovanović in the former's home. We agreed that the future struggle against the dictatorship had to proceed according to a common program. Unfortunately, we did not progress much further, and I left the next day for Zagreb without the encouragement of a concrete achievement in this direction.

A few weeks before, just after the elections, the regime had started a new wave of persecution against Croatian peasants. When gendarmes went so far as to assault the peasants at work on their fields, I issued a directive urging the people to organize a Croatian Peasant Defense, prepared to use force to resist all acts of violence instigated by the regime. This organization was, of course, illegal, but the State authorities refrained from interfering with it. The Peasant Defense was organized on the military pattern and could be mobilized at a moment's notice in an emergency. Its only arms consisted of a few shotguns, but nonetheless it succeeded in almost instantly putting a check to the violent provocations of the gendarmes. In a short time, the function of this defense formation was reduced to occasional appearances at manifestations and parades held by the Party.

I had long been accustomed to celebrate my birthday on July 20 within the restricted circle of my family. This year, however, my followers in Zagreb asked me to celebrate with them in the city. In case I would not heed their wish, several hundred of them planned to invade my farm at Kupinec. I promised to come to Zagreb by an early train on July 20. It was still dawn when my brother-in-law, Ivan Čavlek, drove up to the farm to report that Zagreb was the scene of disorders, caused by the countless Croatian flags with which the city had been illegally decorated. Clashes were reported here and there between the police and the excited population, and nobody could tell what might happen. Notwithstanding this news, I got ready for the trip to the city, profiting by Čavlek's convenient presence to go in his car and thus to enter Zagreb unnoticed. When we reached the bridge spanning the River Sava, one look assured me that the police had beaten a retreat. Almost all the houses were adorned with Croatian flags waving gaily in the light morning breeze; the whole scene before us emanated peace and quiet. At my house I was met by a great number of callers who offered me their heartfelt congratulations. Their number soon increased to such an extent that I found myself obliged to welcome in the street the diverse groups of villagers who had arrived from the surrounding country, equipped with their *tamburizan* orchestras. At quitting time in the shops and factories, the crowd swelled into a mass meeting, the initial ovations made way for a real political manifestation, during which I delivered a number of political speeches. To receive individual congratulations was out of the question. I could merely shake the hands of the few who had managed to push their way to my window. They were mostly workers from the suburbs, with their wives and children. This, after six years of dark dictatorship, moved me to tears.

The police all the while kept discreetly in the background. That day, the Croatian national flag reconquered its right to be raised when and where the Croats saw fit to do so. It proudly displayed its red, white and blue throughout the Croatian lands where, without any previous arrangements the population was joyfully celebrating my birthday by lighting bonfires. This grew into a custom, for the celebration was repeated year after year until the Axis occupation of Croatia. Yet none of the later pre-organized festivities had the value of the spontaneous enthusiasm of 1935.

Prince Paul and Police Minister Korošec were in part responsible for the police's non-interference with the colorful display of Croatian flags; they also deserved credit for terminating the persecution under which the Peasant Party had again begun to suffer. Korošec was fundamentally a federalist, and although he did not hesitate to collaborate with most of the centralistic governments, he firmly believed that whatever

THE BOOM OF THE PARTY 167

the Croats could extract through obstinate fighting would also benefit the Slovenes in the end. Moreover, the impossibility of shattering the resistance and unity of the Croats had been incontestably demonstrated at the elections of May 5, 1935, and in the time that followed.

The elections of 1935 had given new impetus to the Croatian patriotic spirit. Now, every Sunday, the Peasant Party was organizing public meetings in various villages and simultaneously was inspiring the peasants throughout the country in cultural and economic activities. Even before the proclamation of the Royal Dictatorship, the Croatian Peasant Party had been supporting its own cultural organization, the "Seljačka Sloga" or Peasant Union. Its activities had been limited, then completely suppressed by the dictatorship. Re-awakened, it now became extremely active under the leadership of its president, Rudolf Herceg, one of the finest disciples of the late Antun Radić. The Peasant Union made tremendous exertions in the cultural field. It had great success in conquering illiteracy through a series of special reading and writing courses for adults. It also dug out long forgotten national costumes. Women in the villages set to work, as of old, sewing their own traditional garbs. Even linen was woven again in peasants' homes, as their ancestors had done, to supply family needs. Old folk-songs and dances emerged out of the past, and the different branches of the Peasant Union that had sprung up in most villages competed with one another in singing their popular tunes and performing their picturesque dances in the national costumes of each region. To stimulate these competitions, the Peasant Union organized many festivals in which the contrasting skills of its best branches were shown to good advantage. Zagreb was the annual center of the most outstanding festival during which the Peasant Union showered the Croatian capital with the finest flowers that native peasant culture had brought forth. This general revival of deep-rooted customs and traditions was taken up on a considerable scale by the bourgeoisie. Women of all ages appeared, as often as the occasion seemed to justify it, dressed in the colorful traditional peasant garb—the garb which had been looked on with contempt only twenty years earlier.

In addition to the Peasant Union, the cultural subdivision of the Croatian Peasant Movement, another such organization came into being under the name of "Gospodarska Sloga" or Economic Union. Its program was shaped in the course of time by the exigencies of rural life. For many years the great economic crisis stamped its cruel marks on the peasant, who was principally afflicted by the outrageously low prices for his cattle and hogs. These reached a scandalously low level during the wane of winter and the early spring, the very time when the peasant's supply of fodder was running out, and he was compelled to sell his animals at humiliating prices. The Economic Union put an end to these abuses in March 1936. It pledged all peasants not to lead a single head of cattle to market; the well-to-do peasant held his surplus fodder at the disposal of the less fortunate, either on loan or on credit. This brought unexpectedly quick success. In fourteen days, cattle and hog prices had risen 50%—for certain valued breeds even 100%. The new price level remained stabilized as long as the Economic Union exercised its beneficial activities. A similar situation had affected the wine growers of Dalmatia. Many of them kept quantities of between 50 and 100 hectolitres of excellent wine in their cellars but nearly starved because they could not find buyers, so low were the prices. The Economic Union once again managed to help by effecting an exchange of Dalmatian wine for much-needed wheat, one hectolitre of wine for a hundred kilograms of wheat. Later on, the Union even succeeded in exporting the wine to Austria.

The peasant of Hercegovina made his living mainly by growing tobacco, supplemented by a little stock-breeding and some viticulture. The purchase of tobacco, however, was a

State monopoly which paid very low prices. The population of this rugged mountain region had to import, on the other hand, the corn which constituted its principal food besides milk and home-made cheese. The corn trade had hitherto been handled by a small number of middle-men who had made inordinate profits. The Economic Union, by transporting through its own means tens of wagon-loads of corn to Hercegovina, dropped the price of the latter to a normal figure. It did not have to intervene again.

In all the villages, our movement helped install arbitration committees, chosen "from among the good and honest people." These settled all sorts of disputes and minor conflicts among the peasants, only a few of whom preferred to seek justice in court. The arbitrators ended decisively many a lawsuit that had been dragging on for years in the State Courts. A number of County Courts were thus left with practically nothing to do. The authority of the arbitrators was so great that it never entered anybody's mind to appeal to the State Police in order to solve minor crimes. They invariably discovered the guilty person with minimum effort; in most cases he was ashamed to be found out by the other villagers. A thief had to return the stolen goods at once or pay damages, the amount fixed by the arbitrators. Their decisions were generally respected, out of the villager's fear of being socially boycotted by his neighbors, the worst thing that can happen to a peasant.

While all these activities were going on, the Croatian Peasant Party was theoretically nonexistent.

During my numerous interviews with Western reporters at that time, I had occasional difficulties in clarifying the social and economic aims of the Croatian Peasant Party. The West was then—and still is—divided between two ideologies, the capitalist and the Marxist-socialist. Many of my foreign visitors wanted to know if the Croatian Peasant Party accepted either of those ideologies. Others could see that the peasant movements of Eastern Europe did not adhere to either camp, but thought that they represented a compromise between the two. But this is quite incorrect; the ideology of the Croatian Peasant Movement is not something between but something quite apart from the other two. It will perhaps be useful to quote a few excerpts from an interview I gave to a correspondent of the French paper *La République* in 1935:

"Today two economic systems are clashing in Europe—capitalism and Marxism. . . . Neither of them answers our needs. We are a peasant people. Here, the peasant is both a capitalist and a worker. He owns his land, his house; he works himself with his family. It is in this frame of reference that we must place ourselves in order to solve the social problem.

"Before the war two pair of boots could be bought for 100 kilograms of grain; today, one can get only one pair of boots for 300 kilograms of grain. . . . Do you know that in Upper Croatia the peasant must give 100 kilograms of grain for 100 dinars, but by the time this grain comes to the peasant in Hercegovina he has to pay up to 300 dinars for it? On the other hand, the same Hercegovinian can obtain only 14 to 15 dinars for a kilogram of wool for which a Czech merchant must pay 160 dinars.

"All our economic policies strive to correct this situation and it can be corrected by means of cooperatives.

"Our family program, our social and cooperative program is founded on the principle of equality. A minority cannot hold the prerogatives of luxury, while others witness a continuing lowering of their standards, which are too low to start with; it cannot be that some wear English tweeds, while others walk around in rags."

"Here is the content," my interviewer concluded, "of a peasant social and national program. It seemed to me that, from the wall, Leo Tolstoy's portrait was approving."

Yet, it must be pointed out that the Croatian Peasant Party never put forth a detailed social program; its leading idea was the emancipation of the peasantry from both foreign and domestic domination. It never attempted to set up any Five Year Plans which, even in Communist countries where power is highly concentrated (much more so than the peasant ideology would ever allow)—did not turn out to be feasible. We believed that a well organized peasant economic union would always be able to cope pragmatically with any economic problem that might arise.

A tenet of our social ideology was that, basically, every family had to work out its problems for itself. If, however, the problem was such that the family could not work it out, it was first up to the village community to do it. If the village community could not do it, it was a job for the county. And if even the county could not do it, then the state would have to step in. This emphasis on the decentralization of power explains why our social program could not be considered as something apart from our political program for national freedom.

Between 1935 and 1941, when the influence and activity of the Croatian Peasant Party reached a maximum, one of our educated adherents suggested a detailed and specific formulation of our social program. A lengthy discussion followed. Diverse views were expounded before a prominent peasant stood up and said, "Men, what do we need a program for? Don't you see that our program is dictated by our everyday life!"

Once again I remembered Montesquieu and agreed with the peasant who had crystallized an idea present, no doubt, in the minds of many of his colleagues. Today, I still think that they were right.

In my capacity as head of the Peasant Party I directed all political activities personally, and a considerable part of my time was spent on interviews with the many journalists flocking in from the different corners of the world. During each of these interviews I explained patiently that the maintenance of Yugoslavia in its present form was unthinkable for the Croats who, with mounting dissatisfaction, saw their justified demands unfulfilled. Besides, I held daily meetings at Zagreb and on my farm at Kupinec with men from every part of Croatia. At these meetings we worked out ways and means of solving the everyday political problems, principally the organization of passive resistance on the part of the Croats toward the regime. I felt somewhat relieved at the return from exile of August Košutić, on whom I was now able to discharge half the burden. Košutić concerned himself in the first place with the Croatian Workers' Alliance, a labor organization affiliated with our Party, which was founded in 1921 to oppose the General Workers' Alliance of Yugoslavia, at the time controlled by Communists. The great majority of the Croatian workers preferred to join the ranks of the Croatian Workers' Alliance, which of course often entered into conflicts with its employers, entailing sporadic strikes. Košutić intervened more than once and adroitly warded off threatening clashes. His help became even more valuable after the death in 1937 of Ivan Peštaj, the leader of the Croatian Workers' Alliance. Peštaj had possessed an almost unerring sense of justice, and his keen discernment in judging contradictory facts enabled him to nip many a developing social conflict in the bud. His death was an irreparable loss. His successors proved far from equally gifted; thus the Peasant Party, in the person of August Košutić, was compelled to intervene more often.

The many conferences between our party and the representatives of various Serbian parties claimed my special attention. A common base had to be established to permit some sort of cooperation for definitively terminating the Croato-Serbian controversy or, more correctly, the discordance between hegemonic Serbia and oppressed Croatia. These conferences, though devoid of practical results, served, nevertheless, to let some steam off on both sides. The Serbian parties (Radicals,

THE BOOM OF THE PARTY 173

Democrats and Agrarians) would have, on the whole, been inclined to come to an agreement, if their different views on how to proceed had not formed an obstacle. Besides, everyone was afraid of any concrete agreement with us lest after "yielding to the Croats" he would be accused by the rest of being a "traitor to the Serbian cause."

In the autumn of 1935 the Frankists set out to follow a different course from ours. Although their leader, Ante Pavelić was never a member of the Croatian Peasant Party and had gone as an exile to Italy, his followers continued to cooperate to a certain extent with the Peasant Party. Pavelić's right hand, Mile Budak, had signed our Resolution of November 6, 1932. When in the autumn of 1935 Mussolini launched his aggression against Ethiopia, I learned that a group of students from the University of Zagreb had prepared a series of manifestations to acclaim the Italian dictator's greedy adventure. They doubtless followed instructions received from the Frankist leaders in Italy. I used all my powers to forestall them and prevented the manifestations from taking place. For this, the Frankists immediately launched a fierce campaign against our party and against me. The majority of the people ignored this strife between the Party and the limited circle which wanted the Croats to follow the emulators of Mussolini rather than the disciples of Antun and Stephen Radić. But the alienation of the two parties became an accomplished fact in the autumn of 1938.

Mile Budak, acting as Pavelić's deputy, returned in July 1938 from Italy and almost at once paid me a visit at Kupinec. He wanted to let me know he had come back because he had gradually arrived at the conclusion that to prolong his exile made no sense. The only policies worth pursuing were those of the Croatian Peasant Party under my leadership. He told me that Mussolini kept their men in camps, like a chained pack of hounds. When in need of them he would set them free for a spell to serve his own purposes and afterward bind them again as tight as ever. I voiced my approval of Budak's changed attitude and asked him merely to repeat his story to his followers at Zagreb. But of course, he assured me emphatically, this was exactly the reason he had come. He spent the whole day at Kupinec, and on our strolls about the farm I informed him of my conversations with Prince Paul and with members of the Serbian Opposition. Three weeks later, he called again at Kupinec and still persisted in his new belief; at least I did not perceive a change of opinion in what he said.

The end of August and the beginning of September found me at the Slovenian health resort of Rogaška Slatina, where I used to spend a week or two each year. The Sudeten crisis had begun, and Hitler was urging all the Sudeten Germans to leave Czechoslovakia and join the Third Reich. On this occasion, Budak came to see me for the third time. He tried to convince me, as he was himself convinced, that the approaching war would result in victory for the Axis Powers and that the Croats ought to side with the victors this time. He felt, he said, that the moment had arrived for the Croatian national leaders to declare themselves openly for the Axis.

With some surprise I replied that my thoughts were not yet focused on immediate war, as his were; besides, who could guarantee this presumed victory of the Axis? So far as I was concerned, Hitler and Mussolini were sure to lose a war with Great Britain. However, I allowed for a slender possibility to the contrary. Just this ought to caution us, as a small nation, against taking rash steps, I said; rather we should try to keep out of international conflicts primarily involving the great powers. Personally I had not the slightest intention, and this to my knowledge was even more true of the Croatian National Representation, of making such a declaration—certainly never in favor of the Axis.

"Well, if you view the situation from this angle, there is nothing more to say and we are forced to go our own way,"

THE BOOM OF THE PARTY 175

concluded Budak firmly. What else could I reply but, "Alright, then get going."

Before closing this chapter I feel that I must mention a tragic incident which has troubled me ever since.

On April 16, 1936, Kerestinec castle, the residence of the former Ban of Croatia and Slavonia, Antun Mihalovich, became the theatre of a bloody attack. But this time the Croatian peasants were the assailants for once, and their victims the Serbian supporters of the Stojadinović regime. When Stojadinović had assumed power, he had created a fascist organization of "blue shirts," headed in Croatia by Antun Mihalovich. On the fateful day, six of them came to Kerestinec, situated about half-way between Zagreb and Kupinec, to see their leader. They imprudently made themselves conspicuous on their way through the Croatian villages with loud-voiced manifestations, hailing Stojadinović and shouting "down with Maček." Somehow the word got around that they were going to Kupinec to raid my home and kill me. Several hundred peasants abandoned their work on the fields and, armed with pitchforks, axes and hoes, set out in pursuit of the troublemakers. After finding out that the men were headed for Kerestinec castle, the peasants followed and besieged the castle in order to force the "assassins" to surrender. Quite logically, Mihalovich, an elderly gentleman, refused to comply; he even stepped forth to face his besiegers with a gun in his hand. Probably he had no intention of using it, but the gesture sufficed to arouse the ire of the peasants. They rushed at him and quickly disarmed him, not without inflicting slight injuries. They now invaded the castle in search of Stojadinović's men, whom they killed one by one as they were discovered.

As soon as I heard at Kupinec about the siege of Kerestinec, I asked two of our deputies, Ljudevit Tomašić and Ivan Banković, to drive to the village, ten miles distant, and try to calm the excited mob. They arrived too late to prevent the tragedy, for five of the unfortunate men had already been butchered. They at least succeeded in saving the life of the remaining man, who was just being pulled out of his hiding-place. The authorities afterward opened an inquiry, but none of the assailants could be identified or, therefore, be put on trial. Mihalovich, who knew that on his lordly country seat he lived surrounded by peasants, thought it advisable not to recognize any of them.

Four years had elapsed since the incident, when I chanced to talk to Mihalovich's daughter, then married to Antić, Minister of the Royal Court, about the tragic incident. She seized the occasion to mention how that peasant mob, despite the cruelties committed, had preserved to the last a certain courteousness towards the castle's household. For more than half an hour the mob had been absolute master of the place with its riches of gold and silver, yet not a single object was found missing. They had carried off, instead, whatever could be classified as a weapon. A collection of pistols and ancient swords dating from the Middle Ages, which was of purely historical interest, had thus disappeared. Mihalovich later had appealed to me through an intermediary to use my influence on the peasants and to induce them to return these antiquarian arms. After I had put the functionaries of the Croatian Peasant Party in charge of the matter, Mihalovich had the pleasure, one morning, to find all the pilfered weapons lying on his doorstep.

CHAPTER XII

Reconciliation

$\mathcal{I}$N THE EARLY FALL of 1936, Professor Milorad Stražnicki, of Zagreb University, a former schoolmate of mine, informed me that Prince Paul wished to have a private talk with me. I was willing, but fell ill before the meeting could take place. Suffering from an inflammation of the middle ear, I had to undergo an operation which made it necessary to postpone the interview until November.

Prince Paul invited me to his summer residence, Brdo Castle in Slovenia, which I reached before noon after a three-hour drive from Zagreb. We at once embarked in conversation and remained absorbed in it until interrupted by a small lunch, served at 1 P.M. We enjoyed this meal in the company of Antić, Minister of the Royal Court, and an officer of the Royal Guard. As soon as lunch was over, Prince Paul and I withdrew to an adjacent drawing-room for an additional two hours. For obvious reasons (police search, etc.), I habitually refrained from keeping written notes of my political conversations, which makes it very difficult today to reconstruct the precise words exchanged between the Prince and me. At any rate, the subjects were selected from a wide range, including domestic and foreign policies, as well as philosophy and art. We discussed domestic policy less than anything else, for the interview had evidently been arranged for the sake merely of establishing contact between us. I am, of course, unable to guess what sort of impression I made on the Prince Regent. He, however revealed himself as a man to whom aristocratic thinking and aristocratic bearing were innate and who, in spite of a certain autocratic streak, was thoroughly cultured in the best European tradition. Furthermore, he was free of even a trace of that Serbian chauvinism which, unfortunately, was noticeable in his late cousin, King Alexander. Prince Paul made no effort, either, to conceal a certain disinclination toward some Serbian politicians. While we were enumerating and comparing the respective advantages of a monarchy and a republic, I did not conceal my republican views—but I readily conceded that I and many other Croats would not object to a monarchy on the British pattern. At this he smiled sympathetically and replied: "Rest assured that I, too, regard the British form of the monarchy as most desirable. But, to begin with, I should like to ask whether ———— (here he mentioned several familiar Serbian politicians) appear very British to you!" I was obliged to admit that there was little chance for the gentlemen in question to be taken for British.

This first talk had no political sequel; nor did subsequent meetings at Brdo Castle in 1937 and 1938.

At the first meeting, Prince Paul had suggested that I meet at least once with Premier Milan Stojadinović. A meeting was arranged for January 27, 1937 at the Slovenian hunting lodge of a Zagreb industrialist, Mr. Deutsch-Maceljski. The estate was situated about forty miles from Zagreb. We met there only briefly for lunch, which was graciously served us by our host.

Evidently, Stojadinović and I merely were carrying out the request of the Prince. The Premier lectured me at length on his foreign policy and stressed the importance of good relations with the adjoining countries. I responded that this was quite true. These words, it seems, were the only ones of the entire conversation he cared to retain, for in the end he recapitulated: "A pity, we did not agree on domestic policy as well as we did on foreign policy." With this bland remark, the interview closed, leaving me without a chance to explain to him that we did not exactly agree on foreign policy either.

During a discussion of domestic policy, Stojadinović had tried hard to persuade me to enter his Government, using a somewhat unusual argument. "I hardly agreed with former Premier Jeftić," he confided, "but I joined his Government anyhow. I did not do this to support him, far from it. I aimed at his overthrow by working from within. Why don't you follow my example?" The game Stojadinović and the previous dictatorial regimes were playing was perefectly clear to me. They all wanted me to become involved in their Government in order to destroy my reputation among the people; the rest did not matter much.

On May 9, 1937, the town of Senj on the Upper Coast of Croatia was again the site of a bloody political incident. Senj that day held a musical festival, in which a group of young people from the neighboring town of Gospić participated. The group belonged to an association named the "Križari" (Crusaders) which at the time was still predominantly of clerical orientation, although it was already strongly influenced by the Frankists and the "Ustasha" (Insurgents) of Pavelić. The festival ended with dancing and merry-making in the town's principal square, and many Croatian patriotic songs were sung. The singing doubtless emboldened the young "Križari" to loud criticism of the State; for they issued a series of revolutionary shouts. The insignificant detachment of gendarmes, witnessing this, did not dare intervene in the presence of the sizable crowd assembled in the square. Instead they lay in ambush just outside the town, waiting for the truck that returned the young "Križari" home. It had hardly come in sight, when they opened fire without warning. Six young men and a girl were killed on the spot; ten others received more or less serious wounds. I felt pretty certain that Stojadinović and his Government could not be held responsible for this ruthless attack. That Government possessed absolutely no authority over the Gendarmerie, which had been placed under the direct command of the Army. What could not be overlooked, however, was the grave injustice committed by the Stojadinović Government when it issued a communiqué which made Communists out of the victims and stated, moreover, that these unarmed young people had assaulted the gendarmes first who then had fired back in sheer self-defense. I hastened to publish a special pamphlet on the case signed personally, in which I made Stojadinović and his regime the target of severe reprimands. I concluded with these words: "In any country where honesty is at all esteemed, such a Government ought to muster up enough courage to resign in the face of these accusations, or else be eager to obtain satisfaction in Court by suing me for libel." The pamphlet was distributed all over Croatia, and I mailed a copy each to Premier Stojadinović and Prince Paul. Only the latter deigned to acknowledge its reception through his chancery; otherwise nothing happened.

Our negotiations with various Serbian parties progressed only in one respect: We mutually agreed to call for a revision of the existing electoral law and for the election of a new Constituent Assembly. Settlement of the Croatian Question had to be deferred until after elections, when a new democratic Constitution would provide the mechanism for a just solution.

In an attempt to convince the public of the political rapprochement between the Croatian and the Serbian Opposition, the leaders of the latter offered to come to Croatia for a joint meeting. They would avoid Zagreb, of course, but any place in its immediate surroundings would do. I got in touch with an old friend, Ante Irgolić, the parish priest of the village of Farkašić. He promised to do his best in playing host to such a party for a day. Farkašić lies some forty miles from Zagreb, only ten miles away from the Zagreb-Belgrade railroad. Većeslav Vilder, Independent Democratic deputy, a schoolmate of

Irgolić and myself, took charge of the necessary arrangements for the meeting.

On the appointed day, August Košutić, Vilder, myself and a few other members of our Coalition travelled from Zagreb to Farkašić where Ljuba Davidović, Miša Trifunović, Joca Jovanović and their companions arrived from Belgrade. Friendly talks filled the remainder of the day. They did not lead to any practical results.

Time and again I had urged Prince Paul to heed the views of the Opposition, but he had refused even to consider them, on the grounds that he could not sanction important political changes; it was his duty to surrender the State to the young King when the latter came of age, as it had been entrusted to him on King Alexander's death. I tried to explain that a guardian taking over the administration of his ward's property would be guilty of serious neglect if he left that property in a muddled state, prone to insecurity and hazardous risks; he is expected instead to do everything in his power to safeguard his ward's interests. These words had been to little avail.

To defend his position, Prince Paul also declared more than once that an understanding between the Croats and the Serbian Opposition was meaningless, because the various parties forming the latter frequently disagreed and, worse still, visibly lacked the support of the people. During my meeting with the Prince in July 1938, I made known my intention of going personally to Belgrade to return the visit of the Serbian Opposition to Farkašić. He said he was glad to hear this, that it would give me an opportunity to realize that the great majority of the Serbs had remained staunch supporters of the regime headed by Stojadinović.

My visit to Belgrade had been fixed for August 10, but on the request of the Serbian Opposition leaders was postponed until Sunday, August 14. The holiday, it was explained, would render it possible for a "large circle" of the Opposition to welcome me. I had no objections and therefore came to Belgrade that Sunday. The public reception I received surpassed all expectations. The station at Belgrade was crammed with people, and along the streets, leading to my assigned quarters, a crowd of more than 100,000 had gathered to greet me. Surrounded by the different Serbian political leaders, I stepped out several times on the balcony of the house in which I was lodged to address the swaying multitude below. I stayed in Belgrade two days, and returned home on the third full of optimism.* I now believed that Serbia was ripe, if not quite yet for an equitable agreement with the Croats, at least for the definitive abolition of all dictatorship. My optimism was to be undone by those very citizens of Belgrade barely four months later.

On my trip to Belgrade and back, throughout Croatia from Zagreb to Zemun, I received acclamation from vast crowds of people who thronged the railroad stations. Upon my return, I for the first time requested an audience with Prince Paul, who was again staying at Brdo Castle. I wanted to inform him of the hostile attitude among Croats and also among Serbs toward the government. Yet, the Prince neglected to send me an invitation. I let a few days pass, then sent a letter in which I formally withdrew my request, mailing it just before I departed for Rogaška Slatina to undergo my annual treatment. At 10 P.M., the evening after my arrival at the resort, the local Chief of Police came to call on Šubašić, who was with me, and delivered an oral message. It was from the Prince, who urged him to come and see him as soon as possible. Through Šubašić the Prince sent apologies to me: He had been prevented by

* A special session of the Opposition was held on August 15. Present among others were: Radical Party leader Stanojevic, Democratic Party leader Davidovic, Agrarian Union leader Jovanovic, Independent Democratic Party representative Kostic and myself. During the session a resolution was drafted and signed by all of us. I regret that I do not have the complete text. The resolution was important for us Croats, because, for the first time since 1918, representatives of Serbian parties recognized, at least in theory, the Croatian national individuality and the right to a Croatian political territory.

work from sending his invitation sooner and would be pleased to receive me at my convenience on any of the following days. Šubašić told the Prince that I had no intention of interrupting my medical treatment, but that I would be at his service as soon as I returned from Rogaška Slatina. The day I left the resort, I received an invitation to join the royal train at Zidani Most and to make the trip to Zagreb in the company of the Prince. I noticed immediately that the Prince was avoiding being left alone with me because he had also asked Antić, Minister of the Royal Court, and Šubašić to the interview. We were hardly seated when his butler started to lay the table for dinner, and the short journey of an hour and a half thus came to an end before a single political topic could be discussed. When I attempted to bring the conversation around to politics the Regent in a few words intimated that it was difficult to talk with me because I did not recognize "reality." After this failure, I did not ask for another audience, nor was I bidden to one. Some time later, elections for a new National Assembly were announced—to be held according to the old electoral law that had been effective in 1935.

We lost no time in getting ready. The Serbian Opposition considered it natural to have my name at the top of the common list again, since I was still the representative of the most powerful opposition party. In Serbia, as well as in other parts of Yugoslavia with a mixed population, the Serbian Opposition launched a large-scale electoral campaign, while in Croatia things were quiet, as though no one were thinking of elections. There was no need for excitement, for everyone knew beforehand how to vote. Trumbić was lying on his death-bed following a stroke, and the Peasant Party representative, Juraj Šutej, executed the legal part of our list which in due time was accepted by the Belgrade Supreme Court.

In the Croatian parts of the country the elections on December 11, 1938, went quite smoothly. Although voting again was public, the Stojadinović ticket was generally defeated. In the villages nearly a hundred per cent of the votes had been cast for the Opposition. This time even persons dependent on the Government voted for our candidates. In some districts, the Opposition obtained 7,000 or 8,000 votes against a half-dozen or dozen for the Government. Leading in this respect was the district of Pisarovina, where the Opposition candidate received 4,248 against 2 cast for the Government man. The two votes were those of the District Chief and his clerk. The results in the Croatian towns were comparable. In Zagreb, for example, the Opposition defeated the regime by 46,480 votes to 3,912.

In regions overwhelmingly populated by Croats—Upper Croatia and Slavonia, Dalmatia, Bosnia and Hercegovina, the Opposition won 943,964 votes against 429,332 for the government. The large majority of the Opposition votes (791,333) went to the Croatian Peasant Party.

Msgr. Aloysius Stepinac, Archbishop of Zagreb and now Cardinal, also voted on this occasion for the Croatian Peasant Party. A characteristic regime tactic was the "report" by Radio Zagreb, in the hands of the Government, that the Archbishop had voted for the Stojadinović list. The regime next sought to provoke mass indignation and to incite the heated population to storm the prelate's residence. Fortunately, I had been tipped off by a telephone call and was able to dispatch a detachment of the Citizens Defense Organization to the scene in time. It succeeded in making the angry crowd understand that the radio announcement had been fabricated by the Government. The ringleaders of the plot suddenly vanished, and the intended demonstrations against the Archbishop transformed themselves into equally fervent acclamations. Stojadinović apparently had been trying in a modest way to imitate Hitler's Reichstag fire in a different setting to furnish himself with an excuse for persecuting his adversaries at will.

The election returns were less favorable for the Opposition in the Serbian parts of Yugoslavia. Obviously the Serbs did not dare vote openly against the regime, and neither did the Macedonians, Germans and Magyars. I was especially disappointed by the voting in the city of Belgrade. After the big demonstration against the regime during my visit four months earlier in which at least 100,000 people had taken part, I foresaw a sure Opposition victory. To my dismay, Stojadinović received more than 40,000 votes against about 10,000 for the Opposition.

It is interesting to note that Germans in Vojvodina, on direct orders from Hitler, voted unanimously for Stojadinović. As for the Germans in Croatia, whose great majority had voted in 1935 for the Peasant Party, about half abstained, and the rest divided evenly between regime and opposition. The Croatian Frankists, Pavelić's followers, had announced abstention, too, doubtless to conform to instructions from Berlin and Rome. (They could not, after all, declare themselves pro-regime.) Yet, the Croatian Peasant Party had displayed such strength that finally even the local Frankist leaders, with the exception of the worst die-hards, ended by voting for the Opposition.

The final elections returns, as at previous elections, cannot be regarded as accurate; I am sure they credited the Government list with more votes than had been cast for it. The official totals: Stojadinović 1,643,783, Maček 1,364,524.

It soon became plain to me that the tense international situation would not permit Yugoslav internal affairs to continue in their hitherto customary course. This view was promptly confirmed when Prince Paul sent me a message through Šubašić in January 1939, declaring himself ready to do everything compatible with the Constitution to satisfy Croatian demands. The Prince Regent emphasized again, however, that he would still oppose any changes in the Constitution itself under any circumstances. With the international situation rapidly deteriorating, I felt I could not be indifferent or fastidious toward the least sign of goodwill coming from the other side. I felt considerable apprehension for the safety of the Croatian people who, should war break out, were hopelessly at the mercy of the Serbian military clique. I, therefore, declared myself willing to enter an agreement. Through Šubašić I proposed to the Prince the union of the present banovinas of Savska, Primorska and Vrbaska (including the district and city of Dubrovnik) to form the single Banovina of Croatia under a separate status within the State of Yugoslavia. According to Šubašić my proposal had filled the Prince with enthusiasm. "Believe me," he told Šubašić, "tonight, after a long time, I can go to sleep without worrying." When Šubašić went to see him again a few days later, however, Antić, the Minister of the Royal Court, was present and vehemently protested the inclusion of Vrbaska banovina in Croatia, calling it "exclusively Serbian territory," and objected in equally strong terms concerning Dubrovnik. The Prince, who had listened in silence and with apparent resignation, flared up and cut in sharply when Antić mentioned Dubrovnik. "That's enough, please, stop it," he said, "you certainly would not dare assert that Dubrovnik is not truly Croatian." When Šubašić reported this scene to me, I advised him to refrain from further visits to Belgrade. The situation had to be left to ripen spontaneously.

On February 5, the Stojadinović Government fell. Dragiša Cvetković, a member of the defeated Government, became Premier. In an introductory speech outlining his program, Cvetković announced solution of the Croatian Question as one of the important tasks facing his Government. For the first time since Yugoslavia had been created, the very existence of the Croatian Question had thus been officially recognized. I did not react publicly to this and continued to wait for Belgrade to take the initiative.

After the fall of the Stojadinović Government, Italy tried to establish contact with me. Count Bombelles, whose acquaintance I had never made before, came to see me. He introduced himself as a "man with political principles oriented toward England" who had come to put me on guard against a secret agreement concluded during a recent hunting party at Belje by Stojadinović and Count Galeazzo Ciano, Italian Minister of Foreign Affairs: In the event of a world war, Italy would be given the right to occupy part of Gorski Kotar and the whole section of the Adriatic coast extending from Sušak to the south of Split. In return, it would recognize all the rest of Yugoslavia as Great Serbia. All this did not sound altogether improbable, inasmuch as the envisaged frontiers scarcely deviated from those attributed to Italy by the London Treaty in 1915. But I did not attach much importance to Bombelles' communication, because I knew that Stojadinović had been forced out of power precisely because of his exaggerated approaches to the Axis Powers. (He had personally adopted Hitler's and Mussolini's methods by forming organizations of "blue shirts," etc.)

In March 1939 Carnelutti, a building contractor from Zagreb whom Ciano has mentioned in his "Diary," paid me a visit. In spite of his Italian origin (his father had once been acting Italian consul at Zagreb), Carnelutti was thoroughly Croatian and, moreover, a member of the Peasant Party. He told me that he was a friend or relative (I forget which) of the Italian Deputy Foreign Minister, Dino Alfieri, with whom he had had a recent talk. Alfieri had pressed him with questions about Croatian affairs, as well as about my person. They would meet again shortly, Carnelutti added, and wanted to know whether I had anything special for him to transmit to Alfieri. I had no message, but asked Carnelutti to sound Alfieri out on whether there really had been a secret Ciano-Stojadinović pact. He promised to try, but never did come back to tell me what, if anything, he had learned, and I did not ask him about it.

Toward the end of March, Premier Cvetković informed me of his intention to come to Zagreb to open negotiations with me. He arrived on the evening of April 1 and paid me a short visit that night which I returned half an hour later. Our negotiations began the following day. I realized that the situation at last was becoming ripe for mutual understanding. I nevertheless declared at once to Cvetković that in view of the long relations my party had maintained with the Serbian Opposition, including joint participation in two elections with a common list, I considered it unfair to enter any agreement without the Serbian Opposition. I suggested that we adjourn our meeting for ten days, until after the impending Easter holidays. During that time, I would try to persuade the rest of the Opposition to take part in the negotiations. Cvetković consented, but considered it a waste of time since it was impossible to reach any kind of agreement with the Serbian Opposition.

While Cvetković left Zagreb, I sent Košutić to Belgrade to inform the Serbian Opposition leaders of my preliminary agreement with Prince Paul and the negotiations about to open with Cvetković. I offered them a choice of two procedures: Either to leave it to Prince Paul to represent Serbian interests; or to negotiate first with me until we all had reached an understanding, after which I would endeavor to conclude an accord with Prince Paul and Cvetković on behalf of the joint Opposition. Košutić returned from Belgrade having accomplished nothing. The Serbian Opposition had rejected both proposals. The time had been wasted as Cvetković had predicted, and he and I were obliged to resume our negotiations alone in the middle of April.

We reached an agreement concerning basic principles. The banovinas of Savska and Primorska and the district and city of Dubrovnik were to be united *a priori* as Croatian territory. The rest of Slavonia (Eastern Srijem, which was part of the Dunavska banovina), as well as the rest of Bosnia and Hercegovina, were to decide by plebiscite whether they would join Croatia or Serbia. For my part, I consented to the common administration of Foreign Affairs and National Defense, but said that further joint government would have to be decided on when a final document was being prepared for signature. This understanding was not recorded in protocol, inasmuch as Cvetković said he lacked the requisite powers to enter into anything on binding terms. He first had to give a full accounting of our talks to Prince Paul, who reserved the right of final decision. Nothing, therefore, was disclosed to the press before Cvetković left to report to the Prince. When for some days I received no news, I sent Šubašić to Belgrade to find out what had happened. He talked with the Prince as well as with Cvetković, but was unable to get an unequivocal response from either. There remained only one interpretation, the one indicated in the German proverb *Keine Antwort ist auch eine Antwort*—no answer was a negative answer. I no longer felt any need for restraint and placed a notice in the semi-official Party paper *"Hrvatski Dnevnik"* (Croatian Daily), stating that the Prince had declined to recognize the settlement between Cvetković and me. At the same time, I called together the Croatian national deputies at Zagreb, to give them a detailed account of my negotiations. There was a great deal of excitement during the meeting but I succeeded in persuading the assembly against committing itself politically with rash actions.

The moment must evidently have appeared propitious to the Italian Foreign Ministry to get in touch with me. While the negotiations with the Belgrade government were in suspense, Carnelutti came to see me at Rogaška Slatina on May 28, submitting to me the draft of an accord between the Croatian Peasant Party and the Italian Foreign Ministry. Contrary to the account in Ciano's diaries, this draft made no mention whatsoever of the idea that I would pledge myself to prepare a revolution in Croatia. Nor was there any suggestion of financial support on the part of Italy.

But the draft did propose that the Croatian Peasant Party take the obligation, in the event of war, to proclaim an "independent" Croatian State and seek the immediate backing of the Italian Army. This "independent" Croatian State and the

Kingdom of Italy would then establish joint Foreign Affairs and a joint Army. Finally, the Croats were asked either to acknowledge the Italian King as Croatian ruler, or to select their own King from among the princes of the House of Savoy. Should any of these conditions be unacceptable to me, Carnelutti explained, he would readily convey my counter-proposals.

Of course, I declined the offer unconditionally, as Ciano confirms in his "Diary." I preserved a copy of this unsigned draft and entrusted it to a reliable person in Zagreb for safekeeping. Nevertheless, the "affair" soon became known, and the Frankists bombarded me with criticism. They called my refusal of the Italian offer "another treason" to Croatia, since I had pushed aside the "independent State of Croatia" allegedly presented to me on a platter.

Several weeks later, I received an invitation from Cvetković to resume our negotiations. We met at the home of Šubašić at Vukova Gorica near Karlovac. This time we agreed that the Croatian territory should include, apart from the Savska and Primorska banovinas, the districts of Ilok and Šid in Slavonia; Brčko, Gradačac, Derventa, Travnik and Fojnica in Bosnia; and the district and city of Dubrovnik. The equitable division of administrative competence between the Croatian autonomous government and the Central government in Belgrade was a complex matter requiring detailed negotiation by experts. I nominated Juraj Šutej, national deputy, Ivo Krbek, university professor, and Ljudevit Filipančić, financial expert, to represent the Croats in these matters, while for the Serbs Cvetković sent Konstantinović, Ilić and Tasić, all university professors. The six men assembled without delay at Rogaška Slatina to undertake the division of competence affecting all Ministries into the two categories of common affairs and Croatian affairs. On the points that were settled a special protocol was drawn up, while those on which they could not come to terms were left in suspense to be dealt with later between Cvetković and myself. The task was rather thorny, since the Serbian experts

RECONCILIATION 191

tried to retain greatest jurisdiction for the Central Government, while the Croatian experts tried to reserve as much power as possible for the Croatian Autonomous Government. Negotiations deteriorated at the beginning of August, and it looked as though they would come to a standstill without any positive results.

The Independent Democrats, our partners in the Peasant Democratic Coalition, made one last attempt to bring the Serbian Opposition into the conference while the experts were at work. Sava Kosanović, Independent Democratic deputy, brought Milan Grol, leader of the Serbian Democrats to Kupinec. Grol and I talked for more than two hours together. I was again convinced that it was much easier to deal with Prince Paul or Cvetković than with the representatives of the Opposition. Grol did not (perhaps he did not dare) touch a single of the crucial points that formed the real problem. He lost himself in meaningless talk, with repeated references to "lofty concepts, profound concepts, broad concepts" and similar phrases. When he and Kosanović took their leave, the latter turned toward me behind Grol's back and shrugged his shoulders in resignation, as if to say "I have long since despaired and am sadly aware that nothing is to be done."

At the beginning of August, when the negotiations among the experts had reached a deadlock, I received a report from Krnjević in Geneva. I gathered from its contents that the outbreak of a new world war was imminent. This news prompted me to seek to bridge the abyss which separated the Croats from the Serbs as quickly as possible. I anticipated the terrible sufferings in store for both the Croats and the Serbs, should the war surprise them disunited. (Unfortunately, fate confirmed my early apprehensions despite my strenuous efforts to ward off the disaster.)

At a subsequent meeting with Cvetković in his parlor car at Zidani Most, Slovenia, I told him that I was willing to accept a temporary agreement which could always be revised later. He was visibly pleased with my sudden complaisance, the more so because I did not disclose my pressing reasons for this attitude. (I did so later when I was Vice-Premier of his Government and we had become friends.) We decided to meet on August 16 at the State model farm at Božjakovina near Zagreb with our six experts, resolved to stay there until an accord had been drawn up. We stuck to our decision. The experts worked for five days during which Cvetković and myself were called on to act as arbitrators whenever complications arose. We did so by mutual comprehension and sacrifices, intent on accomplishing our task with the utmost speed. On August 20, 1939, we moved with relief to the Palace of the Ban in Zagreb where the accord received its final touch by midnight.

Under the terms of the agreement, a new banovina named *Banovina Hrvatska* (Banovina of Croatia) came into being. Its territory had already been determined by Cvetković and me at our earlier meeting at Vukova Gorica. The Banovina of Croatia obtained its own parliament *(Hrvatski Sabor)* which had the power to vote all autonomous laws sanctioned by the King, and its own government headed by the Ban. The latter had to be nominated by the King but was responsible to the *Sabor* alone. His nomination by the King required no countersignature besides his own. The autonomous affairs of the Banovina of Croatia comprised: Interior Administration, Justice, Public Education, Social Policy, Agriculture, Forestry and Mining, Commerce and Industry, Finance, Construction, and Health.

Foreign Affairs, including Foreign Commerce, National Defense, Post, Telegraph and Telephone, and Transport remained in the hands of the Central Parliament and Government, which also kept control over the important Belgrade-Sušak highway. The agreement stipulated that Croatian autonomy could be extended at any time by means of incorporation of "other joint affairs" into its own administration, but that it could not be reduced without the consent of the Croatian *Sabor*.

The financial problem was solved by a proviso covering the expenses of the Croatian autonomous agreement till the end of the budgetary year (March 31, 1940) from the State's budget; in the meantime, it would be determined which revenues would go to the State and which to the Banovina in order to establish separte budgets. The question of the Gendarmerie was a hard nut to crack. The Corps formed part of the Army. I fought stubbornly to have it removed from the sway of the Army and placed under the authority of the Ban. Yet, I fought in vain. We agreed, at last, to leave it for the time being under the Army's command, provided it was held at the Ban's disposal. Just before the fall of Yugoslavia, the Gendarmerie came under the complete control of the Ban of Croatia.

The text of our agreement was not published immediately, because Prince Paul had to confirm it first. He did so two days later, on August 22, 1939. That day, Stanoje Mihaldžić, Acting Ban of Savska banovina, called on me at Kupinec and informed me of the Prince's unreserved approval of the accord. He simultaneously announced a visit from Cvetković for the next day to make his official statement. After the Premier's visit on August 23, I travelled to the Alpine resort of Bled in Slovenia and from there to Brdo Castle for an audience with Prince Paul, in the company of Cvetković, to decide on the composition of the new Government. The Prince Regent insisted that I join it, although I would have preferred not to do so at that time. He argued that without my participation the agreement would lose its *raison d'être*. I yielded by accepting the position of Vice-Premier offered to me. It was agreed that I would have a free hand in nominating the Ministers of Finance, Commerce and Industry, Post, Telegraph and Telephone, and Social Policy. Three members of the Serbian Opposition also joined the government: Laza Marković and Boža Maksimović of the Radical Party, and Branko Čubrilović, of the Serbian Agrarian Union.

When the question of the Central Government was settled, the Prince asked me as a special favor to propose to him the appointment of Ivan Šubašić as Ban of Croatia. Šubašić had distinguished himself in the course of the past year as the intermediary between the Prince and me, but, in spite of this, I must admit that I was somewhat adverse to his choice. Although I highly valued Šubašić as a personal friend, I thought that he did not have the required prestige among the people; besides, I had a highly qualified candidate of my own in the person of August Košutić, vice-president of the Croatian Peasant Party. But, considering the host of difficulties to be overcome in the course of the transfer of authority from the central to the autonomous Croatian Government, I reflected that, perhaps, it would be wise to have a Ban who fully enjoyed the confidence of the Prince while we were striving to smooth away unavoidable conflicts. This actually turned out to be so. Although because of a slightly autocratic approach and a poor choice of subordinates Šubašić never became very popular, he rendered valuable service to the Croatian cause by consistently and courageously resisting reiterated attempts at meddling in Croatian affairs on the part of certain Belgrade officials.

That evening I returned to Zagreb, but was back at the Brdo Castle two days later, where I met the newly appointed ministers. The new Yugoslav Government was composed as follows:

Premier: Dragiša Cvetković, Serbian Radical Party.
Vice-Premier: Vladko Maček, Croatian Peasant Party.
Finance: Juraj Šutej, Croatian Peasant Party.
Defense: General Milan Nedić, non-partisan.
Foreign Affairs: Alexander Cincar-Marković, non-partisan.
Interior: Stanoje Mihaldžić, non-partisan.
Justice: Lazar Marković, Serbian Radical Party.

Commerce and Industry: Ivan Andres, Croatian Peasant Party.
Agriculture: Branko Čubrilović, Serbian Agrarian Union.
Social Policy: Srdan Budisavljević, Independent Democratic Party.
Transport: Nikola Bešlić, Serbian Radical Party.
Construction: Miha Krek, Slovenian Populist Party.
Post, Telegraph and Telephone: Josip Torbar, Croatian Peasant Party.
Education: Boža Maksimović, Serbian Radical Party.
Forests and Mines: Džafer Kulenović, Yugoslav Moslem Union.
Physical Culture: Jevrem Tomić, Serbian Radical Party.
Without Portfolio: Bariša Smoljan, Croatian Peasant Party, Mihalo Konstantinović, non-partisan.

The first act of the Government when it was sworn in was to promulgate the new law establishing the Banovina of Croatia. Two days later, the Regency appointed Ivan Šubašić Ban of Croatia and asked him to sign his nomination in the same manner as was customary for the Prime Minister.

Now that the agreement had become effective, I convoked the Croatian National Representation for its formal ratification. A single national deputy, Lovro Sušić, rose to read a statement he had prepared in advance which objected strongly to ratification. The agreement was then ratified by the Croatian National Representation by over eighty votes to one.

A few days later Krnjević came home after 10 years of exile. He immediately eased my work load by taking over a large portion of party activities.

CHAPTER XIII

The Gathering Storm

FROM THE START, the new Government confronted many obstacles. The Pan-Serbian extremists, led by the military clique, as well as the Communists and Frankists, used every opportunity to obstruct peaceful development. And the signing of our agreement preceded by only a few days Germany's sudden aggression against Poland on September 1, 1939, which began the Second World War.

Increasing fears that Italy was planning a similar attack on Yugoslavia caused a partial mobilization of the Yugoslav Army. Troops were levied in greatest numbers in Croatia and Slovenia, the areas closest to Italy. The Frankists and, to an even greater extent, the Communists circulated among the mobilized troops, disseminating the tale that they were being sent to France to fight in the front lines. I had to send several of our national deputies to join the troops to combat these false rumors and reassure the upset men. Although the military authorities, God knows why, did their best to prevent the deputies from contacting the men, they nevertheless succeeded in their task. At Karlovac, the soldiers of an infantry regiment refused, because of such fears, to board a troop-train which would take them to the frontier. After twenty-four hours of repeated efforts by influential members of the Croatian Peasant Party, the unfounded fears of the regiment were finally dissipated without bloodshed. Yet, the military authorities seized on the incident to demand martial law in the Karlovac Military District. Prince Paul energetically and successfully opposed this ominous Army demand. Nevertheless, the Army in reprisal sent the rebellious regiment to Macedonia and the Bulgarian frontier.

The military authorities found other ways to sow discontent among the Croatian people. The Army started to commandeer draught-horses and -oxen without compensation, which, of course, touched the peasants at a very vulnerable point. I went through many acrimonious encounters with General Nedić, the Minister of National Defense. "When a State is in peril," he contended, "all individual interests, even the most vital, must be sacrificed to the general interest of survival." To this, I retorted that it was unjust to make the peasants do all the sacrificing, simply because it was they who possessed what the Army needed most. The defense burden had to be borne by all citizens alike, certainly also by well-to-do people who had hitherto escaped their share of responsibility. After much debate, we finally compromised on an ordinance giving the Army the right to buy draught animals from the peasants for specified prices. Disregarding the fact that Finance Minister Šutej was allotting the Army ample funds, the military authorities too often went on confiscating the peasants' indispensable horses and oxen without offering any compensation whatsoever.

The mobilization itself, poorly planned, haphazardly organized and extremely partial, exasperated the population. The same men often remained under arms for a year and a half, while others were never called up. Frequently every able-bodied male in a household was called up, whereas not a soul was disturbed next door. I fought in vain for an impartial distribution of military duty.

During this first mobilization, the total unpreparedness of the Yugoslav Army for any serious action manifested itself in a spectacular manner. About 700,000 men were under arms when winter knocked at the door; the Army, despite an annual expenditure of about three billion Dinars, could supply them barely 200,000 blankets. Some of the soldiers had brought their own blankets, but those who had to depend on army blankets nearly froze to death in their tents.

The Army was guilty of other unimaginable stupidities during all of 1940. Fortifications devoid of any conceivable strategic purpose were erected. In our modern era of planes and fast, heavy tanks, the Yugoslav Army proceeded to dig trenches three feet deep across arable farmland and to drive piles, scarcely three inches thick, into them. These, knitted together with thin barbed wire, were supposed to be effective obstacles to an invader. These incongruous "barriers" cost the State, to my knowledge, more than a billion and a half Dinars, while depriving many a peasant of the few acres that constituted the source of his livelihood. No wonder bitterness mounted against the authorities!

Prince Paul, whom I asked more than once to intervene, did not dare oppose the decisions of the omnipotent Army. The latter had become redoubtable, first in the old Serbia, then in all Yugoslavia, as the decisive force in politics. Seizing the right to dominate the domestic affairs of the State, it failed to concern itself as passionately with the security of Yugoslavia and its defense against foreign intruders. Prince Paul intensely resented the encroachment of the Army and often expressed these feelings in intimate conversations with me. "Woe to the country that is ruled by officers or priests!" he once exclaimed. The Prince's remark, no doubt, was aimed at the Orthodox clergy who, some time earlier, had prevented the ratification of a Concordat with the Catholic Church.

In addition to the difficulties with the Army, another political incident threatened to provoke a Government crisis, three months after the agreement with Cvetković had been signed.

An annex to that document provided for the dissolution of the present Parliament, elected on the basis of an iniquitous electoral law, and the election of a new one under different and more equitable regulations. The Parliament had duly been dissolved. The Senate had followed suit, and elections for a new Senate took place according to the previous electoral law, which was fair from our point of view. The crown enjoyed the privilege of nominating a certain number of senators in addition to those who had been elected.

Toward the end of November 1939, my Chief of Cabinet, Ilija Jukić, transmitted a message to me from Antić, Minister of the Royal Court, inviting me to propose to the Regency several Croats whom I would like to have nominated as senators. I was in Zagreb at the time, and replied that I would be in Niš the day after next to attend the "Krsna Slava" (family feast) of Premier Cvetković, and would consult with him first. With astonishment and displeasure I therefore read in the papers, on reaching Belgrade the following morning, that the Regency had already nominated the Serbian senators. My first impulse was to return instantly to Zagreb, send in my resignation as Vice-Premier, and break all relations with Cvetković. However, Jure Šutej, who met me at the station in Belgrade, explained that Cvetković was not to blame. This outrage was the result of an intrigue on the part of Antić alone, whose implacable antagonism toward any kind of agreement with the Croats was notorious. Through this incident, he hoped to separate Cvetković and me and thus call our recent agreement in question. Knowing the facts, I let the incident pass in silence, especially since the Senate without the support of the Parliament had no importance whatsoever. Soon I was on my way to Niš, where I received a public welcome in grand style from a huge crowd convoked by Cvetković himself. During my visit the Premier and I decided that Antić had to be removed as Minister of the Royal Court, but our common efforts were doomed to failure. Until this day I do not understand what motives prevented Prince Paul from dismissing him.

In spite of all obstacles, the Banovina of Croatia developed according to the terms of the agreement. Of the many difficulties that were dealt with at cabinet meetings, the people at large remained blissfully unaware. I was now working three to four days a week with Konstantinović drafting the various ordinances prescribing procedures for the transfer of powers from the Central Government to the Government of Croatia. During this period of concentrated work, we emptied numerous cups of black coffee and smoked our cigarettes in chains. While Konstantinović was anxious to keep what he could under the Central Government, I directed my efforts toward the opposite goal. He proved a tough adversary, but a fair one. I could rely on Konstantinović that, whenever a particular regulation had been agreed on between us, its draft would be composed correctly, without any of the tricky interpolations some Serbian politicians were wont to smuggle into their documents.

One of my first tasks was drafting the electoral law for the Croatian *Sabor,* using the electoral law for the Constituent Assembly of 1920 as a model. The new law contained some changes for the purpose of permitting the various political parties more effective supervision of proceedings and thereby reducing the possibility of falsification. Every 40,000 inhabitants would be entitled to one deputy, and every list of candidates would require registration with the county courts. The ballot was to be secret, by means of placing rubber disks in boxes numbered to correspond with the lists presented. The seats were to be distributed according to the proportional-representation system. There would be universal suffrage for males over 24 years of age. This last clause may seem reactionary to some people. But I was convinced then that young people do not have enough experience to size up a given political situation and objectively decide intricate political issues.

The fact that Hitler, Mussolini, Pavelić and the Communists recruited their most ardent followers among immature youngsters has done nothing to change my opinion.

On January 14, 1940, Prince Paul and his wife, Princess Olga, visited Zagreb. Large crowds of peasantry and bourgeoisie paid tribute to them on their arrival. During his stay Prince Paul, with the Ban as co-signatory, signed the electoral law for the Croatian *Sabor*. Unfortunately, elections for the *Sabor* never took place: the military authorities, through permanent mobilization, made them impossible.

Shortly after the promulgation of the electoral law for the *Sabor*, a similar electoral law was issued for the Central Parliament. Although Serbian members of the government had told me they shared my views on raising the minimum age for voters to 24, they did not dare assume responsibility for such a change; the right to vote for the Central Parliament was given to all males over 21.

I also tried unsuccessfully to prevent the adoption of another stipulation in the electoral law, which made it unlawful for the county courts to accept Communist lists. With much concern I strove to divert the Serbian politicians from the principle that political parties could simply be pronounced illegal. The law which barred the Communists from election was potentially a direct threat to democracy itself. If a regime is given the right to pronounce one political party illegal it can easily extend this practice to all the parties except its own. The existence of political parties in a nation is a forceful fact which must be respected by every democrat.

Furthermore, this particular electoral stipulation was, in a practical sense, ridiculous. Lists were never submitted under a party's name but under the names of the candidates. And the courts were required only to check the lists on purely formal grounds, *i.e.* to see if they showed the requisite number of candidates and if those nominating them were duly registered voters. They were in no way authorized to examine the candidates' political records. The law did not permit them even to ascertain whether a candidate had attained the prescribed age, let alone find out to which party he belonged.

The general outlook in our domestic affairs was encouraging and filled us with hope in the gradual evolution of the State from a dictatorship to a parliamentary system to a new Constituent Assembly. The new Constituent Assembly would then serve as the key to a definitive solution not only of the Croatian Question but of other national and regional problems of Yugoslavia.

Our foreign politics were less serene; in fact, a storm was brewing on the horizon. After swallowing Bohemia and Poland, Hitler applied more pressure than ever on Yugoslavia and did not conceal his designs to occupy Rumania. Mussolini, meanwhile, occupied Albania and was preparing to attack Greece.

As in other countries, the foreign policy of Yugoslavia was dictated by the Ministry of Foreign Affairs, and the Government had to content itself with the information Foreign Minister Cincar-Marković saw fit to disclose at cabinet meetings. Premier Cvetković regularly informed me of many current events, as did the Prince Regent to an even greater extent. But to gain a better insight into our foreign relations I insisted on the nomination of Jukić, my Chief of Cabinet, as Third Undersecretary in the Foreign Ministry. Jukić had previously been in the diplomatic service, but was dismissed during the dictatorship of King Alexander. As Third Undersecretary, he rendered me appreciable services by procuring much interesting and supplementary news.

Before relating the diplomatic developments of 1940-41, I should like first to set to rights an erroneous belief, commonly held in Yugoslavia as well as abroad—namely, that Prince Paul was chiefly responsible for the gradual strengthening of ties between Yugoslavia and Nazi Germany. The truth is that Prince Paul had tried to put a brake on the country's rapprochement with the Axis. One consequence of his efforts was the unexpected resignation of Stojadinović (who had been Premier and Foreign Minister for four years) following Ciano's visit to Yugoslavia in 1939. Officially Stojadinović's fall was ascribed to his unwillingness or incapacity to come to an agreement with the Croats, but in reality the cause was quite different. Although Stojadinović, a convinced Pan-Serbian, had not the slightest desire for an understanding with the Croats, it was his foreign policy alone that provoked his sudden resignation. Talking with me on the subject one day, Prince Paul told me that Stojadinović had been forced to relinquish power because, little by little, he had passed from trivial political tactics to a well-defined policy of rapprochement with Germany and Italy, a policy that in his view led down a one-way street. The situation Stojadinović had left behind was grave, the Prince said to me, and would give the Government and himself many headaches.

Alexander Cincar-Marković, former Ambassador to Berlin, replaced Stojadinović as Foreign Minister. On another occasion Prince Paul commented that we were lucky to have found in Cincar-Marković at least one man who enjoyed the confidence of the Germans; for the Nazis looked upon the other members of the Government, and upon the democratic Croats in particular, with pronounced misgivings.

When I became Vice-Premier, the heads of all the diplomatic missions accredited in Belgrade paid me formal calls, among them German Ambassador von Herren. Returning these visits I had an opportunity to entertain myself for some time with von Herren. His views, I discovered, differed widely from those of a confirmed Nazi, although he carried out his mission in the perfect manner of a well-trained diplomatic official. I had a strong feeling that he was merely the ornamental head of the German Legation and that the decisive word in politics was spoken by the Commercial Attaché, Neuhausen, a sworn Nazi who exerted heavy pressure on our commercial relations with Germany. He often tried to influence even strictly Yugoslav affairs. I had one long conversation with Neuhausen or, more correctly, I listened for more than half an hour while he poured out a tirade on the incomparable advantages of National Socialism and the military superiority of the Third Reich.

With the fall of France in June 1940, the fact had to be faced that no power remained in Central Europe to match the overwhelming German military machine. Diplomatic means offered the only hope of staving off catastrophe. I recommended such a course to Prince Paul. Soon Germany was asserting a decisive political influence over Rumania and Bulgaria and to a large extent over Hungary. Members of our Government eyed the succession of meaningful events with great anxiety.

Meanwhile, Zagreb and Belgrade had become the theatres of fifth column activity by pro-Axis Forces as well as by Communists. On November 30, 1940, three time bombs exploded simultaneously in different parts of Zagreb: one in the courtyard of the Palace of the Ban, another in my backyard, the third in the apartment of Juraj Krnjević. They caused only minor damage and there were no casualties. The 12 year-old son of Krnjević escaped with his life by a sheer miracle. Without any foreboding he had stepped into the corridor from the very room where the bomb exploded seconds later, destroying the door the boy had hardly had time to close behind him. The culprits were never discovered.

In the beginning of 1941 another time bomb was placed in the British Consulate in Zagreb. This time, Miss Schwartz, the daughter of a lawyer, was so seriously injured by the ensuing explosion that both her legs had to be amputated. The criminal, a waiter, was caught, but escaped legal prosecution, due to the military defeat of Yugoslavia a few weeks later.

No bombs exploded in Belgrade, but the fifth column there was busy publishing and distributing different kinds of pamphlets directed against the Government and, above all, against Prince Paul and his wife, Princess Olga. It was generally known in Zagreb that the activities of the fifth column were being supervised by Pavelić's followers living in exile in Italy. Some of his partisans in Croatia were, therefore, arrested in Zagreb and sent to a special camp in the Travnik District. The activities of the fifth column in Belgrade, meanwhile, were organized by Dimitrije Ljotić, a former minister of the royal dictatorship and now leader of the Pan-Serbian fascist movement "Zbor."

In the field of foreign policy, most of the activity of Prince Paul, Cvetković and myself (insofar as I could influence such developments) was directed toward keeping Yugoslavia out of the war—or at least deferring a military engagement until such time as we might be of real assistance to the Allies. In 1940 and 1941, we knew only too well that Yugoslavia lacked the most elementary readiness for war. The fate of the people had to be defended by diplomatic means, and this—it was painful to realize—could be done only by a certain amount of economic appeasement of Hitler. Our entire foreign policy, in fact, was one big race for time. Our situation was best illustrated by my co-worker Jukić, who, when I asked what he and his fellow diplomats were doing, replied enigmatically: "We are teaching the camel to speak." Noticing my puzzled look, he told the following story.

"Once upon a time, a powerful Sultan reigned over Turkey. It came to pass that he condemned a man to death and ordered his head to be cut off. The condemned man pleaded with the Sultan and begged to be granted just one more year of life, during which time he would teach the Sultan's favorite camel to speak. The mighty ruler liked this proposal. He let the man come out of prison, surrounded him with kingly luxury and entrusted his camel to the care of its audacious teacher. Soon friends came to see the reprieved man and reproached him with stupidity. To cut a head off, they argued, is but a question of a single, tiny second; yet at the end of a year, when the Sultan discovered that the camel could not speak a word, he would expose the poor man to horrible tortures. 'My friends!' exclaimed the man with a faint ring of hope in his voice. 'Think of what can happen in a year: I could die from a natural cause; the Sultan could die; the camel could die; or maybe, with the help of Allah, the camel could start to speak!' "

This was, in truth, our hope.

The Croatian peasants whole-heartedly shared the Government's opinion that we must stay out of the war at all cost. When I was in the Opposition, I used to interview daily a great number of peasants; I continued this practice after entering the Government. Of course, I could devote less time to these interviews, being compelled to go to Belgrade three or four days a week, but I still had a special day reserved to keep contact with peasants from all parts of Croatia. After the defeat of France, I perceived that the peasants were less interested in domestic politics and showed more concern over the question of whether war could be avoided. They wanted me to use all my weight as Vice-Premier to prevent Yugoslavia's participation.

In July 1940 I visited some of the districts around Zagreb. The people everywhere gave me an enthusiastic welcome, and in one village a peasant girl of sixteen honored me with a touching poem she had written. (In the Croatian villages lyric verse is customarily written by young girls.) Needless to say, I was profoundly moved when I discovered amid a bouquet of fragrant flowers a note bearing the following imploring lines:

Save our fathers, save our brothers, save our sweethearts!
Think of the blood and the tears that will flow
If you don't save us from war and sorrow.

I quoted the words to Prince Paul and he vowed that he would do everything possible to avoid being drawn into the war, but he admitted he had little faith in our efforts being rewarded. To justify his pessimism, he referred to the so-called *prophecy of Cremona,* which he said had accurately predicted all the major events in the old Serbia and then in Yugoslavia over the past seventy years, and which now foresaw a catastrophe so terrible for our people that our blood would curdle if we knew the details. The prophecy was kept in a secret royal archive, Prince Paul told me, and said that he would give it to me to read sometime. Despite the fact that I had always been fascinated by mysticism, I never managed, in the realistic atmosphere of daily business, to ask the Prince for the document. Today I wish I had done so.

Toward the end of January 1941, William Donovan, a special unofficial envoy from the United States, arrived in Belgrade for a short visit. His mission was to find out the attitude of Yugoslavia in the event of a Nazi military assault on Rumania and Bulgaria. When he asked me this question I frankly answered that insofar as it depended on me, Yugoslavia would not intervene. I told him further that I had no doubt Great Britain would defeat Hitler in the end, but that we had to preserve our own skins until that British victory seemed assured.

German pressure grew stronger from day to day. Premier Cvetković and Foreign Minister Cincar-Marković left Belgrade on February 14 for Berchtesgaden where they arrived on the 15th to confer with Hitler. After their return, Cvetković encouraged me to be more optimistic. He had gained the impression that the German advance toward Greece and Turkey would bypass Yugoslavia for two reasons. On the one hand, Germany's road to the south across Rumania and Bulgaria already lay open before her; on the other hand, she was determinded to avoid the rivalry of Italy whose occupation of the eastern shores of the Adriatic Sea (Greece and Albania) was a thorn in Hitler's flesh. All the Führer had asked was a guarantee that Yugoslavia would not join his enemies at the critical turning-point of the war. At the time of this meeting at Berchtesgaden, Hitler's desire for Yugoslavia to join the Tripartite Pact had not yet taken the shape of a definite demand. Hitler had contented himself with asking merely for a Yugoslav guarantee to maintain strict neutrality. It was later, in March, that he specified the exact nature of this guarantee by demanding that Yugoslavia join the Tripartite Pact.

CHAPTER XIV

Crisis and Coup

$\mathcal{I}$ WAS IN ZAGREB on March 18, 1941 when *Ban* Šubašić informed me that Prince Paul had passed through the city on his return from a conference with Hitler. The Prince had looked very harassed. He had kept repeating to Šubašić, "My dear Šubašić, I am at a loss what to do," without a hint of the nature of his worries. After inquiring where I was, he charged Šubašić to tell me to be sure I was in Belgrade the next day. I took the evening train.

The first session of a special Royal Council was opened on March 19 at 11 A.M. at the Prince's Palace. It was attended by Prince Paul, Radenko Stanković and Ivo Perović, the members of the Regency; Prime Minister Cvetković, myself, Foreign Minister Cincar-Marković, Defense Minister General Petar Pešić, Minister of the Royal Court Antić, and Minister Fran Kulovec. In a preliminary address, Prince Paul emphasized the extreme difficulties of our international situation, whereupon he invited Foreign Minister Cincar-Marković to make his report. After a brief political introduction, Cincar-Marković submitted to the Council the German request that Yugoslavia join the Tripartite Pact. In return, Germany offered to guarantee the inviolability of Yugoslav territory, protecting it against any invader and Italy in particular. Moreover, Berlin guaranteed that neither German nor Italian soldiers (not even any convoys of wounded) nor transports of arms would enter Yugoslav territory; and that Yugoslavia would never be asked to enter the war against any country. On top of all, Hitler threw in his oral promise that after the war, he would try to arrange that the Greek city and port of Salonika fell to Yugoslavia.

Cincar-Marković concluded that, on the whole, these promises simply meant the mutual acceptance of Yugoslav neutrality. Yet, Yugoslavia could not evade the necessity of joining the Tripartite Pact, for respect for its neutrality could hardly be enjoined on Italy otherwise. There was only one flaw in the proposal, in the Foreign Minister's opinion. The Germans had no intention of including in the text of the Pact the two clauses guaranteeing that no German soldier would enter Yugoslav territory and that Yugoslavia would not be compelled to go to war on the German side. Berlin was ready, though, to lay down these guarantees in special letters not to be published.

When Cincar-Marković had finished, Dragiša Cvetković began to speak. He declared himself neither for nor against the German proposal but merely enumerated the positive and negative angles of it. He expressed his doubts of Hitler's good faith, reminding the Council of the many pacts he had broken and pointing out as suspicious Hitler's reluctance to publish the two important clauses on Yugoslavia's neutrality in the text of the Pact itself.

Minister Kulovec, representative of the Slovenes, who were most directly exposed to a German invasion, was the first to suggest that the German offer be given serious consideration. It would, at any rate, afford us time if nothing else, and time is life. Yugoslavia had plenty of time yet to enter the war, which would mean her certain destruction.

I then asked Cincar-Marković what the consequences would be if we were to reject the German proposal. He replied: "I should say that for the time being there will be no consequences, but nobody can be blind to the fact that the Germans are apt to renew the pressure under less favorable conditions for Yugoslavia, which will leave us only one choice in the end, either to heed their demands or to wage war against them." "Then, if I have understood you correctly we must choose between the pact and war?" I observed in turn. "That is correct," answered Cincar-Marković imperturbably.

I then turned to the Defense Minister, General Pešić, and asked his opinion of our chances in a war with Germany. General Pešić explained that, in case of a German offensive, Ljubljana, Zagreb, Belgrade and the entire north of Yugoslavia would fall into German hands within a week. We could retreat into the mountains of Bosnia and Hercegovina and resist for four to six weeks at most, but then we would be forced to capitulate. Surrender on our part was inevitable, inasmuch as our arms and ammunition were for the most part of German make. Our supplies would soon be exhausted and even if the British wanted to send us ammunition they would not be able to procure the sort we needed.

A member of the Regency, Radenko Stanković, next took the floor. He declared that he understood the compelling reasons against our active warfare, but he felt that we ought to enter the war, if in no other way than symbolically, in order to make clear our position in regard to the European struggle. There was no doubt, he said, of the final victory of the Western Powers who, on the day of reckoning, would destroy Yugoslavia for not having fought with them against the Axis.

I agreed with him insofar as his belief that Britain was bound to win the war was concerned (the United States and Russia were not yet involved), but found his inference that this must bring the dissolution of Yugoslavia a little farfetched. "I do wonder to whom they will give us, seeing that our neighbors are all in with the Germans, the Magyars and the Italians closest of all," I remarked.

"I am not afraid of the Italians, or the Magyars, or the Bulgars, but of the Hapsburg. . . . the Hapsburg. . . ." he exclaimed heatedly.

General Pešić interrupted this outburst to say that he was a soldier who had had time to ponder strategic theories all his life but he had never heard of such a thing as a "symbolic war." Therefore, he would be grateful if Stanković explained what he meant by this expression.

Stanković had no trouble in making himself clear. "But it is very simple," he said. "King, Government and some 200,000 soldiers will retreat to Greece and there join the British with whom they will link their destiny. If the British retreat, our men retreat with them; if they advance our men will advance, too. In short, we shall retreat with the British and come back with them." Stanković doubtless believed that historical dramas, like plays, could stay on the repertoire and be repeated without change. He was, in fact, urging the re-enactment of the Serbian play in World War I. Then the King, Government and part of the Serbian Army, after leaving Serbia and the Serbian people to the mercy of the Germans in 1915, returned unscathed three years later to their ransacked country.

After listening carefully to Stanković, General Pešić commented: "In the present circumstances war seems bad advice, but if it cannot be avoided it will be my duty to die on the shores of the Danube or the Sava, or perhaps in the mountains of Bosnia and Hercegovina. Whatever my fate may be, of one thing I am sure: I do not know how to wage a 'symbolic war'."

Now Premier Cvetković declared that he would not take the responsibility of joining the Tripartite Pact as long as the secret clauses, stating that Yugoslavia was not bound by any military agreement with Hitler, could not be published simultaneously with the text of the Tripartite Pact to make it plain that the latter was merely a form adopted to preserve the neutrality of Yugoslavia. Upon this, the session of the Council came to a close. Foreign Minister Cincar-Marković was charged to continue his negotiations with the Germans and to urge the publication not only of the text of the Pact but of the secret clauses as well.

Cincar-Marković spent the next day, March 20, negotiating with German Ambassador von Herren who as a result made a number of telephone calls to Berlin.

The next meeting of the Royal Council took place on March 21. Cincar-Marković immediately took the floor. He reported that he and the Germans had agreed that the secret clauses would not be put in the text of the Pact itself, but that the German Government had no objections if we published them in our newspapers; it had no intention of repudiating them. Cvetković gave his consent to this arrangement, and Yugoslavia's joining the Tripartite Pact under these conditions was accepted unanimously.

Prince Paul terminated the meeting by saying approximately the following: "Thank you, gentlemen. I realize how hard it is for you to do this, since it is no less hard for me. You know very well that I was once a British student, and many of today's British statesmen were my school-fellows. My sister-in-law is married into the British royal family and my wife is a Greek princess. These few simple facts alone make it easy to guess where my heart belongs. But I have a conscience, too, and I cannot lead my people into a war when I know in advance that it will bring us sure defeat."

After the meeting, I was standing with Cvetković when Regent Stanković came toward me and observed: "Thank God, we passed the ordeal better than we could have expected."

The same evening, the issue of Yugoslavia's adherence to the Tripartite Pact was submitted to the Cabinet. The Cabinet accepted it by 16 votes to three. The dissenters were Budisavljević, Čubrilović and Konstantinović. The first two immediately resigned from the Government; Konstantinović waited until the following morning to hand in his resignation but Prince Paul persuaded him to retract it. A day later, I tried to reason with Čubrilović, who admitted that the course we had taken was well-founded, but insisted that he could under no circumstances abandon his own position, as it might actually endanger his life. I did not think it worthwhile to bother with Budisavljević, who during this whole period was in a state of near hysteria.

Occupying the vacant places with new ministers turned out to be quite a problem. The Government's foes did their best to mislead Serbian public opinion by suggesting that we were preparing to drag Yugoslavia into the war on the side of Germany. Cvetković engaged in an unpromising search for men who dared assume responsibility. On Sunday, March 23, he finally succeeded in securing the collaboration of Časlav Nikitović and Professor Dragomir Ikonić.

At 9 P.M. that Sunday I was with Šutej in Cvetković's office, awaiting the Premier's return from an audience with Prince Paul, when Konstantinović burst in on us. He threw himself into an easy chair and, taking his head between his hands, he moaned: "Catastrophe, catastrophe!" We urged him to tell us what had happened. He explained that a plot was in the making in certain officers' circles which aimed at a *coup d'état*. He went into other details but was interrupted by a phone call from Cvetković, who asked us all to hasten to the Court without delay.

On our arrival, the Prince, visibly nervous, told us that General Dušan Simović of the Air Force had just left him, after having declared that, if the Pact were signed, he would no longer be able to restrain his officers from bombing the Royal Court and the Government buildings before flying off to Greece. Cvetković and I told the Prince that he should place Simović under arrest at once. We advised Prince Paul to summon Defense Minister Pešić to the Court as quickly as possible. General Pešić came and, upon hearing the story, reproached Prince Paul for having received officers like Simović over his head; this implied that the Prince had no confidence in him, and he would, therefore, tender his resignation. I interrupted and reminded Pešić that the situation was too serious to play the game of resignation. If his conscience allowed him to accept a responsible position in ordinary circumstances, he should also be prepared, as was his duty, to stay at his post in hard times. Pešić let himself be convinced and then minimized the danger by dismissing the whole story as irresponsible gossip. He said he knew Simović as an unbalanced but completely harmless type, and he, Pešić, was the man to answer for the Army's doings.This ended the affair.

The following day, March 24, Cvetković and Cincar-Marković left for Vienna to sign the Tripartite Pact. I stayed in Belgrade as Acting Premier. The Pact was to be signed on March 25, and "The Official Gazette," fresh from the press with the text of the Pact and the attached "secret" clauses printed in full, lay ready for distribution.

About 10 A.M. Drinčić, Governor of the city of Belgrade and chief of the Yugoslav Police Force (outside Croatia), came to warn me that the opposition had convoked a protest meeting against the Pact at Kragujevac. Several thousand men had gathered there and he feared that this would be the signal for the outbreak of a revolution. He had sent a battalion of gendarmes to scatter the assembly and was now belatedly asking my permission. I ordered him to stop the battalion immediately, and instead to fill a truck with copies of "The Official Gazette" containing the Pact and the related clauses and distribute them to the gathered crowd. I was convinced that treating the matter this way would achieve better results than bringing the Gendarmerie into play. The people would read and realize for themselves what had actually been going on behind the scenes. It worked. Most of the crowd dispersed quietly after having glanced over the text of the Pact and the "secret" clauses. Only a few hundred lingered on and cheered the ringleaders as they tore up copies of "The Official Gazette." That marked the end of the "revolution."

As soon as "The Official Gazette" had disclosed the authentic text of the Pact and the related clauses, the general nervousness in Belgrade subsided to a great extent. A vast relief could be perceived among the people, who were glad to escape from war at least for a moment. Filled with satisfaction myself, I announced this observation to Prince Paul in the evening. The next day, March 26, I met Cvetković at the station on his return and informed him that I intended to return to Zagreb that afternoon.

That evening, meeting my train in Zagreb, *Ban* Šubašić informed me that the people in Croatia had regained some confidence after the week of fear. I myself shared in this fresh current of optimism, but not for long.

At 6 A.M. on March 27, I was awakened by my son who, with the telephone in his room, reported an urgent call for me from Belgrade. I was startled, then felt sure that the news must be bad—nobody had ever phoned me from Belgrade at that early hour. It was Jure Šutej, calling me from the Defense Ministry, where he was in the company of Smoljan, Andres and Torbar. He told me that the officers under the lead of General Simović had forced the overthrow of the Government, proclaimed the 17-year old King Peter-II of age and asked them to enter the Government under the new Premiership of Simović. Šutej had replied that they could not do this without consulting me and, therefore, had been permitted to contact me. It was obvious that Šutej and the other ministerial colleagues had become the prisoners of the putschists. I told him that I could not make a decision before I had time to consult my political co-workers.

I had scarcely had time to ask Košutić and Krnjević to my house and get into my clothes, when Vikert, Chief of the Zagreb Police, brought news that Prince Paul had arrived in the city on the Royal train and wanted me to join him by car at Brežice in Slovenia, about 25 miles distant, where he was now headed. I instructed Vikert to telephone the station and say I would be there in five minutes if the train had not left. I could not see why I should meet the Prince at Brežice when I could do it just as well in Zagreb.

Košutić, who had hurried to my place, accompanied me to the station. General Petar Nedeljković, Commander of the Fourth Army, was pacing up and down in front of the royal train. He told me not to enter the train because the Prince was asleep, but I went straight ahead into the sleeping car where I bumped into a servant who announced that the Prince was expecting me. I found him lying on his bed, dressed in shirt and trousers only, without a jacket or coat; he was eager to hear what had happened. I gave him a brief account of the latest events and then suggested that he dress in order to hold council in the Palace of the *Ban*.

While the Prince was getting ready I waited in the adjoining drawing-room with General Nedeljković, Košutić, Krnjević and *Ban* Šubašić. When Prince Paul appeared, General Nedeljković received him with the customary but under the circumstances hardly appropriate salute: "Your Highness, everything is in order." The Prince shook hands all around and then drove with us to the Palace of the *Ban*. General Nedeljković followed in his own car. At the station I had drawn Police Chief Vikert aside and asked him how many armed policemen were at his immediate disposal. The answer was about eight hundred. When I asked if he would dare arrest General Nedeljković should it become necessary, he replied: "Why not?"

At the Palace of the Ban, Prince Paul, Košutić, Krnjević, Šubašić and I entered the Ban's office while General Nedeljković waited in the ante-room. After reviewing the situation, I told the Prince that according to information received by Vikert the affair in Belgrade was not yet over. I advised him to arrest General Nedeljković and, in his capacity as Supreme Commander of the Army, to give the command of the Fourth Army to General August Marić, the assistant commandant and a Croat. Due to the mobilization, Zagreb and its environs were full of Croatian regiments, constituting a force strong enough to challenge the rebels in Belgrade. Prince Paul reflected on this for a while, then inquired whether I did not think such a move would mean revolt against the legitimate King. I did not think so but saw it merely as an attempt to save the young King from the hands of irresponsible mutineers. (Indeed, it became known later on that even the young King's proclamation early in the morning of March 27 was falsified; it was actually read over the radio by a young officer who was imitating the King's voice.) The Prince then said that I had not considered that his wife and children were in the hands of the insurgents. Besides, he had had already too much of all this; the only thing he wanted was to be allowed to go with his family to Greece.

I realized then that further argument would be senseless. General Nedeljković was bidden to enter the cabinet and deliver his message to the Prince. In polite form, he expressed the new Government's wish that Prince Paul should return to Belgrade where everything was bound to have a "nice and peaceful" end. The Prince told him drily that he would be on his way back to Belgrade that very morning.

While we were still assembled in the Ban's office, General Simović reached me by long-distance telephone. Declaring that all the other political parties were represented in the new Government he advised me to enter it together with all the Croatian ministers. He added that the new Government would not only acknowledge the Croato-Serbian agreement concluded between Cvetković and myself, but would extend Croatian powers by giving consideration to all my requests.

After thinking for a moment, I consented to the participation in the Government of the Croatian ministers who were in Belgrade, but I reserved for myself the right to wait and see how the political situation developed.

At noon that day Prince Paul left Zagreb with *Ban* Šubašić, whom he had asked to accompany him. On returning from

Belgrade on the morning of March 29, Šubašić told me that Prince Paul had been escorted straight from the Belgrade station to the Defense Ministry where he had been constrained to sign his abdication. Šubašić then lost sight of him until the evening, when he got permission to say good-bye to the Prince and his wife before they were off to Greece.

When the overthrow was an accomplished fact, I had the opportunity of hearing practically all the Western journalists and statesmen exuberantly praise the putschists and simultaneously condemn Prince Paul and his Government for having signed the Tripartite Pact. British Prime Minister Winston Churchill even declared that "Yugoslavia had found her soul" in this revolt. I hope that many of these gentlemen, who have since stomached a good deal to avoid even a risk of war, have changed their opinion and acquired a better understanding of Prince Paul and his Government. We did all we could to preserve our peoples not merely from a risk of war but from certain annihilation.

As soon as Šubašić returned from Belgrade, Košutić went there to open negotiations with Simović on the proposed increase of authority for the Banovina of Croatia and, especially, on the transfer in Croatia of the Gendarmerie from the Army to the exclusive control of the Ban. I also asked Košutić to see whether there was a chance of keeping the country out of war. I had preserved a spark of hope, since the German newspapers had commented that the *coup d'état* was a purely internal affair of Yugoslavia and that, regardless of Yugoslav Government changes, Germany would honor all the obligations imposed on her by the Pact.

Košutić was back in Zagreb on the morning of March 31. He brought good news as far as the new Government's willingness to grant more power to the Banovina of Croatia was concerned, but considerably less reassuring news when it came to preserving the peace. A church service had solemnized the proclamation of the King's majority, and German Ambassador von Herren had been insulted by a mob while emerging from the church and barely escaped physical injury. Although the Government, represented by the new Foreign Minister, Momčilo Ninčić, informed von Herren that it would recognize without reservations the Pact signed by the Cvetković Government and at the same time apologized for the public demonstration against him, von Herren, nevertheless, left Belgrade after this incident, ostensibly to make a report in Berlin. It seemed quite probable, however, that he would not come back.

Meanwhile Mittelhammer, the correspondent of the German DNB News Agency, transmitted to me the advice of the German Foreign Ministry to "keep away from Belgrade."

On April 2, when Šutej arrived from Belgrade, I conferred with him, Košutić and Krnjević, and decided to join the Government. I sent Šutej to Belgrade to announce this to Simović and to tell him I would be there on April 4.

I feel that it is necessary to explain this decision. Like most of the Croats, we had no doubt that the insurrection of March 27 had been aimed at Prince Paul who, according to Serbian opinion, had "yielded too much to the Croats." The signature of the Tripartite Pact was just a convenient excuse to get the stone rolling. Yet for us there seemed no other choice than to join the new Government. Persistent refusal to do so would automatically place us in Hitler's camp. Quite apart from our democratic and anti-Nazi convictions, we firmly believed that Hitler must finally lose the war and that we Croats could only find our salvation with the Western Democracies. We were far from guessing then that neither Hitler nor the Western Allies would emerge victorious, but that the Soviet Union alone would enjoy this privilege.

On the afternoon of April 3, just before I was to leave Zagreb, Maletke, a special emissary from von Ribbentrop, brought me a message that the time was at hand to sever Croatia from Serbia. I was offered German aid in carrying out this project. I answered that such a separation would be possible only through the medium of war, and that, therefore, I would undertake no such thing; on the contrary, I was determined to use all my resources to prevent war. I told him to report this to von Ribbentrop and at the same time explain to him that there was no need for Germany to declare war on Yugoslavia, for in spite of the proclamation of the King's majority and the formation of a new Government nothing had changed very much. I tried to convince him that nobody in Yugoslavia, apart from some youthful hotheads in Belgrade, desired war. This was true if the reports of Košutić and Šutej on the situation in Belgrade were to be believed. Maletke regretted very much that he had not been able to rouse my interest in their scheme, but agreed to communicate to the competent authorities my opinion that a declaration of war upon Yugoslavia was absurd.

At our parting Maletke presented me with a "souvenir," a loaded gun. I thanked him for this peculiar gift, and wondered about its meaning. A short time later, Count Paul Teleki, Premier of Hungary, committed suicide shortly after having signed a Pact of Friendship and Non-aggression with Yugoslavia. Hitler had thereupon demanded that he let German troops march through Hungary to attack Yugoslavia; in case of refusal he threatened to fight. Count Teleki found himself in a terrible dilemma: Either he would plunge his own people into a desperate war or he would have to betray his given word. He rejected both alternatives and the only way out he saw was self-inflicted death. He was an aristocrat of the old school and adhered to the antiquated notion that a gentleman was bound by his word, even in politics.

As soon as I arrived in Belgrade on April 4, I went to see Premier Simović, anxious to discuss with him the subject nearest my heart, namely, whether there was still a possibility of averting war. Simović assured me that such a possibility existed. The Italians did not favor a military conflict between the Axis and Yugoslavia at the moment, because they feared they would be forced out of Albania by the Yugoslav Army before the Germans could send reinforcements. They had, therefore, volunteered to act as mediators between us and the Germans. At any rate, the next day a special meeting of part of the Cabinet would take place, at which Foreign Minister Ninčić would submit a report before we decided on our course. I also asked Simović how much time he thought the Germans would need to prepare an attack against us and he said: "If they want to attack us well prepared, they need at least two weeks to concentrate the necessary troops in Hungary. But if they don't mind taking a chance they can start immediately as they already have a considerable number of troops stationed in Bulgaria for the invasion of Greece, which they might easily turn against Yugoslavia."

I then asked Simović for permission to visit my friend Dragiša Cvetković, interned since March 27, and went to see the latter in his apartment. He was held in his former residence (a small villa) under the guard of an officer and a detachment of soldiers. He was very depressed, of course, and begged me to procure him a permit enabling him to go to his property at Niška Banja. I promised to do so, and Cvetković was released the following morning and instantly left Belgrade.

On the afternoon of April 5, the meeting of part of the Cabinet was held. Foreign Minister Ninčić reported the latest communication received from Italian Ambassador Mamelli. The Germans were willing to respect the obligations of the Pact on the condition that the Yugoslav Army occupy the Yugoslav-Greek border for the purpose of covering their right flank during their advance into Greece. Of course, this new condition made the Pact of March 25 less digestible, but I reflected that by accepting it Yugoslavia would not actually violate her neutrality. We would merely bar the foreign troops from crossing our territory. I expected Simović to oppose this stipulation, but was amazed to hear him say that he had no objection to a Yugoslav occupation of the Greek frontier. On the contrary, he went even further and proposed to occupy Salonika at the same time. Ninčić pronounced himself neither for nor against the Italian proposal, but stressed that a demand to take Salonika inevitably meant war. The other ministers advised using the Italian proposal as a basis for negotiation and dropping the claim on Salonika. Then Simović began to speak. His speech had no political content whatsoever and consisted entirely of patriotic phrases and martial slogans. It became plain that Simović wanted to enter the war at all costs. I am surprised even today that Simović as a professional soldier had no capacity to visualize the complete debacle a war would entail. Probably he was aware of the imminent debacle but hoped against his better judgment, as did Regent Stanković, that the events of 1915-1918 might be repeated. 7 P.M., the appointed time at which we were supposed to give Mamelli our answer, arrived too soon. Ninčić was charged to ask Mamelli for a respite until noon the next day, and we separated with the intention of meeting again at 8 o'clock in the morning.

CHAPTER XV

War and Fascism

ON THE MORNING of April 6, I was torn from my sleep by loud knocking at the door of my hotel room. It was a police official who had come to tell me that Germany had declared war on Yugoslavia barely an hour ago. I rushed out of bed and had just reached the adjoining bathroom when I heard bombs falling on the city. I dressed in a hurry and sought shelter in the hotel basement. Judging from the detonations, the bombs were aimed at something close by, probably the Belgrade railway station. The bombing ceased after a short time but was resumed with equal violence twice within the next fifteen minutes After the third attack, I went up to the first floor where the coffee shop and restaurant were located. All the window panes had been smashed, although neither the hotel nor its immediate vicinity had suffered a direct hit.

The Croatian ministers Šutej, Andres and Smoljan were staying at the same hotel, and we tried to decide what to do next. We were still hesitating when an Army officer came to tell us to go directly to the residence of General Ilić, the Defense Minister, who would give us more precise instructions.

Driving through Belgrade I got a first-hand view of the terrible devastation caused by the German bombing. The Belgrade station, which I passed, was still standing, but all the surrounding buildings, some as high as eight stories, had

WAR AND FASCISM 225

been levelled, reduced to dismal heaps of bricks and construction material which lay scattered all around in utter confusion. I was sad at the thought of what had happened to the tenants. Half an hour had elapsed since the last bombs, yet there was nobody digging about in this tumble of ruins.

General Ilić told us that Prime Minister Simović had left Belgrade in search of a secure refuge for the young King. He advised us to head for a certain spot near Avala Mountain, a fashionable suburb south of Belgrade, and wait there for Simović. While we waited more than two hours at the indicated place near Avala, we witnessed repeated air-raids on Belgrade by several German squadrons. No serious riposte came from the totally unprepared Yugoslav Army. As there was still no sign of Simović, I took the lead and guided our party, which included the Croatian ministers and some of our Serbian colleagues, through Rudnik and Užice toward Bosnia. The other Serbian ministers, I was told, were at Vrnjačka Banja, where, apparently conforming to a preconceived plan, the Government was to establish its new residence. Of all the ministers, only my Slovenian friend, Fran Kulovec,* was killed in the first raid.

In the afternoon we reached Rudnik, where we stopped another two hours. It was there that we decided to go to Užice. Meanwhile, I managed to reach Stanoje Mihaldžić, *Ban* of the Drinska Banovina, by telephone in Sarajevo. He could still communicate with Zagreb and assured me he would call our families and let them know we had safely escaped from the Belgrade raids.

We entered Užice after dark and had scarcely been there an hour when Radio Budapest announced in a news broadcast that the Yugoslav Government was in Užice. The German Intelligence Service seemed, indeed, very up to date.

* Kulovec had succeeded Korosec, who had died in December 1940; he was second Vice-Premier of the Government, and was, in turn, replaced by Miha Krek, general secretary of the Slovenian Populist Party.

We passed the night at Užice and called a Cabinet meeting for the next day, April 7. At this meeting we decided that the Government had no reason to stay on at Užice. An order was issued to General Ilić, Šutej and Trifunović (Užice was the latter's home) to remain while the rest of the Cabinet members would disperse over various localities between Užice and Višegrad.

In the company of Minister Smoljan, I joined Premier Simović and Vice-Premier Slobodan Jovanović at Banja Koviljača. Young King Peter had been provided with quarters in the vicinity. As soon as I met General Simović, I made it clear to him that under no circumstances would I consent to go into exile. Both of us were well aware that the King and Government would be compelled to leave the country at short notice. I informed him of my resignation and my decision to drive by the shortest route to Zagreb. Krnjević, who was to fill the post of Vice-Premier I left vacant, would take my car in Zagreb and continue on to wherever the Government was. (During a previous conference on April 2 in Zagreb, Krnjević had promised to take my place in the Government should it involve the necessity of going into exile.) Simović complied reluctantly but asked me to keep my resignation secret. For the time being Krnjević would be nominated a Minister Without Portfolio, until circumstances would permit me to take some other Cabinet post and Krnjević would then become Vice-Premier.*

* According to my arrangement with Simovic, Krnjevic accepted the position of vice-premier of the Yugoslav Government-in-exile. He was, however, to have insurmountable difficulties with his Serbian colleagues. First, they attempted to make the Croats and Slovenes appear responsible for the military defeat of Yugoslavia. And then, although during its first session in exile (in Jerusalem), the government did resolve that the Macek-Cvetkovic agreement would continue as the basis of Yugoslav internal policy, when the government was invited by the Allies to adopt a resolution on the future internal settlement of Yugoslavia, the Serbs rejected Krnjevic's demand that such a resolution include the Jerusalem statement. The leader of the Democratic Party, Milan Grol, declared that this would be "the worst insult to the Serbian people!" And the Radical Party leader, Misa Trifunovic, resigned as Premier, because he did not wish to "make concessions to the Croats."

Leaving Banja Koviljača, I journeyed toward Zagreb. On the right bank of the River Drina, across from Zvornik, I stopped to pay a call on the King at his temporary quarters, set up with the help of a group of young officers. I then drove on without interruption arriving at Banja Luka at 2 A.M. on April 8. There a halt became imperative since my driver had not rested in twelve hours. I learned in Banja Luka that German planes had strafed the nearby camp of an infantry regiment the preceding day, and had caused heavy losses among our men.

Leaving Banja Luka at 6 A.M. we passed through northwest Bosnia, and reached Kupinec shortly after noon. My family, which had arrived from Zagreb the day before, greeted me there. Košutić, Krnjević and Šubašić also joined us before long. They observed that the Croatian people were terribly upset and resentful against the Serbs for unnecessarily bringing this war on us. We decided that I would make a brief speech to calm the people over the telephone, which was broadcast by Radio Zagreb. I told the people that the greatest misfortune which could befall a small nation had befallen us, namely war. I asked them to observe strict discipline and to perform their duties conscientiously in the Army and elsewhere. This was all I could do under such trying circumstances. This appeal was, it happened, my last speech on the radio.

The next day, April 9, I went to Zagreb. At the Palace of the *Ban* I met Army General Jurišić who seemed surprised to see me in Zagreb. What was I doing here, he asked, and then wanted to know why on earth I did not solicit some sort of peace. I had done what was in my power, I said resignedly, but now it was too late.

According to General Jurišić's information, the German troops had crossed the Bulgaro-Yugoslav border on April 7 without encountering much resistance and advanced to Skoplje the next night. At the moment we were talking, they had in all probability pushed as far as the Albanian border and united with the Italians. In the north, German troops had conquered the firm land between Croatia and Hungary. They had been hindered, however, in their efforts to cross the Drava by Croatian troops defending the banks of that river—even though two Croatian regiments had refused to go to the front, disarmed several Serbian superior officers and returned to the town of Bjelovar. General Jurišić did not know how long our positions on the Drava River could be maintained in the face of the superior German forces. He asked me to send an appeal to the two regiments in revolt, which I did, although I was aware of the futility of further resistance against overwhelming Axis power. Whether my appeal ever reached the regiments in question I do not know, at any rate results were equal to nothing. (Later I was to learn that a reserve captain named Ivan Mrak had instigated the revolt and for this was rewarded with a promotion to the rank of colonel by the *Ustaša* Government. He was, however, ultimately killed by the same hands which had promoted him.)

April 10 again saw me in Zagreb, where Šubašić told me that the Germans had crossed the Drava and could be expected in the city within twenty-four hours. The *Ban* made preparations, along with some officials, to retreat to the southern extremity of the *Banovina* of Croatia. I said good-bye to him and his wife and went home. Šubašić left Zagreb with his party at 1 P.M.; he was gone only an hour when the first German tanks began to roll into the streets of Croatia's capital.

After lunch Košutić and I conferred about the fate of the Peasant Party's press. With a heavy heart we decided to suspend all publications during the German occupation rather than write under compulsion. It meant the end of our weekly paper *Dom* (Home) and of the *Hrvatski Dnevnik* (Croatian Daily).

I was about to go to Kupinec when two Germans suddenly appeared at my door. One of them was the Austrian Dörfler whom I had known before. He had formerly done electrical research in the Croatian mountains for an Austrian firm. The name of the other man has slipped my memory. They had come to inform me that the German Army had invested Slavko Kvaternik, a Croat and former Austro-Hungarian colonel, with full powers over Croatia, and that he had in accordance with the plans of the German Reich proclaimed the "Independent State of Croatia." They wanted me to surrender the "leadership" (*Führertum*) of the Croatian Peasant Party and the Croatian people to him. I retorted that the Germans had acquired the power to confer rule over Croatia to whomever they liked, but that the Croatian Peasant Party, and the Croatian people likewise, were not a property of mine. "The Croatian people and the Croatian Peasant Party do not belong to me, I belong to them." The confidence shown me by the Croatian people after the death of Stephen Radić could be withdrawn only by this same people. After a lengthy haggle, we agreed that I would issue a proclamation to the people stating that the Germans had occupied Zagreb and the better part of Croatia and given power to Colonel Kvaternik who, in his turn, had proclaimed the "Independent State of Croatia." I would furthermore appeal to the people to accept these new facts peacefully, since there was no other choice. When this was settled, the two telephoned Kvaternik to come to my house to obtain the text of a proclamation to the above effect.

Driving back toward Kupinec that day, I got as far as the bridge spanning the Sava River when a German guard signalled me to stop. He detained me an hour; then a German officer arrived to take me back before the German Commanding General in Zagreb. Confronted with the latter at the Hotel Milinov, I noticed that he seemed at a loss as to what to do with me. He offered me a seat and asked me to wait until he had finished with some more pressing matters. I sat there waiting for another hour before I was called into the next room to face a member of the Gestapo by the name of Nassenstein. He promptly undertook to persuade me that my policy, which excluded the thought of possible collaboration with the Germans, was unrealistic. Quite naturally, he said, they preferred to work with persons who were sincerely devoted to Nazism and therefore could be counted on as wholly reliable, but they would not be disinclined to see me assume the leadership of the newly proclaimed "Independent State of Croatia." I extricated myself as well as I could from the situation by underlining my reputation as an incorrigible pacifist who had no desire for any political activity during the war. He finally asked me where I had been heading for when they stopped me on the Sava bridge, and I replied truthfully that I intended to join my family at Kupinec. "Very well," he answered, "but it is too late to start out today. I suggest you go to Kupinec first thing tomorrow morning. And remember," he added, "that it will be in your own interest to stay there without venturing forth— and under no circumstances to Zagreb."

I followed his advice. From the moment I again set foot on Kupinec on the morning of April 11, I remained there until October 15, 1941, the date of my arrest.

Within a few days the Yugoslav Army had been dispersed throughout Yugoslavia and on April 18, the Government's plenipotentiary, General Danilo Kalafatović, sat down to sign the military capitulation. The conspirators responsible for the coup of March 27, under the slogan "better war than the Pact," safely escaped the country by plane, having fled first to Greece and then to more distant points, leaving the Yugoslav Army and the peoples of Yugoslavia at the mercy of the German Nazis and the Italian Fascists.

A wave of enthusiasm pervaded Zagreb at this time, not unlike that which had swept through the town in 1918 when the ties with Hungary were severed. Many people thought it a great advantage to be freed from Serbian domination. The fact that the Germans had gift-wrapped their occupation under the euphemistic title of "Independent State of Croatia" blinded and intoxicated many. Quite a few of my former followers and friends seriously believed me to be shortsighted to say the least not to have jumped at the opportunity for a timely arrangement with the Germans to give me complete control over Croatia. Such opinions were prevalent in Zagreb and most other cities.

In the villages the situation was quite different. As in 1918 the peasantry had accepted the new order with profound depression, so now the peasants understood, without being deceived by first appearances, that their struggle over the past thirty years to become masters of their homes and their country had suffered a tremendous setback.

On the fifth day after the proclamation of the "Independent State of Croatia," Ante Pavelić arrived in Zagreb from the Italian zone of occupation escorted by two hundred well-armed and rigorously disciplined members of the "Ustaša." The undermining activities of the German-Italian fifth column was crowned with special success in Zagreb where almost the entire Civilian Defense Organization put itself at the disposal of the Ustaša Government. The latter sent the members of this organization to Bosnia for the purpose of maintaining order there. They traversed without resistance a part of Bosnia where the population consisted mainly of Serbs and then turned back after having reached the Drina River. On their return to Zagreb they were halted at the city gates and disarmed by Ustaša troops.

From the very beginning the Peasant Defense Organization refused to collaborate with the Germans who, therefore, seized the first opportunity to disarm its men with the aid of the Ustaša Government. Their last shotguns were thus confiscated. The only peasants who did not conform to this otherwise reserved pattern were the peasants of Hercegovina. In the middle of April, news reached Zagreb of terrible massacres that had blotted out two Croatian villages there. Those responsible for the gruesome deed were Serbian Chetniks* who had raided the villages two days after the proclamation of the "Independent State of Croatia." Soon many refugees from Hercegovina poured into Zagreb and were promptly enrolled by Pavelić in the militia which he had previously organized in Italy. This Ustaša militia was well armed and included several thousand rigorously trained men.

The wave of general enthusiasm in Zagreb subsided after May 18 as suddenly as it had begun. For on May 18 the Pact of Rome was signed which compelled Pavelić to abandon to Italy nearly all the Croatian islands, the lion's share of Dalmatia and a substantial slice of the hinterland backing Rijeka. The Axis divided all of Slovenia; the Northern part was incorporated into the German Reich, the Southern part into Mussolini's Italy. At the same time Hungary, with Hitler's approval, annexed Bačka, Baranja, Prekomurje and Medjumurje, the last of which was 100 per cent Croatian. The remainer of the "Independent State of Croatia" was divided into German and Italian zones of occupation. The line of division between the two zones cut through Croatia from the north towards the south-east, passing between Zagreb and Jastrebarsko (the Croatian capital was part of the German zone) and ending at the frontier of Montenegro. To top it all, the Ustaša regime had to accept an Italian prince, the Duke of Spoleto, as "King of Croatia." A common practice in European history was thus reversed: Instead of regaining the territory lost to Italy after

* Chetniks was the name of the members of a Serbian terrorist organization, employed before the Balkan War of 1912-13 on Turkish territory, especially in Macedonia. After 1913, when the mentioned territory had become Serbian, the Chetniks resumed their terrorist activity in Macedonia with the aim of quenching the troublesome national aspirations of the Macedonians. This continued in the inter-war Yugoslavia. After the Yugoslav defeat, it would appear that the principal task of the Chetniks was to fight the occupation troops within the country. But most of their activities were directed at exterminating the non-Serbian population, especially the Moslems of eastern Bosnia and the Croatian Catholics in Dalmatia. The Fascist troops in the Italian zone of occupation greatly favored the Chetniks.

1918 (the towns of Zadar and Rijeka and the province of Istria with islands) in return for the recognition of the sovereignty of a foreign prince, Croatia had to cede additional large parts of her territory and population.

This was too much even for many of those who several weeks earlier had acclaimed Hitler, Mussolini and Pavelić as liberators. After the publication of the text of the Pact of Rome, a moral depression descended upon the inhabitants of Zagreb. The widespread discontent, however, remained below the surface since even mild expressions of opposition were punished by death or detention in a concentration camp from which few ever returned. Thus, for instance, among those sentenced to death was the Very Reverend Josip Lončar, canon of the Chapter of Zagreb and a professor of theology. Several of his students had denounced him to the authorities for having spoken disapprovingly of Pavelić in a conversation with them. The sentence passed on him was suspended, out of regard for his social standing, but examples of this kind were sufficient to deter the people.

The Ustaša Government, undertaking to carry out the Nazi program, at first contented itself mostly with bloodless persecution. Jews were compelled to wear a yellow ribbon pinned to their clothes, and Jews and Serbs were banished from certain sections of the city. I was told that even a Catholic nun of Jewish extraction had to go to church with the conspicuous yellow ribbon on her black habit. When the generally esteemed surgeon, Dr. Gottlieb, was on one occasion summoned for a consultation by a member of the Ustaša Government, he too displayed the large yellow sign on his chest. The minister, overcome by a surge of shame, exclaimed: "By God, doctor, there is no need for you to go around with this thing." Gottlieb, however, replied that he was proud of wearing the discriminatory mark as long as his co-religionists had to wear it.

Approximately a hundred of the most devoted followers of the Croatian Peasant Party had been among the first arrested, but still all this was child's play compared with what ensued after the Ustaša had securely gripped power. Soon Jews were arrested in vast numbers, and Orthodox Serbs and a great many Croats, especially those reputed to be Anglophiles, were rounded up and sent to concentration camps. Some of these victims had been arrested directly by the German Nazis who toward the end of May had also seized Žiga Šol (National Deputy of the Croatian Peasant Party), Hinko Krizman (National Deputy of the Independent Democratic Party), Stanoje Mihaldžić (former Minister in the Cvetković Government) and Andrija Štampar (university professor) and interned them all at Graz in Austria. Šol had gotten on the Gestapo black list back in 1938 when, as a candidate in Osijek County (where Germans were a strong minority) he clashed with pro-Hitler elements during the election campaign. The reasons for the arrest of the other three are unknown to me. Actually, the Germans unwittingly rendered them service, for their lot was not half as bad as that endured by prisoners in the various Ustaša concentration camps. Žiga Šol was wounded during a subsequent air-raid, migrated to South America and died in Buenos Aires, Argentina in June 1957. Krizman and Štampar returned to Yugoslavia after the war, offering their services to Tito and his Communist regime, while Mihaldžić remained in Austria where he died ten years later.

After the towns had been pacified to some extent, the Ustaša turned with terrible vehemence to the systematic extermination of Serbian villages in Upper Croatia and northwest Bosnia. In June 1941 a frightening number of Serbs were slaughtered in the village of Gudovac near Bjelovar. At the same time several hundred Serbs, who had gathered within the sanctuary of a church at Glina, were pitilessly murdered. But the notion that the Ustaša forced mass "conversions" of Serbs to Catholicism is entirely false. The idea of such a conversion apparently arose among the persecuted Serbs themselves.

Serbian Orthodox peasants from near and far came to Kupinec to seek my advice as to how to protect themselves from Ustaša persecutions, inquiring whether conversion to Catholicism would guarantee them safety. I had to confess my doubts, but told them, nevertheless, to try. I cannot tell how many, if any, succeeded in buying freedom from persecution by becoming converts, although I know of a good many Orthodox peasants who appealed to Catholic priests to take them without delay under the wings of their Church. There were priests who did not hesitate to meet the peasants' wishes—some perhaps to increase their parish, others merely to aid the people during this period of trial—without examining whether such "conversions" were sincere. Still others strictly observed the religious regulations and required the prospective converts to learn in the course of several weeks the dogmatic differences between Catholicism and Orthodoxy. The latter category was severely censured by Orthodox Serbs for refusing help to their neighbors in need.

After the war the Communists did not bother to inquire about the reasons which induced the priests to accept converts, and proceeded to persecute all of them bloodily. Very striking is the case of a priest in the Sarajevo diocese who told a number of Orthodox people: "Children, you see that your mother (Orthodox Church) is in grave distress and she cannot take care of you. Come to your aunt (Catholic Church) and when your mother recovers, you will return to her." As a reward, the priest was sentenced to death.

While a number of the Catholic Clergy had adopted the bloody Ustaša movement with lamentable eagerness, they were relatively few in the Zagreb diocese, where Archbishop Stepinac was known and greatly admired for his courageous opposition to terrorism. The story goes that Monsignor Stepinac, who had just learned of a fresh massacre of Serbs, appeared one day without notice at Pavelić's door, addressed him with the words, "Remember the Fifth Commandment: Thou shalt not kill," then walked away without further comment. His sermons against racial discrimination and Nazism, delivered during the occupation of Hitler's troops in the Cathedral of Zagreb, were famous with the Croats. His nomination to the dignitary rank of Cardinal was certainly well deserved.

The best proof that the Ustaša did not persecute the Serbs for religious reasons is that later on, in 1942, they themselves founded a Croatian Orthodox Church, headed by a Russian emigre bishop. Soon afterward, the planned mass killings of the Orthodox population subsided.

Meanwhile, the general slaughter of men, women and children went on. While the Ustaša pursued their insane policy of Serbian extermination in Croatia, their equally fanatical Serbian counterparts, the Chetniks, undertook to kill off the entire non-Serbian population occupying the territories which they considered theirs. The inevitable fierce clashes and ensuing slaughters are beyond description. Possessed by unspeakable hatred, both sides were equally contemptuous of their own lives and consequently equally cruel in their dealings with the enemy. ("My head for a penny and all the others' for a half-penny.") The whole extent of their fanaticism can be measured by the meaningful songs that enjoyed general popularity in the relative camps. The Ustaša were singing: "It is green on Trebević mountain, where Pavelić is sitting, drinking wine, roasting lambs, killing Serbs," etc.; whereas the Chetniks revelled in: "Oh Croats, we shall kill you when Pero (King Peter) comes back from London. . . ." Their hordes were not satisfied with attacking each other, but loosed their fury over entire Croatian and Serbian villages. Aged people and terrified women and children paid with their lives for passions they hardly understood.

Confined to Kupinec while all this misery befell my people, I was reduced to the role of a helpless onlooker. Croatian and Serbian peasants came daily to my door seeking advice and help. The only solace I could offer them was the thought that such a horrible state of affairs could not last for long. I drew the attention of the Croatian peasants living in mixed regions to the humanitarian principles that had guided Stephen Radić, encouraging them to extend whatever help they could to their Serbian fellow-peasants.

I also dispatched a series of peasant messengers to various parts of Croatia with similar advice to the population. Among them were Perić from Hercegovina, Blažak from Moslavina and the National Deputy Andrija Pavlić. Perić was caught and shot in Hercegovina by the Germans. Blažak was killed by Communist partisans. Pavlić was taken to an Ustaša concentration camp, where he was mistreated so badly that he barely stayed alive.

After the German onslaught on the Soviet Union in June 1941, the ranks of the Chetniks were swelled by a steady influx of Communists. The number of the latter was small in Croatia, consisting mostly of University of Zagreb students who soon were persecuted by the Ustaša. Apart from the students, the Communists had recruited a small following among the younger so-called "progressive" intelligentsia. Common peasants and workers responded to Communism in some measure only in the regions around the Adriatic coast. In Serbia, particularly at the University of Belgrade, the Communists were considerably stronger.

I had occasion to observe, however, that most of the Communists in Croatia (which was not atypical) belonged preponderantly to the upper social strata. The Communist youth consisted primarily of the children of the rich and some young intellectuals, who on the whole had moderately good incomes. I believe accordingly that those Western writers and statesmen who advocate fighting Communism merely by raising the living standard of the common man are very much in error. One of the compelling motives for the amazing expansion of Communism is, in my opinion, the marked desire of the young to emancipate themselves from the moral restraints dictated by the already established generation of society.

While the Germans marched into Russia, and the latter defended herself with enormous sacrifices, a certain amount of sympathy toward the USSR developed in Croatia. People began to think that, after all, Communism was not so bad—"the devil is not as black as they paint him."

For a long time the Communists among the guerillas, hiding behind the patriotic title of National Liberation Front, did not openly display their true colors. Surreptitiously they worked their way to the top in half a year, suddenly asserting their absolute mastery over the movement in 1942. They were greatly helped by the Ustaša and the Chetniks, who with their mass slaughter of both the Croatian and Serbian population had driven countless individuals into Tito's arms.

CHAPTER XVI

Prison Again

ON OCTOBER 10, 1941 a German officer arrived at Kupinec and parked his car in my farm yard. He handed me his calling card but asked me to keep our conversation secret. I tore the card to pieces in his presence without looking at his name or rank. He introduced himself as a spokesman for the competent German military authorities, who had arrived at the conclusion that the situation in Croatia could not be allowed to continue. They had merely asked the country to be quiet, but the Ustaša had gone on creating new disorders which would soon bring complete chaos. Once, when he had visited Bosnia, he had fallen into the hands of the insurgents. They let him go free, because they had understood they had little chance against the overwhelming German force. Yet, they would not stop fighting Pavelić's Ustaša until their last drop of blood. The Germans thought that the population, Croats as well as Serbs, would calm down if I were to assume power in Croatia. He had been authorized, he continued, to ask me whether I was ready to do so. I replied that, although I felt it was urgent to stop the needless bloodshed, I could not assume control over the country under the present conditions of restraint. I suggested that the Germans try to supersede the Ustaša and entrust one of their own generals with the delicate task of ruling. With the collaboration of local officials, as well as with a just rule, he could soon establish peace and order.

I actually do not believe that Hitler would have let the Ustaša down so easily, even had I accepted this offer. From the very beginning of the occupation, a distinct antagonism had made itself felt between two leading German personalities in Croatia. The Commandant of the German Army of Occupation, General Edmund Glaise von Horstenau (an Austrian), realizing that the Ustaša terrorists would plunge the country into utter chaos, advised Hitler to remove them from power. But the real master of the Independent State of Croatia, the German "Ambassador" Siegfried von Kasche (an S.A. *Obergruppenführer*) considered the Ustaša, not without reason, as the only reliable element as far as the Nazis were concerned.

To stem the Communist Partisan Movement, spreading rapidly over all Yugoslavia, the Germans had placed at the head of occupied Serbia the former Yugoslav Defense Minister, General Milan Nedić. It is probable that von Horstenau wanted to place me in a similar manner over Croatia, but wished to be sure of my acceptance before submitting his plan to the Führer. It is also probable that the Ustaša had received intelligence of von Horstenau's intentions and, therefore, decided to arrest me at once.

Early on the morning of October 15, exactly five days after the officer's visit, a heavily armed Ustaša detachment of about sixty men invaded my property at Kupinec, burst into my house without ceremony, and formally arrested me, before I had even managed to dress. The men were all equally unknown to me, but the leader gave his name to my wife as Vjekoslav Luburić. I was bundled off into a small car which took off in the direction of Pisarovina. The leader and two well-armed guards were with me. Luburić did not tell me where we were headed until we reached Sisak. Then he finally informed me that Jasenovac, a concentration camp which had already acquired particular notoriety, was my destination. We left Sisak and

Sunja behind and were ferried across the Sava River at exactly noon. After the crossing the car stopped. Luburić got out, murmuring something to the driver, and then walked away. The car with the rest of us headed from Jasenovac toward the little village of Krapje. The road along the banks of the Sava was narrow and muddy, but we exchanged it, once we had passed Krapje, for a small path winding through the middle of a cornfield. At a certain spot where the path broadened somewhat, the car stopped again. With all I had heard about Ustaša methods, I thought my end had come. I betrayed my emotion by no outward signs and only said silently Our Father and Hail Mary, commending my soul to God's mercy. I then smoked cigarette after cigarette, waiting. An hour passed and nothing happened. I had run out of cigarettes and asked one of the men to give me one. He searched but found that he had none. The driver, who had overheard me, left his seat, shouldered his rifle and explained that he would go look for cigarettes but that it was not safe to go around unarmed. He made his way toward a cluster of huts scarcely visible in the distance and returned after some time with twenty cigarettes in an envelope which he gave me. I wanted to pay him for them, but he refused on the ground that he had not paid for them either.

Meanwhile, a thin autumn rain had set in. The driver suddenly broke out impatiently: "Nobody can make me wait here any longer," whereupon he started the motor and without another word drove us back the way we had come. Before reaching Krapje, we encountered a second car from which Luburić emerged and resumed his former seat beside me. We drove on for about a mile through the village of Jasenovac; then the car again left the highway and went on to an old road bordered by ditches overflowing with water. Finally we came to a halt near an abandoned powder-magazine. The building, made of brick, was thirty feet long and twenty feet wide, had an iron door and iron louvered windows and was completely enclosed by a twenty-foot-high mud-wall. It was empty except for some heavy logs lying in a heap near the wall. Three other Ustaša received us there. Luburić now offered to take a few words of reassurance to my wife as he would pass Kupinec again the next day. I wrote a few lines to comfort her, telling her that my predicament was not as bad as she doubtless feared.

When Luburić had left, one of the remaining Ustaša introduced himself as Lieutenant Ljubo Miloš, and said that he had been given charge of me. As long as he were here, he assured me, I would be in want of nothing. (Indeed, although I was to learn that he had become notorious as one of the worst cut-throats, I had no complaints during the period I was entrusted to his care.) After these reassuring words, he disappeared; it was already dark when he came back with a truck full of supplies. He instantly gave me some bread, a couple of boiled eggs, a tin of sardines and a bottle of wine. I had had nothing to eat since morning and attacked the food hungrily. While I was occupied with my meal, the Ustaša men carried in two beds, a couch, a table, a few chairs, an oil lamp, an iron stove and a cupboard with glasses, plates and cutlery. All of this was brand new, presumably just out of some recently plundered furniture store.

As Miloš did not stay through the night, I was left with the three aforementioned Ustaša. I spent the next ten days with them, reading the books I had taken with me and pacing to and fro in my cell as an alternative. I slept alone in one of the beds while two of the Ustaša shared the other (sleeping in their clothes) and the third stood guard near the door. Lieutenant Miloš came twice a day with our lunch and dinner.

The day after my arrival, I was visited by Eugen Kvaternik, Chief of Public Security, who thought it necessary to tell me that my present situation was only a temporary arrangement. As I would most likely remain interned for the rest of the war, my transfer to some other place, where my family could visit me, would render my confinement easier.

At noon on October 24, Lieutenant Miloš informed me that we were to move that very evening to another place where I would feel more comfortable. In fact, Miloš came to fetch me at dusk in a small car which he drove himself, accompanied by two armed Ustaša, to the concentration camp of Jasenovac. This camp had previously been a brick-yard and was situated hard upon the embankment of the Sava River. In the middle of the camp stood a two-story house, originally erected for the offices of the enterprise.

At the entrance to the house, an electric bulb sent a thin beam of light over the yard, revealing that it was empty except for several armed guards patrolling here and there. Miloš led me up a stairway to the second floor where a small corridor divided four rooms into two on the right and two on the left side. A few Jewish inmates, employed in the camp's administration, occupied the rooms to the right; those to the left had been reserved for me. A tiny neglected kitchen completed my quarters. Each room was provided with two beds. The bigger of the rooms, which also contained a table and several chairs, apparently was to serve as the dining-room. Lieutenant Miloš shared the bedroom with me; three, sometimes four Ustaša slept in the two beds in the dining room. The windows in my room were covered with an opaque, dark blue paper to prevent me from seeing what was happening outside and, even more, to prevent my being seen by the prisoners below. This precaution did not, however, prevent me from being aware of the daily tragedies of the camp. The screams and wails of despair and extreme suffering, the tortured outcries of the victims, broken by intermittent shooting, accompanied all my waking hours and followed me into my sleep at night.

Two of the Ustaša were permanent guards who never left my side. The few times I left my room daily were to use the toilet, but even these few steps I did not traverse alone. The

Ustaša guard would first lock the Jewish clerks into their office and post a special watch on the stairway to keep intruders away from the second floor until I was back in my room.

When I developed influenza, I was able to obtain the aspirin or quinine necessary to alleviate my fever in a matter of minutes, but a doctor seemed out of reach, despite the fact that dozens of them were interned but a few paces away. My anxiety was enhanced by the scarce news I received from home. My family did not fare better; only on rare occasions did they receive one of my letters.

A few days before Christmas I began to enjoy the company of a new prisoner, who was Vladimir Singer, an Ustaša Police Commissioner. I had known him during his student days, before he had gone into exile in 1931. Since then he had spent his time in the various military camps which the Ustaša had organized in Hungary and Italy. He was arrested on the grounds of having protected a friend who later planted a time bomb in the Zagreb Post Office. He showed me great sympathy during my illness (influenza and ensuing heart and bile attacks) which left me with kind memories. He remained with me at Jasenovac for the whole period of my confinement and was afterward transferred to the Stara Gradiška Penitentiary, where his Ustaša colleagues finally murdered him.

I stayed in this hellish place of Jasenovac for fully five months. I could not complain of physical ill-treatment or of the food I received, but nevertheless lost close to forty pounds, bringing my weight down to little more than a hundred. My nerves gave way under the anxiety of the prison. They never regained the strength which they had somehow preserved despite twenty years of Belgrade regimes, four years of which I spent in prison. I mentioned earlier how among my prison guards under the dictatorship there had always been more then one, sometimes Croat, sometimes Serb, who had been sympathetic to me and performed innumerable little services. Among my Ustaša guards I also found many with humane feelings, but I could not expect them to impinge in the slightest on the strict orders of their superiors. This was understandable. In prewar Yugoslavia, a guard risked, at worst, his job (two of my keepers in the Mitrovica Penitentiary had been fired for bestowing little illicit services on me); but under the Ustaša rulers a guard could expect a bullet through his head without a preliminary show of formalities. Besides, my guards were carefully selected from among the most fanatical Ustaša adherents. A striking example was my chief guard, Lieutenant Miloš.

As room-mates for some time, we got to know each other more closely after a few evenings of idle chatting. His habit of making the sign of the cross before going to bed naturally did not escape my notice, and one evening I turned the conversation to religion. Pointing out the monstrosity of his actions, I asked if he were not afraid of the punishment of God. He replied quickly and with a bluntness that staggered me. "Don't talk to me about that," he said, "for I am perfectly aware of what is in store for me. For my past, present and future deeds I shall burn in hell, but at least I shall burn for Croatia." Could fanaticism, national, religious or social be better illustrated than by this utterance? In the Middle Ages, people showed this extraordinary readiness to commit atrocious crimes in the name of religion. I once read about a Spanish King who on his deathbed pleaded with God for mercy, because he feared he had not burned enough heretics to please Him. Lieutenant Miloš, on the other hand, recognized his horrible sins for what they were, but his nationalist fanaticism had entirely stifled his conscience.

The Communists are more logical. They commit crimes in the name of "history" and "social justice" and avoid their conscience by denying God's existence altogether, which eliminates all possible notions of heaven or hell, of reward or punishment according to the degree of observance of the divine Commandments. Even the existence of the code of moral ethics that served the pre-Christian philosophers to distinguish between good and evil had to be disavowed in the process of mental adjustment to their doctrine.

At the beginning of March 1942, Luburić communicated to me the decision of the higher authorities that I be confined henceforth on my estate at Kupinec. Escorted by fifty Ustaša men, I was transferred there on March 16. My wife told me after my arrival how this had come about. During my absence people from all over the county kept coming to Kupinec to talk to her. The Ustaša, therefore, thought of confining her, too. The idea of killing two birds with one stone—to intern my wife and simultaneously to keep Kvaternik's promise to me— occurred to them. Luburić then asked my wife to his office in Zagreb, where he informed her that I would be transferred to Kupinec but only on condition that she agreed to the confinement of herself and the children along with me. Thus, from March 16, 1942 until the collapse of the Ustaša regime, my family shared my internment.

My house had two stories. The second was occupied by our family; the first was reserved for my estate-agent, his wife and daughter, as well as the cook and maid. The latter two had been willing to be confined with us. In time it became evident that my wife's acceptance of the new order had been a mistake, because the Ustaša extended the same regulations that applied to us to my bailiff, his family and all the other farmhands. None of them could leave the grounds without an Ustaša escort. The farmhands would not bow to this and left for good shortly afterward. My bailiff and his family, who were more our friends than servants, remained with me, though he was deprived of practically all the farmhands. My son and daughter joined forces with him and the maid to keep things going. They were generously assisted in various odd jobs by some villagers who offered to work, again more for friendship than for wages, and risked incurring the wrath of the Ustaša for helping us out. The Ustaša searched them minutely each time they entered or left my farm. But this was not all. On my birthday in 1942, the bailiff with his family, the cook and the maid came up to my apartment to congratulate me, accompanied by the ubiquitous Ustaša guards, of course. Poor Vera, the cook, was unable to control herself, and between sobs brought out in broken sentences: "Dear President, my most ardent wish for your next birthday is that you may achieve what you yourself and all the Croatian people hope!" These heartfelt words cast the shadow of suspicion on her. When some days later one of the guards tried to molest her in the yard, she slapped his face. He did not react immediately, but shortly after this incident Vera was arrested. For two and a half years she was dragged from one concentration camp to another. She died a month before the end of the war of the dreaded typhus, only one of many hundreds of similar victims.

In Jasenovac I had been used to listening to the Ustaša discussing their fight against the Chetniks. After my return to Kupinec, there was no more talk about Chetniks, but about Communist Partisans. Not far from Kupinec, on the right bank of the Kupa River to the south, and in the Žumberak Mountains to the north, a concentration of Partisan troops were active.

As a consequence, on January 9, 1943, Luburić came to Kupinec accompanied by Ustaša Colonel Ante Moškov and a strong detachment of soldiers. They were preparing an attack on the Partisans in the vicinity, which necessitated my going to Zagreb. It would be only a temporary measure, lasting about eight days, after which I was to go back to Kupinec with my family.

At dusk they put us in two cars and brought us to Luburić's private apartment, at 10 Bulić Street. For the next two months we were kept there in complete secrecy by a couple of Ustaša. Luburić's aged mother and two sisters shared the apartment with us. Luburić himself during this time had moved to some other place. His mother was a quiet and pious woman, treated by her son with tenderness and respect. Notwithstanding this, she confided once with tears in her eyes to my wife: "You see, how my Vjeko is nice to me. But if only a small part of what people say about him is true, I wish I had never seen the day I gave him life." Of course, my wife did not burden her with new intelligence about her son's crimes. On March 9, we were finally sent back to Kupinec.

When Italy capitulated in the fall of 1943, the Western Allies commanded the Italian occupation troops on Yugoslav territory to turn over all of their arms and equipment to the Partisans. Thus the Partisans were greatly strengthened. By the time winter had come, they were again closing in on Kupinec. We were, therefore, dispatched once more to Zagreb by the Ustaša militia on December 9. We remained there until the end of the war. The same day, the Ustaša garrison evacuated Kupinec and the following day the Partisans took the village. Their occupation was quite decent until March 1944.

In the spring of 1943, the Partisans had carried off from his residence the president of the Pisarovina district organization of the Croatian Peasant Party, Ivan Tor. When they occupied Kupinec, they named him their commissary. In this capacity, he protected the people from Partisan plundering as best he could. The inhabitants had to provide lodgings and food for the Partisan units, but only in proportion to their ability to do so. Telling my estate-agent that he had to supply food for the Partisans, he added that it was all right to give corn mush with skim-milk. Should somebody be bold enough to demand something else, my bailiff was to come and tell him about it. To indicate the full measure of his liberality, Tor also permitted the bailiff to send food from the farm to Zagreb for me and my family. For this purpose he issued a special authorization to a man from Kupinec, enabling him to make these regular trips to Zagreb unhampered and to convey whatever he liked from one end to the other. Every second day the man came to the city with fresh butter, and for Christmas he arrived at our house laden with fifteen turkeys. Of course, a ruse was necessary. He was in possession of two identification cards, one made out by the Partisans at Kupinec and the second by the Ustaša in Zagreb. He would walk with the Partisans' card from Kupinec to the station at Zdenčina, where he would leave it for safekeeping with a friend of his who worked at the railway. Then he travelled on by train to Zagreb with the certificate issued by the Ustaša. The next day, on his homeward journey from Zagreb, he again switched papers, this time leaving the Ustaša card at his friend's and continuing to Kupinec with that of the Partisans. He practiced this successfully for three months.

Meanwhile the Partisans tried hard to win leading members of the Croatian Peasant Party over to their own movement. They fixed the term within which the latter were to make their decision for the end of February 1944. When disappointed in their hope of winning the Peasant leaders over, the Partisans removed Ivan Tor from Kupinec. A new commissary performed his former duties. My farm was now thoroughly plundered, for the Partisans took fifteen cows, four oxen, four horses with their harness and wagons, and ten breeding hogs with their litters. They ransacked my house from cellar to attic, carrying off all the furniture including many family heirlooms, precious to me for the memories they evoked of my parents and the days of my happy boyhood.

The peasants, too, were deprived of their cattle, except for a single cow left to each family. The men were forced to fight in the Partisan Army. To fill the bitter cup to the brim, the Germans had sent the Vlassov Cossacks to Kupinec. Notwithstanding their relatively small number, the Partisans retreated without offering the least resistance. A great many villagers were forced to retreat with them. The Cossacks began at once to pilfer what had been overlooked by the Partisans and hung three most noteworthy men as Partisan "collaborators."

It was at that time that the Communists began to show their true colors. Before then, they were hiding behind the label of Partisans. When they occupied a village, for instance, they asked the local priest to celebrate a Mass for the assembled people. They went so far as to name their brigades after Antun and Stephen Radić, and one after Vladko Maček. At the beginning of March 1944, however, they launched a volley of sharp attacks against the Croatian Peasant Party and myself.

The Partisans' tactics differed notably from those of the Ustaša and the Chetniks. They did not indulge in mass killings. But as soon as they laid their hands on one of the Peasant leaders, they tried to persuade him to join them at least in form. In case of persistent refusal, they would liquidate him one way or another. When in October 1944 the Red Army occupied Belgrade and installed Tito as supreme ruler (Tito then declared himself in unequivocal terms to be a Communist), it mobilized several thousand youngsters from among the bourgeoisie, in many instances mere children. These were placed in front of their troops marching into Croatia to serve as fodder for the German and Ustaša machineguns.

Wherever the Germans and Ustaša evacuated the countryside during 1944, the Partisans almost at once replaced them, killing first the representatives of the Croatian Peasant Party whom they hunted up in every village. The Ustaša and Chetniks had perpetrated their mass executions blinded by hatred. The Communists killed, with a cool, calculating mind, all those who were likely to hinder the ultimate establishment of Communism in the country.

In spite of the enormous amount of help that the Partisans were receiving from 1943 on (acquisition of Italian equipment was followed by their recognition, at the Teheran conference, as the only belligerent Allied party on the Yugoslav territory and by continuous help from the Western Allies), they had formed a habit of avoiding all serious fighting against the Germans. Their activities consisted usually in destroying secondary bridges or railway sections, burning official buildings and schools in the totally unprotected villages and sporadic fights with the Ustaša and remnants of Chetniks. The Germans did not attach very much importance to these acts. They defended only the principal railway lines, such as Belgrade-Zagreb-Zidani Most and Slavonski Brod-Sarajevo. The rest of the country was abandoned to the Ustaša, Chetniks and Partisans to fight and kill off each other as they pleased.

The Western democracies naïvely believed the skilfully mounted Communist propaganda which spread the story of twenty German divisions cut off in Yugoslavia by Tito's forces. The untruth of this assertion was most pertinently proved by the retreat, with hardly any impediment, of the combined German forces from Greece across Yugoslavia in the spring of 1945. If important strategic points of the Germans were sabotaged by the Partisans, the former proceeded to hang fifty men who had the misfortune of being discovered in the vicinity, and speedily repaired the damage within twenty-four hours.

A few days after our removal to Zagreb in December 1943, a tremendous explosion shook the outskirts of the city when the Partisans destroyed an ammunition arsenal about two miles out from the center. Nobody bothered to look for the real authors of this act of sabotage, but on the next day fifty persons, without respect to sex or age, were fetched from the prison of Zagreb and ostentatiously hanged on trees in Maksimir Park. Among the victims were some suspected of Communism; but the majority consisted of casually arrested citizens who had violated a police curfew. Their bodies remained strung up until Christmas Eve, when they were at last cut down and buried. A similar occurrence took place in the tiny village of Oroslavlje in the District of Stubica. A shot had been fired at a car containing three German officers. To avenge this, fifty inhabitants of the village were hanged on both sides of the main street.

These cases came to my ears during my confinement and represent but two among hundreds of equal atrocities committed everywhere in the country. As a consequence, after each new act of sabotage entire villages went into the forest, seeking their salvation in the ranks of the Partisans.

I used to listen to all kinds of talk about the Chetniks although their leader, Draža Mihajlović, was little known in Croatia. It was only toward the summer of 1944 that I received a copy of a letter Mihajlović had addressed to me. His messenger was supposed to come to Zagreb with the letter and deliver it personally into my hands. As this was out of the question, he allowed Ljudevit Tomašić (National Deputy) to copy it. Tomašić then succeeded in smuggling it in to me. In this letter Mihajlović unfolded to me a plan, according to which three independent armies (Serbian, Croatian and Slovenian), entitled to the same privileges, would be created in order to fight en bloc against the Communists. Unfortunately, his proposal came too late. The Western democracies had declared themselves decisively in Tito's favor. Many people in the world begin to see reason only when the cause is lost; others, still more numerous, will never see reason at all.

The name of the Communist leader Josip Broz-Tito I heard for the first time early in 1943, when the Zagreb papers printed an offer of reward for his head amounting to one hundred thousand kunas. But later on I recalled an incident which provides a glimpse into Communist clandestine methods between the wars. Most of Tito's biographies inform the reader that he had been active before the war under the assumed name of Walter. But in 1927, while I was president of the Assembly of Zagreb Province, to which two Communist deputies had been elected, I came in close touch with one of

PRISON AGAIN   253

them, Ivan Krndelj.* I respected him for his sober way of debating, whereas he appreciated my conciliatory and impartial attitude toward the Opposition. Once, after the elections of 1935, Krndelj sent me a message, announcing that he wished to see me at Kupinec, but that he preferred the visit to take place in secret. I complied with his wish and asked him to come as early as possible on the morning of whatever day he chose. I advised him to present himself as a German reporter, pretending not to know Croatian. Several days later, before seven in the morning, he arrived and introduced himself under the name of Walter, correspondent of some second-rate Austrian paper. Apparently the pseudonym Walter was quite popular with other Communists besides Josip Broz-Tito.

At first the Ustaša treatment of our family in Zagreb was considerably more lenient than that in Kupinec. We were confined to our own home, Prilaz 9. My apartment took up the whole second floor. It consisted of six rooms of which four served as living quarters and two as my law-office. Apartment and office had separate doors leading out to the stairway. The Ustaša guards settled in my office, as well as in a room on the first floor, while the living quarters were reserved for our private use, with the addition of our maid Katica. The third floor was occupied by the family of my late brother. (We were co-owners of the house.) My wife's mother and sister were allowed to visit us daily, but only in the presence of an Ustaša guard who listened to all our conversations. Apart from this, my wife and children were allowed to go for walks in less frequented streets of the city before dark every day, accompanied by two Ustaša agents. Every Sunday they went to the nearby church to hear Mass.

Dr. Oto Belošević, our family physician, visited us once a

* Not to be confused with Edward Kardelj, today Vice-president of the Communist Executive Council of Yugoslavia.

week and even more often when there was need of him. As Dr. Hinko Kovačić, physician and a Ustaša Major (though by that time quite disgruntled), accompanied him on these calls, the Ustaša guard abstained from joining us. We could talk freely about everything passing through our heads, and thus I was able to obtain valuable information on important political issues.

During this time, Ljudevit Tomašić succeeded in establishing regular contact with me by sending written messages. He would give them simply to some member of my brother's household who would in turn slip them under my door at a propitious moment.

On February 13, 1944, I witnessed the first air raid on Zagreb. There was no strategic damage whatever, but more than a hundred civilian men, women and children were killed. Two months later, on Easter Sunday 1944, Belgrade also suffered a heavy attack by American planes. Again German losses were negligible, but I heard that several thousand civilians lost their lives by it. I cannot refrain from expressing regret that, without any strategic reason, thousands of innocent people were killed merely because they lived on the territory occupied by enemy forces.

Later on, Zagreb was subjected to several more raids, in these instances, however, with justified military purposes. They were aiming at the eastern suburbs of the city where the airfield and the railway yards, with many vital lines newly established by the Germans, were located. The ensuing casualties had all been living close to these targets. A particularly tragic and heroic incident was that of the Monastery of Saint Dominic which stood in the immediate vicinity of the airfield. The Dominican Friars kept a gymnasium for boys in the building. When the sirens signalled an alarm, the Friars led the children hurriedly into the basement but themselves reascended to the first floor since the basement was gorged with children. In a direct hit a bomb killed twelve Dominicans, all professors, while the children and laymen in the basement escaped with their lives.

In mid-summer 1944, Tomašić sent me a short note, announcing that there was definite hope for a change in the very near future. He did not enter into detail, but instead sent me the regards of Ante Vokić, Defense Minister in the Pavelić Government. He assured me that when the change occurred I should be brought with my family to a safe place. Obviously some sort of plot was in the making, but I ignored wholly the extent of its possible ramifications and who else had a part in it besides Tomašić and Vokić.

On July 20, news flashed through the country about an abortive attempt on Hitler's life and about the tragic aftermath of a series of suicides and executions among German officers of all ranks. At once I suspected some connection between Vokić's hint and these recent occurrences. It is amazing how often a trifling coincidence is apt to influence and change radically the course of history. If Hitler had not left his table and retired to the far corner of the room to look at a geographical map a few seconds before the time bomb exploded, the anti-Nazi revolt in Germany would have been a success. In that event, I am convinced, even the growing influence of the Communists and their fellow-travellers could hardly have prevented European history from taking a different course.

A month later, all visitors were barred from my house, my family was refused the privilege of going to church, and even the Ustaša physician, Dr. Kovačić, had been compelled to give up his calls. Our family physician, Dr. Belošević, lay desperately ill in a sanatorium. A couple of days after these innovations, Radio Zagreb announced the arrest of Vokić and of Mladen Lorković, Police Minister in the Pavelić Government.

This news was followed by mass arrests among members of the Croatian Peasant Party. Those arrested were: Ivan Pernar, Bariša Smoljan, Ljudevit Tomašić, Ivanko Farolfi, Josip Torbar and Mijo Ipša—all of them national deputies—as well as Mgr. Pavao Jesih, Branko Pešelj, Bažo Vučković, Dragan Belak and other unswerving followers of the Croatian Peasant Party. I learned later on that, except for Tomašić and Farolfi, none of them was involved in the Vokić-Lorković plot.

Two years earlier, Mihovil Pavlek Miškina, national deputy and poet, had been killed in the Ustaša camp at Jasenovac where Marko Suton, another national deputy, had disappeared without leaving a trace. A third national deputy, Franjo Malčić, was kidnapped from his home in the middle of the night and killed by the Partisans in a near-by wood in the spring of 1944. The Communists also murdered the former mayor of Sušak, Mario Šarinić, as well as young Vojko Krstulović, the latter in the very center of Split. These are but a few of many innocent victims, personally known to me, whom the Ustaša and the Communists had ruthlessly murdered.

The Peasant leaders arrested in August 1944 were first imprisoned in Zagreb and afterward detained in the penitentiary of Lepoglava. They were submitted to most inhuman treatment, including systematic starvation and being forced to sleep on the bare concrete floor. All of them fell prey to typhus and in this deplorable state were left to lie on the concrete without any medical attention. They were set free shortly before the end of hostilities, except for Tomašić and Ivanko Farolfi who had been murdered together with eight colonels of the Croatian Home Defense Army and the two former Ustaša ministers Vokić and Lorković. History will perhaps uncover who was responsible for these murders, committed during the last hours of the war when the Ustaša regime was collapsing and its armies in full retreat. The same destiny befell a host of other prisoners who, bound tightly with wire, were taken away from Lepoglava in April 1945 and were never heard from thereafter.

During these mass arrests, August Košutić crossed over to the Partisans. At first he was fairly well treated, but he was arrested after a week because he had not consented to become the tool of the Partisans. He stayed in a Communist prison for two years without ever being brought to trial and was finally released in September 1946.

With mounting apprehension, I watched the political situatinon deteriorate from day to day. I listened to the London Radio and the Voice of America almost daily. From the early spring of 1944 on I kept noticing an increasingly stronger pro-Tito propaganda. Early in the summer I heard that King Peter nominated a new government, headed by the *Ban* of Croatia, Šubašić. The affair was not quite clear to me immediately. But I understood soon that Šubašić was to play the role of a mediator, with the aim of safeguarding for the Western democracies at least half of the influence in Yugoslavia. This was impossible, of course. The task would probably have been too much even for a stronger man than Šubašić. Recently Vice-President Nixon remarked aptly, that he who would eat with the devil must have a very long spoon.

In September 1944 King Peter—barely 21—invited all the fighters against the Nazi occupation to join Tito. A few months later, in January 1945, I heard that the British Government requested the King to turn all the power in Yugoslavia over to the government set up by the Soviets in Belgrade, adding that if the King did not agree to the request, it would be assumed that he had done so. After a few days of struggle, the King agreed. It became clear that the fate of the peoples of Yugoslavia was sealed for some time to come.

On Easter 1945, which fell on April 1, Radio London transmitted in Croatian the news that the Red Army had invaded Medjumurje and was expected to enter Zagreb in the next twenty-four hours. The information was false, but it was obviously intended to prompt the people to abandon all resistance to the advancing Communists.

At the beginning of May I heard on the German radio that Hitler was seriously ill, and that it was believed he could not live more than two or three days. This was followed shortly by another announcement, announcing his "glorious end in the midst of the battle." The end was obviously imminent, but there was still no change in our condition. Only a day or two before the complete collapse of Nazism were my relatives and acquaintances again permitted to visit me. One of my first visitors was Mgr. Aloysius Stepinac, Archbishop of Zagreb, now Cardinal, who today lives as a virtual prisoner under the Communist Government.

On the evening of May 4, around 9 P.M., Ante Moškov, an Ustaša general, came to inform me of the impending resignation of the Ustaša Government and the withdrawal of its Army from Zagreb and Croatia; the Germans had left them to their fate with literally no ammunition. He advised me to leave the country with my family, since it was quite certain that the Communists would do away with me as soon as they could get their hands on me. He added that the ultimate salvation of Croatia and of the Croatian people was now in my hands alone; thus the first of my duties was to preserve my life. He told me to come to a decision at once, since the possibility of getting out of the country was unlikely to last long, since the Red Army had already crossed the Austrian border. We talked for about two hours; I reserved my decision for the following morning.

During the night I consulted gravely with myself and finally made up my mind to leave the country the next morning and go into exile. I must admit that for the first time in my political struggle consideration for my wife and children had borne weight in directing my steps. My children had become acquainted with life in confinement during the tender years of youth because of my political activities. What will happen to them, I was forced to ask myself, if they fall into the hands of the Communists?

I instructed the guard in command to telephone Moškov and to ask him to see me. Moškov appeared in half an hour. After learning of my decision he looked visibly relieved and ejaculated "Thank God!" I am still not sure whether he expressed relief because he was convinced that the Communists would kill me or whether, perhaps, he thought that the retreating Ustaša would do it for fear that remaining in the country, I would collaborate with Communism. Anyhow, I told him to find Branko Pešelj, whom I had known from his student days. He had been released from the concentration camp of Lepoglava only three weeks earlier. He had spent a year in Paris and a year in London and spoke French and English fluently. He had often served as my interpreter during my interviews with journalists and political personalities who had not known Croatian or German. His American-born wife had automatically retained her United States citizenship. When I asked Pešelj if he was willing to accompany me into exile with our respective families, he agreed at once and undertook the indispensable preliminaries for our journey.

Although visitors could come and see me all day long, the Ustaša guard remained on duty until I entered the car carrying me off into exile. Among my last visitors were the national deputies Josip Reberski and Roko Mišetić, as well as those recently released from the camp of Lepoglava, Pernar, Torbar and Smoljan. I was aghast when I caught a glimpse of the last three. They resembled revived skeletons, nothing but bones and skin of an ash grey hue. They, too, were determined to go into exile. Smoljan changed his mind because of family reasons. When the Communists reached Zagreb he was arrested almost immediately and condemned to forced labor. His fate was similar to that of thousands of other democrats who emerged from Ustaša prisons just in time to enter Communist jails.

On May 6, at 6 P.M., Mr. and Mrs. Pešelj arrived at my house with two cars. After a short prayer we descended the stairs to the street below and took our seats in the cars. Some of the crowd who surrounded us wept, and a voice, raising above the general murmur, pleaded "Save us!"

After a two-hour drive, we passed the small town of Krapina, where I started my legal career forty years earlier, and after the crossing of the Sutla River we left Croatia. The next day, at 1 A.M., we came to Celje, lying in a part of Slovenia then under German occupation. We rested in the waiting-room of the local railway station and then continued in the direction of Maribor. When we had reached Maribor and were eating lunch at one of its inns, lots of people pressed close to me and wanted to know what course of action they ought to take. Unfortunately, I had no advice of any kind to give that could be of some use to them.

Following the left bank of the Drava River, we gradually approached the Austrian border, and at 4 P.M. passed without difficulty from Slovenia into Austria.

CHAPTER XVII

In Exile

We STOPPED that afternoon, May 7, 1945, in the small Austrian town of Villach. The Germans had evacuated it shortly before and had left only about a hundred men behind. A German army doctor told us that even this garrison would be dissolved that night. The British were approaching from the south-west, and the Yugoslav Partisans from the south-east. The British were only thirty miles away, and American troops had already captured Salzburg about a hundred miles to the north-west.

We deliberated whether to go meet the British, whom we could easily reach that night, or to cross the Austrian Alps and join the Americans. Mrs. Pešelj, because of her United States citizenship, favored the American troops, who would surely afford her protection that could be extended to all of us.

That night we embarked on the road to Salzburg, but two or three miles outside Malnitz we ran out of gas and had to remain in the middle of the road until daylight. The German troops, engaged all night in a hasty and disorderly retreat, did not bother us. Now and then a straggling soldier would flash his light into our cars and then proceed quietly on his way. Finally a German truck driver we met in the morning traded us gasoline for a few hundred cigarettes, enabling us to continue.

When we drove into the railway station of Malnitz, a young

man stepped up and greeted me as soon as I emerged from my car. He was a Croat from Bosnia named Halilović. Taken as a prisoner of war in 1941, he had succeeded in escaping from his camp before the capitulation of Germany, He had no desire to return to Yugoslavia but wanted to stay in Austria doing business in the "black market." His case was illustrative of the strange opportunities suddenly thrown in a man's path when the compelling and restraining forces of organized society no longer exist. Among the local population, as well as among a large number of homeward bound German soldiers, this Croatian civilian had managed to acquire such authority as to be obeyed by everybody, even the railway employees.

With Malnitz we had reached the end of the turnpike. The only way to cross the towering mountains ahead of us was through the railway tunnel to Bad Gastein. At this point Halilović's influence came in handy. He ordered and supervised the loading of our two cars onto the waiting train, which would swiftly carry us to the other side of the mountains. After the cars had been unloaded in Bad Gastein, Halilović took us to an inn and ordered lunch for all of us. We then bade him farewell. When I asked him what he would do now, he casually remarked that I should not worry about him! He was going back to Malnitz, for he saw many golden opportunities there in his new line of business. I never saw or heard of him again.

From Bad Gastein we drove to Bischofshofen, where we arrived by nightfall. There was not a single trace of German soldiers. The citizens were organizing some sort of civilian militia to maintain order. It was necessary, because many prisoners of war from the disbanded camp of Pongau were pouring into Bischofshofen. That night, the news of Germany's surrender to the Western Allies was announced.

Although the mayor of Bischofshofen told us that the Americans had barred private cars on the road between Bischofshofen and Salzburg, we paid no heed and continued our journey toward Salzburg. Some distance from Bischofshofen, we met a U.S. Army jeep which passed us without stopping. Driving on a nearly impassable road, we finally drew up before the deep bed of a creek which barred the way completely. All at once the jeep stopped alongside our car, and a U.S. Army Major clambered out. Mrs. Pešelj, identifying herself as an American with the aid of her papers and, even better, her unmistakable Chicago accent, asked for directions to the nearest U.S. command. He amiably told her that it was in Salzburg and gave her instructions about the road.

Before reaching Salzburg we encountered several smaller American detachments, none of which thought it necessary to stop us. Once, though, we were helped by one of them across a damaged bridge.

It was late afternoon when we finally entered Salzburg. The Pešeljs immediately set out to look for the United States Command. After half an hour they came back, announcing that they had reserved two rooms in the hotel where the Command was quartered; for we had to wait until the morrow for the office to open. At the hotel we made the acquaintance of Jenkins, an American lieutenant, who invited us to dinner at the officers' mess. During the meal our little group was joined by a captain.

Next morning I was received by a superior officer, to whom I explained my situation in detail, with the Pešeljs acting as interpreters. He noted it all down very conscientiously, then advised us to stay at the hotel until precise instructions from Supreme Headquarters had been received.

That afternoon two young men came to my room and were soon engaged in an argument with Mr. and Mrs. Pešelj. I did not understand a word, but was told that as alleged members of the C. I. C., they had come to advise us to return to Yugoslavia. They were speedily sent away.

We took all our meals at the officers' mess in the agreeable company of Lieutenant Jenkins. We learned from him that the Supreme Command had ordered our transfer to its headquarters. He did not disclose our final destination, but told us that we would go to Augsburg, Germany, where further orders awaited us. With an ample supply of gasoline and canned food, and a special recommendation addressed "to whom it may concern," we left for Augsburg on May 12.

I later learned that I owed this cordial and speedy arrangement to General William J. Donovan, chief of the U. S. Office of Strategic Services, with whom I had conversed for an hour in Belgrade in 1941. We reached Augsburg at dusk and were well received in the 3rd Division of the United States Seventh Army. A few repairs on our cars were made before we could continue, under the protection of U.S. troops, to Schorndorf and Saarbrücken. Toward evening on May 15, we at long last reached Reims, France, the seat of the Supreme Headquarters, Allied Expeditionary Force (SHAEF).

At Reims, we were given lodgings at a local hotel and had our meals regularly at the officers' mess. Soon we learned that the Army, considering that it had done its duty in our behalf, had referred us to the State Department.

A few days later, Jack Beam, Deputy Ambassador to SHAEF, came to see me and inquired whether he could be of any use. I expressed my wish to go at once to London to meet Krnjević and also said I would be much obliged if I could communicate with Šubašić, then Foreign Minister of Yugoslavia, who was in San Francisco for the United Nations conference. Beam wanted to consult his British colleague with whom he came to see me the next day. I repeated my request to the British Ambassador, whose name I cannot recall. The latter's opinion was that no obstacle could reasonably be placed in my way, but that nevertheless he first had to ask for specific instructions from his Government.

After a week, we were still awaiting news from the British Government, as well as from Krnjević and Šubašić, when Roko Mišetić rejoined us in Reims. At last I went with Pešelj and Mišetić to see Robert Murphy, U.S. Ambassador to SHAEF. He was very kind to me and promised the assistance of his

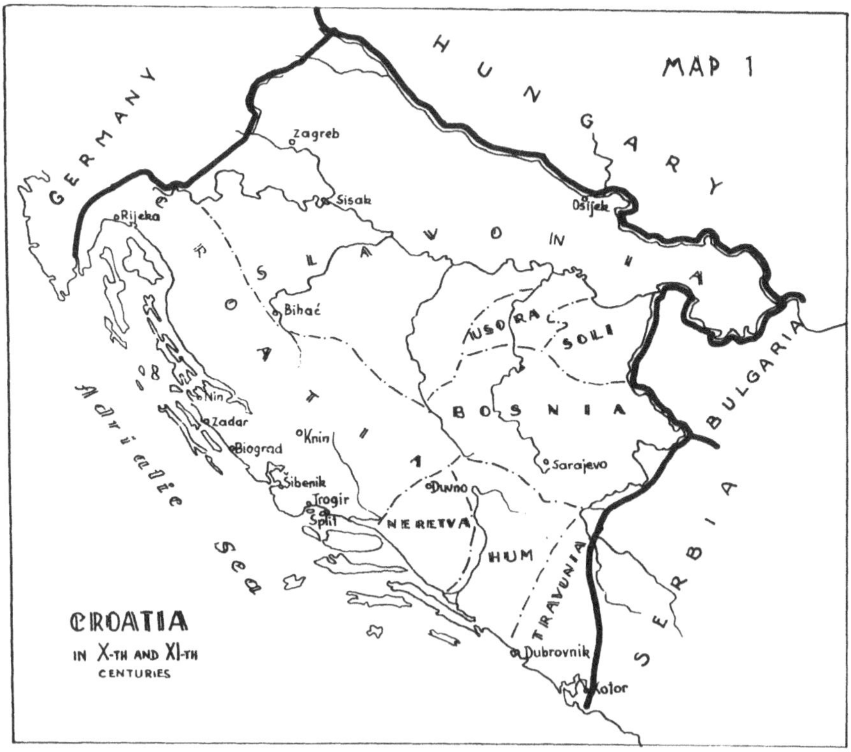
MAP 1
GERMANY
HUNGARY
BULGARIA
SERBIA
CROATIA
SLAVONIA
USORA
SOLI
BOSNIA
NERETVA
HUM
TRAVUNIA
Adriatic Sea
Zagreb
Sisak
Osijek
Rijeka
Bihać
Nin
Zadar
Biograd
Knin
Šibenik
Trogir
Split
Duvno
Sarajevo
Dubrovnik
Kotor
CROATIA
IN X-TH AND XI-TH
CENTURIES

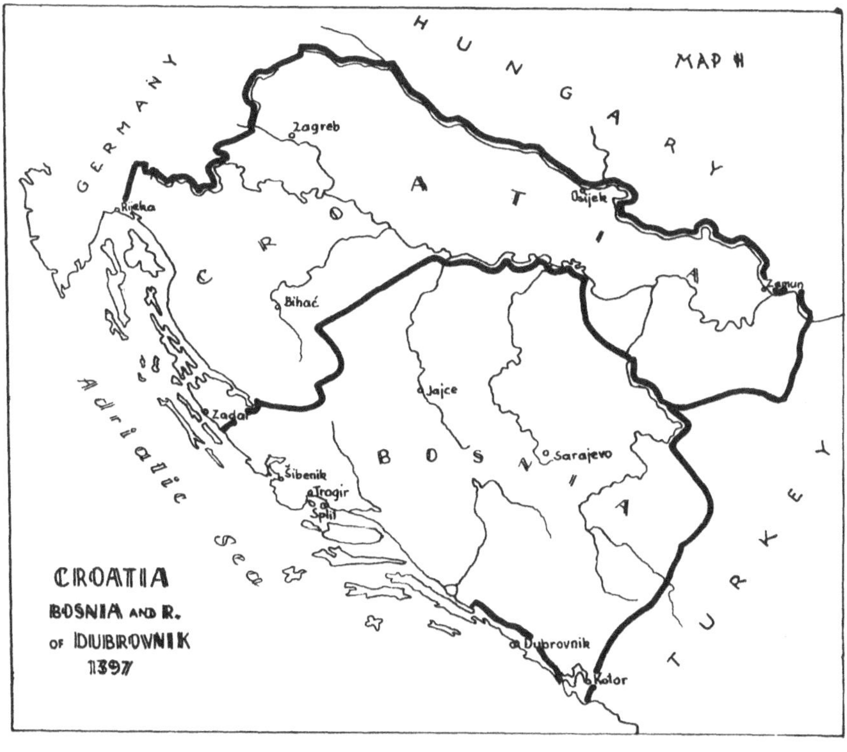
MAP II
GERMANY
HUNGARY
CROATIA
BOSNIA
TURKEY
Adriatic Sea
Zagreb
Osijek
Zemun
Rijeka
Bihać
Jajce
Zadar
Sarajevo
Šibenik
Trogir
Split
Dubrovnik
Kotor
CROATIA
BOSNIA AND R.
OF DUBROVNIK
1397

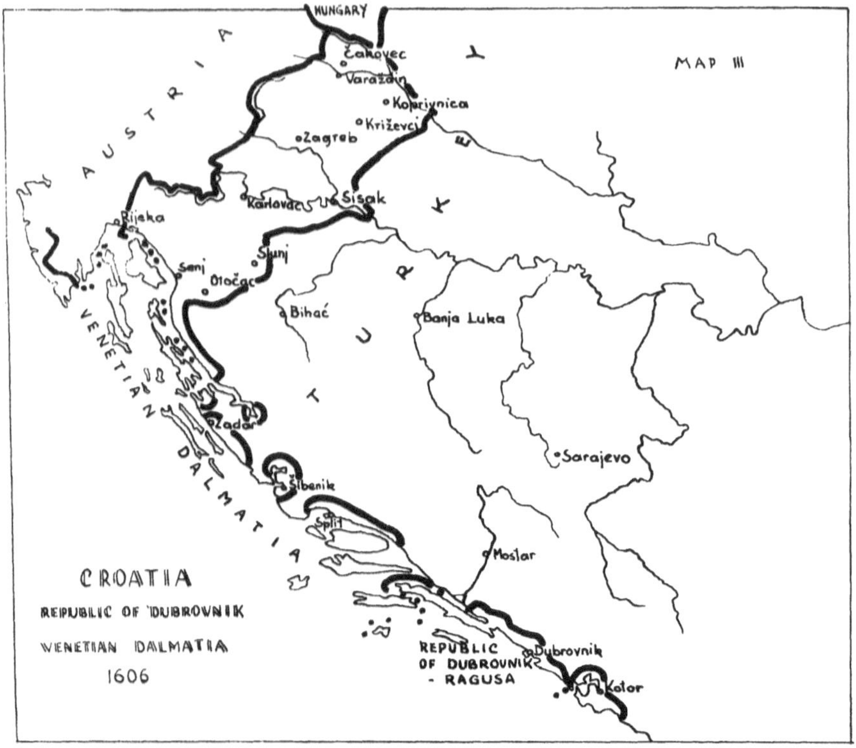

MAP III
HUNGARY
AUSTRIA
TURKEY
VENETIAN DALMATIA
Čakovec
Varaždin
Koprivnica
Križevci
Zagreb
Sisak
Karlovac
Rijeka
Slunj
Senj
Otočac
Bihać
Banja Luka
Zadar
Šibenik
Split
Sarajevo
Mostar
Dubrovnik
Kotor
REPUBLIC OF DUBROVNIK - RAGUSA
CROATIA
REPUBLIC OF DUBROVNIK
VENETIAN DALMATIA
1606

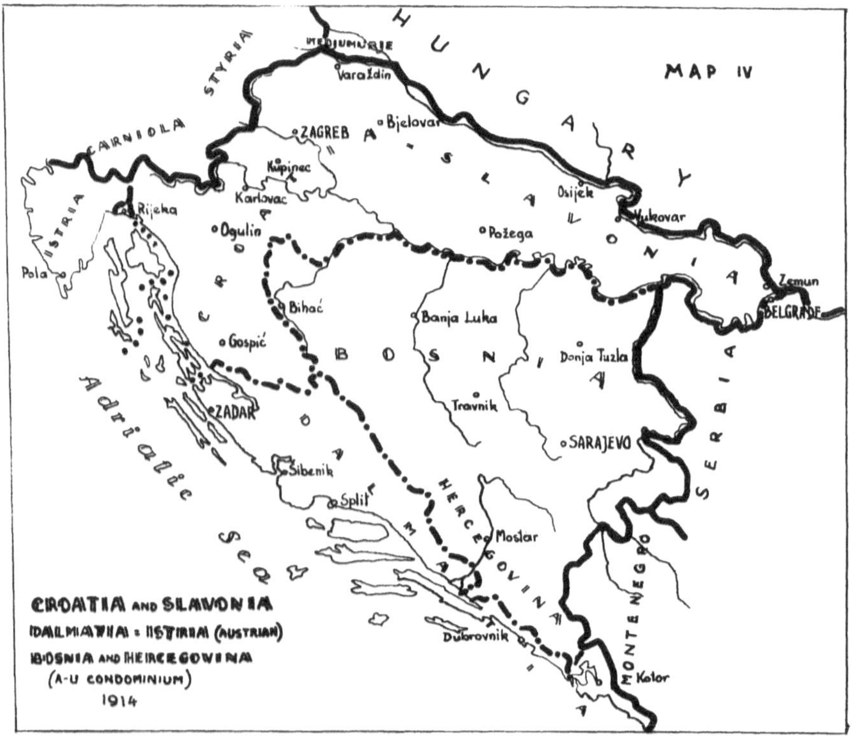

MAP IV
HUNGARY
STYRIA
CARNIOLA
MEDJUMURJE
ISTRIA
CROATIA
SLAVONIA
BOSNIA
HERCEGOVINA
DALMATIA
SERBIA
MONTENEGRO
Adriatic Sea
Varaždin
ZAGREB
Bjelovar
Kupinec
Karlovac
Rijeka
Pola
Ogulin
Osijek
Vukovar
Požega
Zemun
BELGRADE
Bihać
Banja Luka
Gospić
Donja Tuzla
Travnik
ZADAR
SARAJEVO
Šibenik
Split
Mostar
Dubrovnik
Kotor
CROATIA AND SLAVONIA
DALMATIA : ISTRIA (AUSTRIAN)
BOSNIA AND HERCEGOVINA
(A-U CONDOMINIUM)
1914

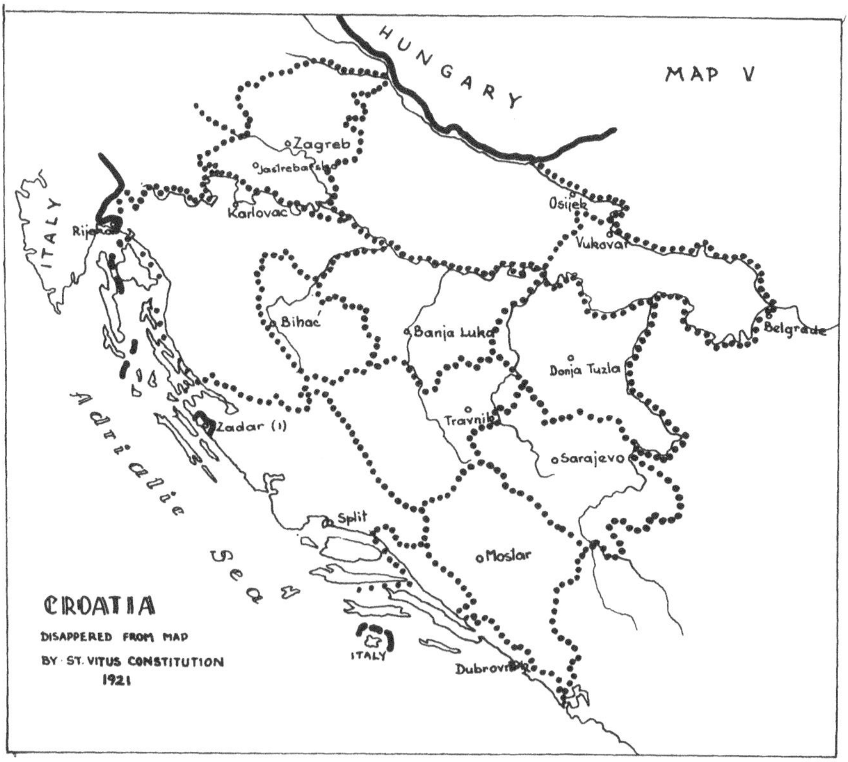
MAP V
HUNGARY
Zagreb
Karlovac
Rijeka
ITALY
Osijek
Vukovar
Belgrade
Bihac
Banja Luka
Donja Tuzla
Travnik
Sarajevo
Zadar (1)
Split
Mostar
Adriatic Sea
ITALY
CROATIA
DISAPPERED FROM MAP
BY ST. VITUS CONSTITUTION
1921

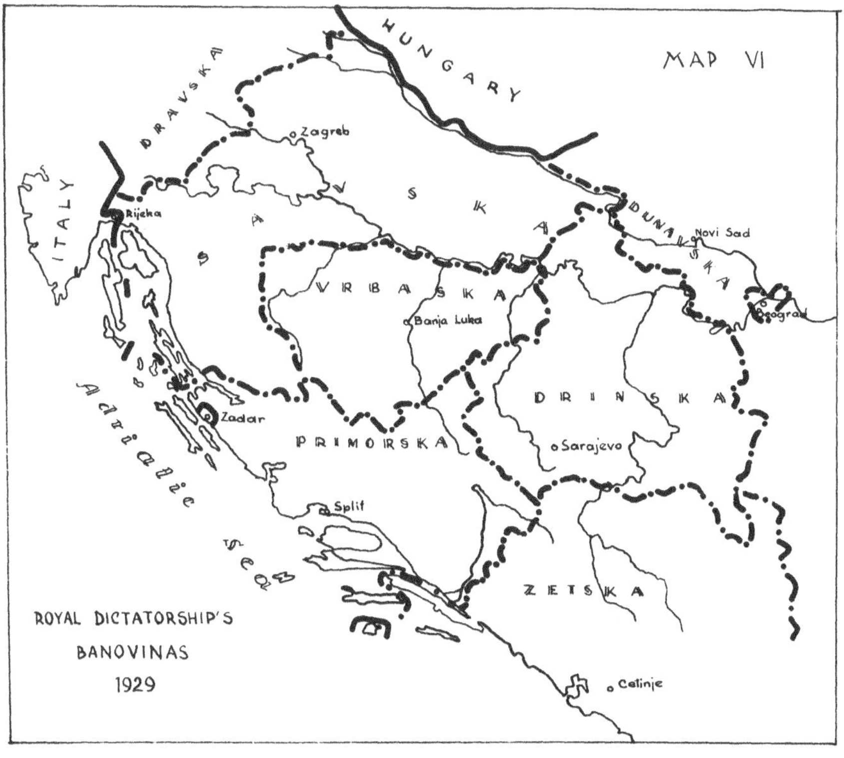
MAP VI
HUNGARY
DRAVSKA
Zagreb
ITALY
Rijeka
SAVSKA
DUNAVSKA
Novi Sad
Beograd
VRBASKA
Banja Luka
DRINSKA
Sarajevo
Zadar
PRIMORSKA
Split
Adriatic Sea
ZETSKA
Cetinje
ROYAL DICTATORSHIP'S
BANOVINAS
1929

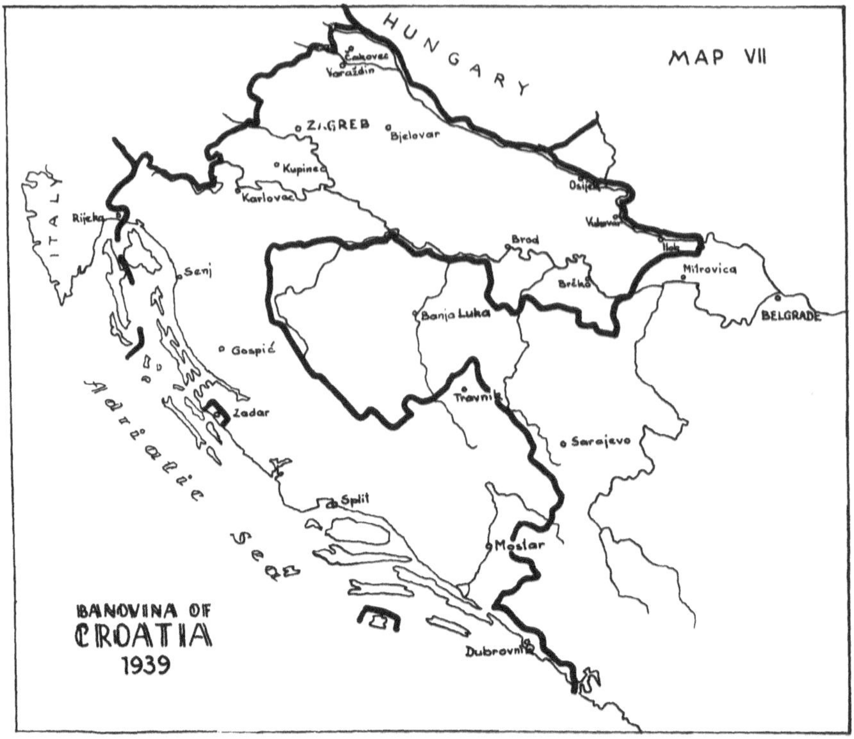
MAP VII
HUNGARY
Čakovec
Varaždin
ZAGREB
Bjelovar
Kupinec
Karlovac
Osijek
Vukovar
Ilok
Mitrovica
BELGRADE
ITALY
Rijeka
Senj
Gospić
Zadar
Brod
Brčko
Banja Luka
Travnik
Sarajevo
Split
Mostar
Dubrovnik
Adriatic Sea
BANOVINA OF
CROATIA
1939

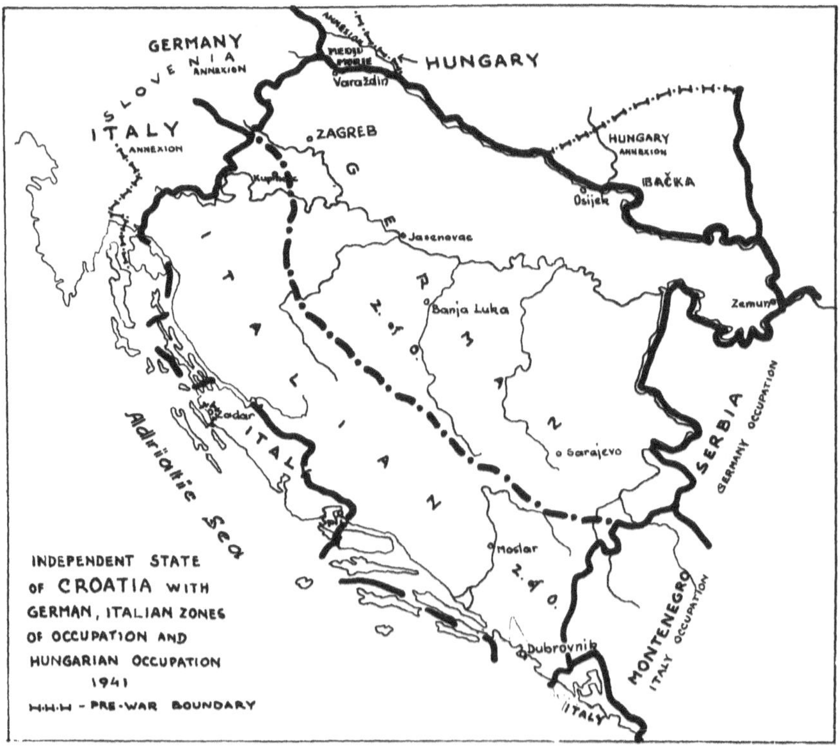
GERMANY
SLOVENIA
ANNEXION
HUNGARY
MEDJU MURJE
Varaždin
ITALY
ANNEXION
ZAGREB
HUNGARY
ANNEXION
BAČKA
Osijek
Jasenovac
Zemun
Banja Luka
GERMAN ZONE
ITALIAN ZONE
Zadar
ITALY
Sarajevo
SERBIA
GERMANY OCCUPATION
Adriatic Sea
Mostar
Dubrovnik
MONTENEGRO
ITALY OCCUPATION
ITALY
INDEPENDENT STATE
OF CROATIA WITH
GERMAN, ITALIAN ZONES
OF OCCUPATION AND
HUNGARIAN OCCUPATION
1941
H·H·H - PRE-WAR BOUNDARY

Government. He had a very favorable report, made by John James Meilly, the United States Consul General in Zagreb at the beginning of the war, outlining my policy.

I had made Meilly's acquaintance in 1938. I was then in opposition and had no official contact with foreign diplomats, although they kept in touch with me through mutual friends. One day Meilly came to see me without prior notice. Speaking German fluently, he had come for the information necessary for a report he was preparing on our movement and on various political personalities within the orbit of his Consulate. He much preferred, he said, to obtain his information directly from myself rather than get it secondhand. I was pleased to put myself at his disposal and tried to explain in minute detail the situation of the Croats and their political aims. This first visit of the United States Consul was the prelude to many more, made and returned between our families. This regular intercourse was upheld until the German occupation of Zagreb. As an observer for his still neutral country, Meilly remained in Zagreb for some time afterward, thus becoming an eye-witness to our debacle. To my great distress, Murphy told me that Meilly and his wife had died in an air disaster during the war.

With still no news from London, Pešelj decided on May 30 to go to Paris and ask Ambassador Murphy to help us move from Reims to Paris. He soon informed us by telephone that all was well and arrived that afternoon at Reims with two American cars to take us to Paris. That very evening we took possession of a house at Neuilly, furnished by the United States Army, which also provided for all our other needs through its representative, FitzPatrick. The latter's uniform gave rise among us to many conjectures as to his rank, for there was no sign or badge to indicate his status.

The American military authorities advised us to arrange our sojourn in Paris with the proper French authorities. I addressed myself, therefore, to Ernest Pezet, National Deputy, whom I had had the pleasure of meeting at Kupinec in 1937.

Pezet obligingly arranged a meeting with the French Minister of Foreign Affairs, Georges Bidault. On other occasions throughout my stay in France, Pezet and Robert Schuman were of great help and moral support to me.

After my meeting with Bidault, the American Ambassador, Jefferson Caffery, received me, and after him Tsien-Tsai, the Chinese Ambassador, General Varnier, the Canadian Ambassador and Duff Cooper, the British Ambassador. As an exile I felt greatly honored by these receptions given me by the Ambassadors of Great Powers, although I knew them to be merely gestures of courtesy; for the unfortunate postwar situation had slowly crystallized into a permanent condition, with which nobody would venture to tamper any more.

The gloomy political outlook was brightened by a faint beam of hope, when Richard Patterson, the newly appointed American Ambassador to Yugoslavia, stopped in Paris on his way to Belgrade. He expressed a desire to meet me, and as I accepted this invitation gladly, the American diplomats in Paris started to look for a discreet place to hold the meeting. Patterson himself saw no need for secrecy and invited me without ado to the United States Embassy. The impression he made on me at this brief encounter was most favorable. I gathered from our conversation that he harbored no illusions with regard to Stalin or Tito. Our meeting coincided with Tito's announcement of "elections." I drew Patterson's attention to the fact that they would be only sham-elections. The Communists had openly and loudly heralded the dictatorship of the proletariat. If the elections were really free, the dictatorship of the Communist proletariat would be instantly defeated. Tito could not have exposed his own game more clearly than when he permitted only one list for the elections. Patterson did not conceal his fierce indignation, and declared that if the elections in Yugoslavia were really carried through with a single list he was convinced that the United States would not recognize a government chosen in this manner. But he was wrong, for shortly after the elections based on a single list the United States officially acknowledged Tito's new Government. Patterson did not remain at his post in Belgrade long.

Toward the end of July 1945 I received intelligence about a most odious crime. The Yugoslav Communists had mercilessly slaughtered the Croatian Home Defense Army and the Ustaša units, along with large numbers of Slovenes and Serbs in a massacre that threw into the shade even the well known Soviet execution of Polish officers at Katyn. The complete details of their criminal act have not been brought to light to the present day, and thus I shall confine myself to mentioning only a few proved facts.

When the Ustaša Government was forced out of Croatia on May 6, the Ustaša units were ordered to follow it, together with three divisions of the Croatian Home Defense Army who had been recruited against their will. In addition, tens of thousands of civilians, men, women and children, had joined the soldiers in their flight from Communist terror. Their common goal was the British, whom they finally encountered in the Austrian town of Bleiburg, close to the Slovenian border. The Army surrendered to the British, and the civilians entreated the latter to protect them. They were, instead, turned over to the Yugoslav Communists.

The exact number of soldiers and civilians who had thereupon been butchered is still a mystery. Yet, a Slovene from Maribor, who came to the United States in 1954, estimates that about sixteen thousand Croats lie buried in the trenches originally cut for tanks and extending south of that town. Within the space of several days during that time, he had seen the bodies of men, women and children, tied securely with wire, floating down the Drava River. From this it may be concluded that many of them had been thrown alive into the whirling waters of that river.

Those who had been spared such a fate were driven in endless columns through Zagreb and on through Croatia and northern Yugoslavia, until they were disposed of in numerous concentration camps. If an individual could drag himself along no more and fell exhausted in the dust, he was promptly shot. Wherever the death march had passed, the road bore evidence of this cruel procedure, and the inhabitants were kept busy for days to come digging graves for their unfortunate countrymen.

A similar fate befell the members of the Slovenian Home Defense Army, which had been founded at the end of 1943 by the former Yugoslav General, Leo Rupnik, to fight the Communists. Ten thousand men of this Army placed themselves in the hands of the British. They were well treated, but after a month were delivered to the Communists who killed them all near the village of Vetrinje. The same happened with two thousand Chetniks of Mihajlović. All this happened after the signing of the armistice. Despite these Communist atrocities, Tito and his accomplices had the boldness to claim the right to pass judgment on other war criminals.

At the beginning of October 1945, I fell victim to a heavy attack of angina pectoris. I spent six weeks in bed and for some months afterward had to shun all physical exertion and mental excitement. With the aid of God and Dr. Faquet I regained some of my former health.

During my illness, Krnjević visited me twice after I had succeeded in establishing contact with him through a Slovene, a member of the Yugoslav Embassy in Paris (who a short time later resigned his post).

In the fall of 1946 I travelled by airplane (for the first time in my 67 years) to the United States and Canada, accompanied by Pešelj. On this trip I had occasion to meet many Croatian immigrants, some of whom had been settled in these countries many years, others of recent arrival.

IN EXILE 269

More than a hundred years have elapsed since the beginning of Croatian emigration to the United States. The first settlers were mostly people from the Croatian coast who had been compelled to earn their living elsewhere after steamships had superseded the old sailing vessels which had been the source of their prosperity. The emigration from the interior of Croatia started somewhat later. I was a little boy when the vine disease ravaged the vineyards around Jastrebarsko, between 1886 and 1889. Almost every family saw one of its members cross the ocean to America in the hope of making good there. The majority of them returned sooner or later, after having worked in mines and heavy industry and after having saved up one or two thousand dollars, which was regarded at that time as a considerable fortune in Croatia. It served in the first place to restore their vineyards and often helped pay, besides, for the erection of a new cottage or the remodelling of the old one. In the course of the next ten years Jastrebarsko county had completely changed its appearance with a multitude of respectable tile roofs having replaced the thatched ones. This example was followed by peasants of other regions. While I was living at Kupinec, from 1932 to 1942, I seldom encountered a peasant over fifty who had not worked at least a couple of years in a United States plant or mine. But most emigrants from the Croatian coast and from the poorer regions of the country never returned. Some of them disappeared into the vast expanse of the new world and were never heard of again; others succeeded in climbing the social ladder a step or two after a prolonged period of hard work and privations. Even they could not easily forget their old homeland. Those who have no immediate family in the old country usually remembered with parcels and gifts of money some distant relatives, people with whom, today, they have nothing in common except the roofs under which they were born and village churchyards which cover the bones of their forebears.

When after the first world war restrictions were placed on

immigration to the United States, the Croatian emigrants went to Canada instead. Among them, some in the prime of manhood, some already advanced in age, more than one has expressed the hope of seeing Croatia again. One of them, for instance, had come to Canada in 1930. When he had saved some money he decided to marry. Yet, he could not bring himself to marry a Canadian girl, not even one of Croatian origin, but wrote to his parents in Croatia to find him a girl they knew would be to his taste. The young woman was duly found and packed off to Canada just before the outbreak of the war, and according to plan became his wife. When I stopped at their place, they treated me with a copious breakfast. They could call their home and a prosperous business their own and they enjoyed most of the modern commodities that characterize the North American standard of life. Their happiness ought to have been complete. When I said so, the master of the house nodded an assent that seemed not wholly convincing. "Everything is fine here, but it was nicer at home," he finally confessed with a little sigh. I then asked his wife what she thought. "You can see for yourself," she told me. "Here, I live better than many a lady in Zagreb. But believe me, I would rather be back in my village even if I had to weave onions into chains until my fingers were bleeding." But these dreams were only expressions of an intense nostalgia for the native land; I am sure that most of these people would find it very difficult to go back to the hard life they had lived at home.

Nearly all the Croatian immigrants in Canada had left Croatia after the first war and consequently knew and have remained faithful to the ideology of the Radić brothers. They have founded in Canada their own cultural organizations which can serve as models to all other Croatian organizations around the world.

Before returning to Paris I met Georgij M. Dimitrov, leader of the Bulgarian Agrarian Union, in Pittsburgh. He proposed that, in the name of the Croatian Peasant Party, I join with

IN EXILE 271

him and Milan Gavrilović, the president of the Serbian Agrarian Union, in forming an International Peasant Union in Washington. I agreed to such a project on principle, but asked him to let it wait until we had secured the participation of like-minded men from the other countries of Eastern Europe.

On my return to Paris I made an attempt to establish contacts with the chief of the Rumanian Peasant Party Juliu Maniu, of the Polish Peasant Party Stanislaw Mikolajczyk and the Hungarian Smallholders Party Ferenc Nagy. Nicolas Caranfil, a former member of the Rumanian government, who lived in Paris, informed me in a short time that he had received an answer from Maniu, who endorsed our plans with enthusiasm although it was impossible for him personally to leave Rumania. The intermediaries through whom I had tried to reach Mikolajczyk and Nagy told me the time was not yet ripe for their parties to join our movement, but I would not have to wait long. And indeed, early in the summer of 1947, Dimitrov wrote me that Ferenc Nagy (who after an unsuccessful attempt to collaborate with Communists on a democratic basis had been forced to flee his country) had arrived in Washington. Shortly afterward the International Peasant Union was founded in Washington on July 4, 1947. Dimitrov, Nagy and temporary representatives of the Rumanian Peasant Party attended the initial meeting. Gavrilović and I acknowledged our membership by mail.

Washington appeared to me as the chosen center for the International Peasant Union's political activities. Thus, I applied for and very quickly obtained a visa for myself and my family to enter the United States. On August 5, 1947, accompanied by Pešelj, we embarked on the French liner, SS *Oregon*, which sailed from Le Havre to New York and docked there on August 18.

Upon my arrival in the United States, Francis Cardinal Spellman, General William Donovan and especially the late Reuben H. Markham were of great assistance to me. I had known Markham for a long time. He had come to Bulgaria as a Protestant missionary as a young man and, later on, remained there as a reporter for many years; hence he was very familiar with the conditions in that part of Europe. He visited Croatia several times, especially during King Alexander's dictatorship. On those occasions he never failed to visit me in Kupinec or in Zagreb. With his sudden death, in 1949, the peoples of Eastern Europe lost one of their finest friends in the West.

On August 30, I moved to Washington where I at once conferred with Dimitrov and Nagy. Together with Stanislaw Mikolajczyk, the leader of the Polish Peasant Party who, after an experience similar to Nagy's, had come to join us, we set up the program of the International Peasant Union, complete with by-laws. We were assisted in our task by Dr. Manuila, the delegate of the Rumanian Peasant Party. (He was succeeded by Nicholas Buzesti; since the latter's death the post was occupied by Augustin Popa.) The International Peasant Union received the additional support of Josef Černy, in behalf of the Czechoslovak Agrarian Party, and Fedor Hodža, in behalf of the Slovak Democratic Party, both of whom had recently come to Washington. They were followed by representatives of the Estonian, Lithuanian, Latvian and Albanian peasants.

Twelve nations are represented today in the International Peasant Union, all of them belonging to the eastern part of Europe that stretches from the Baltic to the Black and Adriatic Seas. There are exceptions though. One of them is the Slovenes, who have no peasant party in their country, and instead are affiliated, under the leadership of Miha Krek, with the Christian Democratic Union. Nor are the Ukrainians represented, due to a permanent disagreement among them over the choice of a delegate.

Soon after its formation, the International Peasant Union entered into a great activity in Europe and Asia, especially in

India and Japan, in the hope of implanting the peasant ideology firmly in the minds of the rural population. To our great distress, the International Peasant Union has had no means of access to the enormous masses in Russia, where, in my opinion, the peasantry would be most receptive toward the peasant ideology and might use it as a means of casting off the Communist yoke.

Unfortunately, the Western democracies still do not sufficiently understand the importance of the peasant parties of Eastern Europe in the struggle against Communism. In particular, they do not appreciate the fact that, after liberation from the Communist oppression, only the peasant parties (providing they are led by responsible leaders) will be able to consolidate Eastern Europe. The peasantry alone will be able to smooth out the national conflicts, made extremely acute by chauvinism. This is because the peasant never was and never will be either an imperialist or a hegemonist.

In September 1914 when the Austro-Hungarian Army invaded the northwestern section of Serbia, I was with them in command of a company. Struggling slowly across a swampy plain, my mobilized Croatian peasants gave vent to their discontent. One of them especially overflowed with bitterness. I overheard him heartily curse the Emperor Franz Josef. "If he is that greedy for land," he growled, "I can give him half my four acres at home, just so he won't make us tread this infernal swamp any longer." That same evening we occupied an almost evacuated Serbian village. I greeted an old Serbian peasant, seated in front of his house, and began to talk to him. He asked me bluntly what we wanted in his country. I assured him that neither my soldiers nor I had planned to come to his village as enemies; but there were others who command. "Yes, yes, the others." he reflected gravely. "They told us too, that we were fighting for Bosnia. What shall I do with Bosnia? I have twenty acres of good land. I had three sons. Two have already died in the war, and I do not know whether the third is alive or not. I have no one to work our own land—what shall I do with Bosnia?" His words made me reflect that a good many fewer wars would be fought if the peasants had more say in world politics.

As the Western democracies do not appear to be aware of this vital factor, they go on in their experiments, to my opinion entirely futile, with so-called "national" Communism. They do not realize that Communism is one and indivisible regardless of the form it may assume under various circumstances. Little thought is being given to the disastrous damage inflicted upon the peasantry by materially and morally supporting their Communist oppressors.

In spite of all this, I am filled with confidence as to the future of the Croatian people and of all other peasant nations.

Once a Croatian aristocrat, to justify exploitation of the peasants, coined the saying "The peasant is like a willow tree; the more you prune it, the greener it gets." There is a bit of truth in these cynical words. For almost no oppression and no force can destroy the peasant's vitality as long as he is connected with his land. This was recognized by the Communists long ago, and they have always done their violent best to tear the peasantry away from the land. Stalin admitted that he had destroyed millions of peasants by murdering them directly or sending them into Siberian mines. Stalin has not succeeded and neither will his pupils.

The peasantry has it in itself not only to live through the worst catastrophes, but also to erode, slowly but surely, every imposed way of life. That is why the peasantry itself is indestructible. Even in the event of a Third World War which, according to some pessimists, would spell the end of our present civilization, I am sure that this green stratum of the peasantry would persist. The peasants will remain; they will continue to believe in God; they will continue to guard spiritual values willed to them by their fathers; they will love and work their land, feed themselves and their families, and create the possibility of progress for the generations to come. Yes, in spite of present and possible future disasters, the peasant peoples will live, and among them my beloved people of Croatia.

INDEX

Alexander I Karageorgevic, King of the Serbs, Croats, and Slovenes (later King of Yugoslavia), 79, 97, 100, 102, 103, 113, 116n., 121-124, 126-129, 134, 136-138, 140, 152-156, 178, 181, 202, 272
Alexander I Obrenovic, King of Serbia, 54
Alexander Karageorgevic, Prince of Yugoslavia, 218
Alfieri, Dino, 187
Andrej Karageorgevic, Prince of Yugoslavia, 154
Andres, Ivan, 195, 216, 224
Ann, 17
Antic, 176, 177, 183, 186, 199, 209

Bankovic, Ivan, 175
Basaricek, Gjuro, 111, 112
Bauer, Dr. Ante, 51
Beam, Jack, 264
Bedekovic, Janko, 127
Belak, Dragan, 256
Belosevic, Dr. Oto, 253, 255
Benkovic, Viktor, 85, 86
Beslic, Nikola, 195
Bidault, Georges, 266
Bismarck, Princt Otto von, 124
Blazak, 237
Bombelles, Count, 186, 187
Boskovic, Dusan, 138
Brkljacic, Karla, 135
Brodar, Janez, 149
Budak, Mile, 138, 140, 141, 147, 173-175
Budisavljevic, Srdan, 195, 213, 214
Buzesti Nicholas, 272

Caffery, Jefferson, 266
Caranfil, Nicolas, 271

Carnelutti, 187, 189, 190
Cavlek, Ivan, 136, 165
Cerny, Josef, 272
Charles V, Holy Roman Emperor, 26
Churchill, Sir Winston, 62, 219
Ciano, Count Galeazzo, 187, 189, 190, 203
Cimic, Dr. Ernest, 95
Cincar-Markovic, Alexander, 194, 202, 203, 207, 209-213, 215
Crnojevic, Arsenije, Serbian Orthodox Partriarch, 32
Cubrilovic, Branko, 194, 195, 213
Cuvaj, Slavko, 57
Cvetkovic, Premier Dragisa, 142, 186-194, 198, 199, 202, 205, 207, 209, 210, 212-216, 218, 220, 222, 226n.

Davidovic, Ljubomir (Ljuba), 90, 93, 98-100, 102, 109, 159, 160, 165, 181, 182n.
Deak, Francis, 122
Deutsch-Maceljski, 178
Dimitrov, Georgij M., 270-272
Donovan, General William J., 207, 264, 271
Dörfler, Herr, 228
Drincic, 215
Drljevic, Dr. Sekula, 110, 123
Duff Cooper, Ambassador Alfred, 266
Dumandzic, Vaso, 143, 144

Einstein, Albert, 135
Elizabeth Karageorgevic, Princess of Yugoslavia, 218
Erdoedy, Count, 19

INDEX 277

Faquet, Dr. 268
Farolfi, Ivanko, 255, 256
Ferdinand I, Holy Roman Emperor, King of Hungary and Bohemia, 25, 26
Filipancic, Ljudevit, 190
Filipovic, 146
FitzPatrick, 265
Folnegovic, Fran, 35, 54
Frank, Dr. Josip, 35, 37, 51, 54, 57, 58, 116n.
Frankopan, Kristo, 26
Franz Ferdinand, Archduke of Austria, 60
Franz Josef I, Emperor of Austria and King of Hungary, 27-29, 33, 34, 51, 56, 68, 122, 273
Austria and King of Hungary, 27-29, 33, 34, 51, 56, 68, 122, 273

Gavrilovic, Milan, 271
Gjuricic, Marko, 96
Gojkovic, Gavro, 100
Gottlieb, Dr., 112, 233
Grandja, Ivan, 111-113
Grey, Sir Edward, 77
Grol, Milan, 191, 226n.

Halilovic, 262
Herceg, Rudolph, 167
Herren, Ambassador von, 203, 213, 219, 220
Hitler, Adolph, 62, 128, 174, 184, 185, 187, 201, 202, 205, 207, 209, 210, 212, 220, 221, 232, 234, 236, 240, 255, 257
Hodza, Fedor, 272
Hodza, Milan, 134
Hohenberg, Duchess Sophie of (*Née* Countess Chotek), 60
Hohnjec, Msgr., 102, 103
Horstenau, General Edmund Glaise von, 240
Hranilovic, 135
Hruskar, Djuro, 84, 85, 87
Hrvoj, Dragutin, 79

Ikonic, Professor Dragomir, 214
Ilic, General, 224-226
Ilic, Professor, 190
Ipsa, Mijo, 256
Irgolic, Ante, 180, 181

Jalzabetic, Tomo, 87
Janjic, Voja, 96
Jeftic, Premier Bogoljub, 156, 158, 160, 163, 174, 179
Jelacic, General Josip, 27, 34
Jenkins, Lieutenant, 263
Jesih, Mgr. Pavao, 256
Job, 145
Jovanovic, Dragoljub, 152, 158, 158n., 159
Jovanovic, Joca, 93, 109, 160, 165, 181, 182n.
Jovanovic, Ljuba, 95, 102-104
Jovanovic, Professor Slobodan, 124, 226
Joza, 70, 71, 73
Jukic, Ilija, 199, 202, 205
Jurisic, General, 227, 228

Kalafatovic, General Danilo, 230
Kardelj, Edward, 253n.
Karl I, Emperor of Austria and King of Hungary, 68, 69
Kasche, "Ambassador" Siegfried von, 240
Katica, 253
Kecmanovic, Dusan, 138
Keglevic, Count, 52
Kemfelja, Djuro, 149
Kent, Princess Marina, Duchess of, 213
Kerdic, Msgr., 116
Kezman, Dr. Ljudevit, 81-85, 87
Khuen-Hedervary, Count Karl, 30-33, 45, 49, 56, 57
Klepac, Dr., 114
Konstantinovic, Professor Mihalo, 190, 195, 200, 213, 214
Korosec, Msgr. Antun, 78, 79, 93, 94, 100, 102, 109, 126, 127, 160, 164, 166, 225n.

Kosanovic, Sava, 138, 191
Kossuth, Louis, 26, 57
Kostic, Dr. Milan, 112, 147, 182n.
Kostrencic, Marko, 164
Kosutic, August, 81, 96, 100, 101, 103, 105, 113, 128, 134, 135, 151, 159, 172, 181, 188, 194, 216, 217, 219-221, 227, 228, 256
Kosutic, Mira Radic, 81, 82, 101
Kosutic, S., 103, 105
Kovacevic, Dragutin, 81
Kovacic, Dr. Hinko, 264, 255
Krbek, Professor Ivo, 190
Krek, Miha, 195, 225n., 272
Krndelj, Ivan, 253
Krnjevic, Dr. Juraj, 81, 95-98, 103, 105, 121, 128, 134, 151, 159, 191, 195, 204, 216, 217, 220, 226, 226n., 227, 264, 268
Krizman, Hinko, 138, 234
Krstulovic, Vojko, 256
Kulenovic, Dzafer, 195
Kulovec, Fran, 209, 210, 225, 225n.
Kvaternik, Chief Eugen, 242, 246
Kvaternik, Colonel Slavko, 229

Laginja, Matko, 78, 87, 88
Ljotic, Dimitrije, 205
Loncar, Very Reverend Josip, 233
Lorkovic, Mladen, 255, 256
Louis II, King of Hungary, Croatia, and Bohemia, 25
Lovrekovic, Vinko, 56
Luburic, Vjekoslav, 240, 241, 246, 247

Macek, Agnes, 137
Macek, Andrej, 106, 137
Macek, Josipa, 156
Macek, Mary, 98, 108
Macek, Paul, 137
Makarije, 145
Maksimovic, Boza, 193, 195
Malcic, Franjo, 52, 256
Malesevic, Lieutenant-Colonel Tosa, 70, 71, 75

Maletke, 220, 221
Mamelli, 222, 223
Maniu, Juliu, 271
Mann, Heinrich, 135
Manuila, Dr. Sabin, 272
Maria, Queen of the Serbs, Croats, and Slovenes (later Queen of Yugoslavia), 154
Maric, General August, 217
Markham, Reuben H., 271, 272
Markovic, Lazar, 193, 195
Marx, Karl, 47
Masaryk, Professor Thomas Garrigue, 37, 45, 128
Meilly, John James, 265
Meilly, Mrs. John James, 265
Mestrovic, Ivan, 76
Mihajlovic, General Draza, 252, 268
Mihaldzic, Stanoje, 142, 143, 154, 156, 193, 194, 225, 234
Mihalovich, Antun, 175, 176
Mikolajczyk, Stanislaw, 271, 272
Milos, Lieutenant Ljubo, 242, 243, 245
Misetic, Roko, 259, 264
Miskina, Mihovil Pavlek, 256
Mittelhammer, 220
Montesquieu, 78, 171
Moskov, Colonel Ante, 247, 258
Mrak, Colonel Ivan, 228
Munich, General, 74
Murkovic, Captain Ivan, 75
Murphy, Robert, 264, 265
Musakadic, 143, 145
Mussolini, Benito, 116n., 140, 173, 174, 187, 201, 202, 233

Nagy, Ferenc, 271, 272
Napoleon I, Emperor of the French, 25
Nassenstein, Herr, 229
Nedeljkovic, General Petar, 217, 218
Nedic, General Milan, 152, 194, 197, 240
Neuhausen, 203, 204

INDEX

Nicholas Karageorgevic, Prince of Yugoslavia, 218
Nikitovic, Caslav, 214
Nincic, Momcilo, 220, 222, 223
Nixon, Vice-President Richard M., 257

Olga, Princess of Yugoslavia, 201, 205, 213, 218, 219

Pasic, Nikola, 77, 79, 91, 93, 95-97, 99, 103, 105, 106, 108, 132
Paskevich, General, 27
Patterson, Ambassador Richard, 266, 267
Paul Karageorgevic, Prince of Yugoslavia, 128, 155, 156, 164, 166, 174, 177, 178, 180-183, 185, 186, 188, 189, 191, 193, 194, 197, 198, 200-207, 209, 213, 214, 216-220
Pavelic, Ante, 79
Pavelic, Ante, 79, 116n., 140, 141, 172, 179, 185, 201, 205, 231-233, 235, 236, 239, 255
Pavlic, Andrija, 237
Pejacevic, Count Theodore, 30, 49
Pejnovic, 135, 136
Peric, Dr. Ninko, 110, 111, 237
Pernar, Ivan, 81, 87, 110-113, 121, 149, 151, 255, 259
Perovic, Ivo, 155, 209
Peselj, Branko, 256, 259, 263, 265, 268, 271
Peselj, Mrs. Branko, 259, 261, 263
Pesic, General Petar, 209, 211, 212, 214, 215
Pestaj, Ivan, 162, 172
Peter I Karageorgevic, King of Serbia (later King of the Serbs, Croats, and Slovenes), 54, 80, 212
Peter II Karageorgevic, King of Yugoslavia, 154, 155, 181, 192, 212, 216, 218, 219, 221, 225-227, 236, 257

Petrovic, Nastas, 99, 100, 102
Pezet, Ernest, 265, 266
Pintar, General Bolto, 62, 63
Popa, Augustin, 272
Posilovic, Archbishop, 51
Potiorek, General, 64
Predavec, Josip, 81, 82, 87, 96, 97, 103, 105, 114, 119, 133, 134, 138, 150, 159
Pribicevic, Svetozar, 77-79, 90, 99, 103, 105-107, 109, 111, 113,-115, 121-124, 126-128, 137, 138, 161

Racic, Punisa, 110-112, 135, 136
Rackoczy, Prince Ferenc, 26
Radic, Antun (Ante), 38, 41-44, 46, 47, 56, 81, 167, 173, 250, 270
Radic, Maria, 62, 81, 97, 98
Radic, Pavle, 105, 112
Radic, Stephen, 34, 44-47, 50-54, 56, 58, 61, 62, 68, 69, 76, 79-81, 83, 84, 87, 88, 90, 92, 95-98, 100-103, 105-120, 152, 159, 173, 229, 237, 250, 270
Ramberg, 30
Rauch, Baron Levin, 29
Rauch, Baron Pavel, 56
Reberski, Josip, 259
Ribbentrop, Joachim von, 220, 221
Rogulja, Stjepan, 150, 151, 153
Roje, Father, 144
Rosic, 135
Rupnik, General Leo, 268

Sarinic, Mario, 256
Schlegel, Toni, 127, 135
Schuman, Robert, 266
Schwartz, Miss, 204
Simovic, General Dusan, 214-216, 218-223, 225, 226, 226n.
Singer, Vladimir, 244
Skrbec, Dean, 149
Skrlec, Baron Nikola, 57
Smoljan, Barisa, 195, 216, 224, 226, 255, 259

Sokolovic, Grand Vizir Mehmed Pasha, 145
Sol, Ziga, 81, 234
Soldin, 135
Soljan, Frane, 130, 149
Spaho, Dr. Mehmed, 93, 94, 100, 109, 160, 164
Spellman, Francis, Cardinal, 271
Spoleto, Prince Aimone, Duke of (Tomislav II, "King of Croatia"), 232, 233
Sreten, 146-148
Stalin, Joseph, 266, 274
Stampar, Professor Andrija, 234
Stankovic, Radenko, 155, 209, 211-213, 223
Stanojevic, Aca, 160, 164n., 182n.
Starcevic, Ante, 28, 30, 33, 35, 37
Starcevic, Dr. Mile, 57, 58, 107
Stepinac, Aloysius, Cardinal, 184, 235, 236, 258
Stojadinovic, Premier Milan, 164, 175, 178-181, 183-187, 203
Stozir, Judge Ivo, 85
Straznicki, Professor Milorad, 177
Strossmayer, Bishop Josip Juraj, 27, 29, 30
Subasic, Ivan, 152-154, 182, 183, 185, 186, 189, 190, 194, 195, 209, 216-219, 227, 228, 257, 264
Subotic, Jovan, 132
Sufflay, Dr. Milan, 135, 140
Suleiman The Magnificent, 145
Superina, Benjamin, 87
Supilo, Frane, 54, 76
Susic, Lovro, 195
Sutej, Juraj (Jure), 138, 144, 183, 190, 194, 197, 199, 214, 216, 220, 221, 224, 226
Suton, Marko, 256

Tasic, Professor, 190
Teleki, Count Paul, 221
Thaller, Dr. Lujo, 153-155
Tito, Marshal Josip Broz, 158n., 234, 238, 250-253, 257, 266, 267
Tolstoy, Count Leo, 170
Tomasic, Ljudevit, 175, 252, 254-256
Tomasic, Nikola, 56, 57
Tomek, 143, 144
Tomic, Jevrem, 195
Tomislav II, "King of Croatia". See Spoleto, Prince Aimone, Duke of
Tomislav Karageorgevic, Prince of Yugoslavia, 154
Tor, Ivan, 248
Torbar, Josip, 81, 195, 216, 255, 256, 259
Trbuha, Josip, 138
Trifkovic, Marko, 96
Trifunovic, Misa, 160, 181, 226, 226n.
Trumbic, Ante, 76, 79, 105, 116n., 130, 138, 151, 159, 161, 183
Tsien-Tsai, 266

Uzunovic, Nikola, 155, 156

Vandekar, Josip, 152
Varnier, General, 266
Vera, 147
Victor Emmanuel III, King of Italy, 190
Vikert, Chief, 216, 217
Vilder, Veceslav, 138, 147, 180, 181
Vokic, Ante, 255, 256
Vuckovic, Bazo, 256
Vujcic, 111
Vukicevic, Velja, 108

Wels, Major, 71, 73
Wilhelm II, German Emperor, 62, 68
Wilson, President Woodrow, 76

Zapolya, John, King of Hungary, 25, 26
Zivkovic, Chief, 144, 145
Zivovic, General Petar (Pera), 124, 134, 136, 155, 156
Zrinski, Peter, 26

www.ingramcontent.com/pod-product-compliance
Lightning Source LLC
Chambersburg PA
CBHW020301010526
44108CB00037B/276